WEALTH PROTECTION, M.D.

The Ultimate Money & Practice Guide
for 21st Century Physicians

Christopher R. Jarvis

David B. Mandell

with

Celia R. Clark

Glenn M. Terrones

2004

Guardian Publishing LLC

Library of Congress Cataloging-in-Publication Data:
Jarvis, Christopher, 1970–
    Wealth Protection, M.D. the ultimate money & practice guide for 21st century physicians / by Christopher Jarvis, David B. Mandell
        p. cm.
    Includes bibliographical references and index.
    ISBN 1-890415-02-1
    1. Executions (Law)—United States.   2. Debtor and creditor—United States
 3. Estate planning—United States.   4. Tax planning—United States   I. Mandell, David B., 1968– II. Title.

Printed in the United States of America

10 9 8 7 6 5 4 3 2 1

About the Authors   vii

Acknowledgments   ix

Preface — Work "On" Your Medical Career, Not Just "In It"   xi

Introduction — Why We Wrote This Book   xv

Part I — Understanding What This Book Can Do For You   1

1. Why This Book Should Cost $10,000   3
2. What Is "Wealth Protection Planning"?   9
3. Finding Your Personal Economy   15

Part II — Customizing This Book for Your Practice And Your Family   17

4. The Risk Factor Analysis (RFA)   19
5. The Questions   21
6. Interpretation Of Your Answers   25

Part III — Asset Protection   35

7. Why Asset Protection Is So Important Today   37
8. Myths About Asset Protection   41
9. Asset Protection Is A Sliding Scale   45
10. Anatomy Of A Lawsuit   49
11. Ownership Forms You Must Avoid   59
12. Using Existing Laws To Protect Assets   65
13. Using Insurance As An Asset-Protector   67
14. Using Exempt Assets   71
15. Family Limited Partnerships And Limited Liability Companies   75
16. Using Trusts To Shield Wealth   83
17. Using International Planning To Protect Assets   91
18. How To Protect Your Home   101
19. Protecting Wealth From Divorce   109
20. How Personal Assets Should Be Owned   117

Part IV — Practice Planning   119

21. Avoiding the Financial Mistakes Of The Typical Physician Practice   121
22. Using Corporations In An Ideal Medical Practice Structure   123
23. Buy/Sell Agreements   127
24. Removing Headaches With PEOs   133
25. Protecting Your Accounts Receivable   137
26. Protecting Your Real Estate and Equipment   143

27. Using Captive Insurance Companies (CICs)   145

28. Advanced Asset Protection For Your Practice   151

29. The Perfect Corporate Structure   157

Part V — Tax Planning   161

30. Make Sure You Don't Foolishly Give Away More Than Necessary   163

31. Uncle Sam's Piece Of Your Pie   165

32. Is Your Tax Advisor Helping Or Hurting You?   169

33. Retirement Plans   173

34. How To Borrow Your Children's Lower Tax Rates   175

35. Deducting Long Term Care Insurance   179

36. Using Charitable Giving To Reduce Income Taxes   183

37. 529 Plans   189

38. Income In Respect Of Decedent (IRD)   195

39. Tax Benefits of Captive Insurance Companies   197

40. Tax Strategies to AVOID   199

Part VI — Retirement   203

41. We Don't Know Where We're Going, But We All Want To Get There   205

42. Defined Contribution Plans   207

43. Defined Benefit Plans   211

44. Variable Annuities   215

45. Life Insurance As A Retirement Tool   217

46. Don't Run Out Of Money (Or Pay Too Much Tax) In Retirement   221

47. Avoiding the 50%–70% Tax On Retirement Plan Balances   225

48. Don't Let Medical Conditions Ruin Your Retirement   227

Part VII — Investing   229

49. Your Money Doesn't Come With Instructions   231

50. Understanding Investing   233

51. Taxes, Inflation, And Your Investments   239

52. When (And How) Do I Get Back Into The Market?   241

53. Variable Annuities   245

54. Life Insurance As An Investment   249

55. Have You Outgrown Mutual Funds?   251

Part VIII — Insurance Planning   257

   56. Avoid The Biggest Pitfall   259

   57. Life Insurance   261

   58. Pay Up, Self Insure, Quit Medicine, or Go Bare   267

   59. Disability Insurance   269

   60. Long Term Care Insurance   277

Part IX — Estate Planning   281

   61. Making Sure Family Assets Aren't Lost To Disinheritance, Courts Or The IRS   283

   62. The Truth About The Estate Tax Repeal   285

   63. Wills & Living Trusts   289

   64. The A-B Living Trust   295

   65. Avoiding Joint Ownership & Disinheritance Risk   299

   66. Double the Value of Your Life Insurance   303

   67. Family Limited Partnerships and Limited Liability Companies   309

   68. Why Your Pension, 401(k) Or IRA May Be A 70% Tax Trap   313

   69. Avoiding the 70% Retirement Plan Tax Trap   319

   70. "Free Insurance"   325

   71. Long Term Care Insurance For Estate Planning   329

   72. Charitable Estate Planning   333

   73. Keeping The Estate All In The Family   337

Part X — Implementing Your Wealth Protection Plan   339

   74. What Is The Wealth Protection Alliance?   341

   75. Working With The Wealth Protection Alliance   345

Appendices   347

   A. The Ten Commandments Of Offshore   349

   B. Fraudulent Transfer Laws   353

   C. Intestacy   359

   D. 2005 Tax Rate Schedule   363

   E. Asset Questionnaire   365

   F. Sample Employee Census For Retirement And Other Benefits Planning   373

   G. Scheduling a CME Seminar for Your Group, Association or Hospital   379

   H. Book Order Form   380

About the Authors

Christopher R. Jarvis has experience as an actuary, entrepreneur and financial planner. As an author, Chris has written four books, including *Wealth Protection: Build and Preserve Your Financial Fortress* (available at **www.mywealthprotection.com**) and over 100 articles and has been quoted in the *Wall Street Journal* and *Los Angeles Business Journal*. Mr. Jarvis has appeared on Bloomberg Television and over one hundred radio programs. Mr. Jarvis has addressed hundreds of medical associations and hospitals, including the AANS, ICS, AAPI, and Cedars Sinai. Chris attended the University of Rhode Island where he received an honor's degree in applied mathematics. He earned his Master's of Business Administration with a concentration in entrepreneurial studies and finance from the Anderson School at UCLA.

David B. Mandell is an asset protection and estate planning attorney who has offices in Florida, New York and California. David has written four books, including *Risk Management for the Practicing Physician*© (accredited for 6.25 hours of Category I Risk Management credits). David has been interviewed on Good Day, New York (Fox-TV in New York) and Bloomberg Television. David has delivered hundreds of seminars to physicians, most recently addressing the American Ophthalmology Association, the American Association of Neurological Surgeons, AAPI and more. David earned an honor's degree from Harvard University and a Master's in Business Administration from UCLA. David also earned his law degree from UCLA where he was awarded the American Jurisprudence Award for achievement in legal ethics.

Celia R. Clark is an attorney practicing in the areas of taxation and estate planning. Ms. Clark has served as an Adjunct Assistant Professor of Law at Benjamin N. Cardozo School of Law of Yeshiva University and is the Chair of the Planned Giving Council of the Arthritis Foundation (NY Chapter) and an active member of the American Cancer Society Planned Giving Committee. Ms. Clark was graduated from the Law School of the University of Chicago in 1979 and received her LL.M. (in Taxation) from New York University in 1988.

Glenn M. Terrones is an asset protection and estate planning attorney in California. Mr. Terrones has specific expertise working with physicians and franchise owners. He was a judicial extern for the 9th Circuit of Court of Appeals. Glenn has been the key legal speaker at the annual meeting of the International College of Surgeons and has been offered a position as an adjunct professor of law at West Coast University. Mr. Terrones graduated Cum Laude from the University of Pennsylvania with double major in English and Sociology. Glenn earned his law degree from the Boalt Hall School of Law at the University of California.

Acknowledgments

We would like to first thank our families for encouraging us to use our knowledge and energy to help others and for supporting our often time-consuming endeavors whole-heartedly. Thank you Dot, Ray, Jane, Charlie, Edgar, Christine.

We want to thank our business partners and staff for all of their outstanding work in supporting our writing and for helping clients when we were otherwise busy putting together this book and our other educational materials. Thank you Peter Hartman, Steve Corzan, Renee Cardriche, Karla Lopez, Christine Edwards, Todd Goldfarb, Tricia Psychas, Dale Edwards, David Wright, and Jenny Piper.

We also want to thank the professionals who were integral in the research and writing of this book and in the implementation of Wealth Protection Planning for hundreds of clients nationwide. Our sincerest thanks go out to our colleagues in the Wealth Protection Alliance:

Pramod Ahuja, Doug Austin, Bob Baker, Chuck Baldwin, Jim Bardash, Barbara Barton, John Baxa, George Becknell, David "Mike" Breedlove, Brian Breuel, Christopher Broyles, Phil Calhoun, Don Camphausen, John Cane, Greg Carroll, Steve Church, Bryan Church, Frank Cochran, Ryan Coker, Tom Collins, Rob Davenport, Tim Dempsey, Rich DiPasquale, Nancy Dreyer, Steve Dunbar, John Ellard, David Ernst, Chris Fay, Rao Garuda, Mike Halloran, Jeff Hamblen, Todd Harris, J. Thomas Hassell, John "David" Hebert, Larry Helmer, Ted Houghton, David House, Russell Jacobs, Jeff Jaskol, Mike Jensen, Ron Jenssen, Fred Johnson, Tom King, Paul Klass, Karen Kolling, Bill Lloyd, Peggy Lombardo, Armond Madirossians, Hugh McDonald, Tom Miller, Keith Mohn, Jeffrey Moormeier, William Muench, Jeff Nesseth, Kevin Perlberg, Bob Rever, Greg Rever, Dennis Sanchez, Steve Scammell, Lou Shapiro, Shaker Sherif, John Steiger, Ernie Stiba, Sandy Stokes, Brian Stump, Scott Syphers, Vance Syphers, Maureen Verduyn, Frank Wong, Rob Young.

Lastly, we want to thank our special friends who helped us build the WPA and develop strategies that help our clients, namely: Arnie Goldstein, Danny Wexler, Vito Lanuti, Alan Brown, Danielle Smith, Bob Sontheimer, Steve Hardee, Jonathan Woods, Jack Howell, Neil Finestone, Mike Jones, Stacy McCauley, Jim Carlin, Jerry Fisher, J.K. McAndrews, Mark Smallhouse, Michael Coulson, Chuck Kissee, George Gifford, Simon Kerruish, Kaushal Majmudar, Allie Miller, Larry Keller, Todd Soll, Kim Michel, Eric Cannon, John O'Connell, Ken Brill, Larry Jones, Josh Hazelwood, Jim Percy, Joe Strazzeri, Deb Hoag, John White, Richard Warner, The Foundation for the Advancement of Research in Medicine (FARM), Dr. Abel Torres, Charles Cleveland II, Daniel Simon, Todd Udall, Joe Zuccolotto.

Preface

WORK "ON" YOUR MEDICAL CAREER, NOT JUST "IN IT"

One of the authors of this book comes from a family of physicians — his brother is a young cardiologist, his father is a radiologist close to retirement, and his grandfather was a general practitioner from the 1930s to the 1970s.

The grandfather worked only for cash, except when he took food from patients who did not have money during the Great Depression. He made house calls and knew all his patients by name. He never uttered the words "managed care," "malpractice crisis," or "HCFA audit."

The father spent nearly 30 years in a lucrative radiology practice. He saw reimbursements *increase* for many years and enjoyed an over-funded pension. He took advantage of numerous tax laws during his career (now gone) that swelled his after-tax income beyond what he had ever expected to earn when he began his career in the 1960s. The idea of going bare for malpractice never occurred to him — premiums were reasonable and personal liability was never a major concern.

As you well know, "the business of medicine" has changed dramatically through these three generations. The young cardiologist now begins his career dealing with a medical malpractice crisis with skyrocketing insurance premiums and legal liability, increasing time demands for administration and paperwork, shrinking reimbursements, and increasing regulation. He thinks about terms like "practice buy-in," "malpractice premiums," and "debt repayment." He wonders if he'll ever reap the financial rewards his father did in medicine — or whether the landscape has just changed too much.

Where do you fit within these generations? Perhaps you are between the radiologist and the cardiologist — in the prime of your career or in its 2nd half. If so, the issues on your mind are likely "retirement" (if and when), "asset protection," "tax reduction," and even "partner buy-out." Certainly, it is a lot to consider.

Treat Your Practice Like a Business

Notice above we used the term "business of medicine." This was not by accident. In fact, we were quite purposeful. In using this book and the national network of consultants that help put it together, you must make a paradigm shift in your medical career. *You must see your practice like a business!*

While we mean no disrespect — medicine is truly a virtuous calling and your primary motivation to become a physician was likely an altruistic one — the hard reality is that there are myriad business issues that affect your practice and personal finances every day of your career. Unfortunately, the vast majority of physicians are completely unprepared for these issues. They suffer from lower incomes, personal legal liability, shorter and less comfortable retirements, acrimonious practice splits, severe financial stress and bankruptcy. As a result, some are forced to exit the practice of medicine.

It is no surprise that 99% of physicians do not properly handle the financial and business issues that affect their career. Why? Because they have had *absolutely no training* in these matters whatsoever. The typical physician may receive over 10 years of clinical training by the time medical school, residency and fellowship are completed. This is over 3600 days. How many days of training have they received on topics such as asset protection, compensation arrangements, taxation, investing, and retirement planning? Zero! How many days on malpractice insurance options, partner buy-outs, or disability protection? Zero! What about employee training, contracts and practice management? Zero!

With this complete lack of non-medical training, it is a wonder that any medical practice survives. Imagine how more economically efficient and less stressful practice would be if you had been properly trained in all of the above fields. How much better protected would your wealth be from lawsuits? How much more income would you bring home? How much smoother would your practice run? *Imagine.*

While we cannot attempt to change how the U.S. medical establishment trains its physicians (although we have often been asked to speak to medical schools and residency programs), we can make the following urgent recommendation:

> **Make today the first day of your self-imposed training program by dedicating time to become educated about the non-medical issues that affect your business and personal financial situation.**

As the subheading of this preface states, you must treat your practice like a business and learn the business and financial issues that are crucial to its success and to your reaching your financial goals. Spend a fraction of your time on these issues — perhaps one day per quarter or one afternoon per month — working ON your practice. For as long as you toil only as the medical worker, you will suffer from the stress and lower rewards that come to people who handle matters "half-way." Only when you step back and act like the CEO of your practice and your career can you hope to achieve the financial and lifestyle goals that you certainly deserve.

Envision Your Ideal Career in Medicine

When you chose to be a physician, you made a decision to rely on your medical practice to provide you with the things you value in life — free time, financial security, and low stress. Think back before medical practice, residency and medical school to your college days. What was your vision of your life as a successful physician? What was your vision when you were toiling in medical school or during all-night calls during residency or fellowship? Did you envision a career that was a pay-off for all the years of hard work and training?

Now, after considering what the ideal vision of your career looked like during different stages of your career, examine your present practice and personal financial situation. How close are you to this ideal vision? Do you think it could be improved? Is it as stress-free, lucrative, and secure as your ideal vision? Is it worth a small fraction of your time to work toward this ideal? The answers to these questions are obvious.

In the generation of the father radiologist earlier, the medical business environment was so easy that physicians could almost totally ignore the business and financial issues described above and achieve these life goals rather easily. Even if they made financial mistakes daily, it did not matter — they simply rode the wave of the financial profitability with minimal regulation. It was truly the "golden age" of medicine for U.S. physicians.

Today, however, nothing could be further from the truth. Like the cardiologist brother, you do not have that luxury. You must be as effective and efficient as possible if you are to enjoy the benefits of a "golden age" today. You must be a physician and a businessperson — or suffer the consequences of today's medical business environment.

Avoid the trap of inertia. Be confident enough to envision your ideal situation and use this book and the advisors who contributed to it to help you achieve it. You have worked hard *in medicine* to get to where you are today. Now, work *on (the business of) medicine* to take you where you want to go.

Be Practical, Not Political

Certainly, many physicians reading this book may get riled up to march on Washington and demand malpractice caps, tort reform, lower tax rates, and greater reimbursements. This may improve your present practice and financial situation, will it not? Whether legislative changes will have a significant impact on your personal situation or not is a matter of debate. Though this is not our area or expertise, we do know that changing laws takes time and you need to change your financial situation today.

We are financial and legal advisors to physicians, not policymakers or politicians. In this book, we will not discuss how the laws regarding non-economic damages in malpractice cases should be limited. We will neither opine on the fiscal policies of the malpractice insurers nor comment on Medicare reform. We will not discuss tax policy or medical education. These elements, and changes to them, are beyond your control as an individual doctor.

While rallying with your fellow physicians into a political group may be effective for the long-term, we will let other voices (like your local medical association) take up that cry.

Our focus here is to show you, in a real and practical way, what you can personally do to move your practice and medical career from point A (financially inefficient, high liability exposure, chaotic financial plan) to point B (efficient, asset-protected, organized for maximum financial success).

Begin a Path

Like any worthwhile endeavor, education is just the beginning of a process. For you, this means reading this book and digesting the general ideas before determining which of these strategies will make sense for your practice and personal situation. This is only the beginning — *education without action is fruitless.*

Like a patient who let the pills you prescribed sit in the medicine cabinet, if you do not implement what you read in this book, your situation will not improve. This book, then, is only the beginning.

When working on this book, an update on their *Doctor's Wealth Protection Guide©* of 1999, Chris Jarvis and David Mandell worked with a series of advisors from the Wealth Protection Alliance (WPA) — a national network of top financial advisors to physicians. These advisors not only have their own successful practices in 50 cities throughout the U.S., but they have also been have been trained by the authors in the areas of asset protection, tax planning, and advanced business issues that specifically impact medical practices.

For your planning, the next step after reading this book is to meet with one of the authors or with a member of the Wealth Protection Alliance to put the knowledge you have gained into action for you. This way, you can ensure that your practice and your life will be as close to your "ideal vision" as possible and you can enjoy your "golden age of medicine" in your career.

Introduction

⊰•—————•⊱

WHY WE WROTE THIS BOOK

Each year, we (the authors) give over 100 CME seminars. Invariably, we begin each talk with a lawyer joke and a brief case study. The lawyer joke usually lightens the mood and the case study illustrates the dangers of inadequate Wealth Protection Planning. As we start this book, we have decided to share our own families' experiences. We are not going to pull any punches or exaggerate in any way. We don't need to.

In fact, what happened to our families motivated us to go into the field of Wealth Protection Planning. To say it bluntly, we entered this field — and wrote this book — to help other families avoid the financial pain and emotional suffering that our very own families endured.

When you read this book, remember we are not only authors and well-known advisors, but we are also members of families who were deeply impacted by positive and negative Wealth Protection Planning. From our stories, you will see why Wealth Protection Planning is fundamental to the long-term security of every family, including yours. If, after you read the book, you are still left with a yearning for good lawyer jokes, attend one of our seminars and you'll be sure to get your fill.

Chris' Story

I must preface this story with the fact that my mother, Dorothy, is a very proud woman. She doesn't like people to know about her problems and rarely asks for assistance. Dorothy is also the kind of woman who cares deeply for everyone around her, has many friends, and will always sacrifice herself for the happiness of others. Her sense of caring won out over her sense of pride. When she heard about my new book, she asked me to use her story in an effort to help others help themselves. For this, I am grateful.

My stepfather Tom was a successful attorney. He came from a wonderful family and had a great sense of family values. More importantly, he loved my mother and treated her with the most respect and admiration I have ever witnessed in any relationship. He also treated his children and stepchildren very well and was extremely generous in sharing his success with all of us. He was a wonderful man, worthy of a relationship with my mother.

My mother's relationship with Tom was particularly rewarding for me because I had watched my mother struggle financially to take care of us (her three small children) for years. She tried so hard to give her children the perfect childhood. She worked multiple jobs to try and pay the bills, but never let us know how bad things were financially (Welfare supported us while my mother went back to school) or how much her divorce from our father hurt her emotionally. It wasn't until after I saw how happy Tom made her that I realized how stressed, frustrated and unhappy she was before she met him.

Like most children, especially one in high school who still idolizes his father, I didn't know how to react to a new stepfather. But, when Tom swept my mom off her feet and made her truly happy for the first time in over a decade, I couldn't do anything but embrace him. I was thankful that someone was able to make my mother as happy as she made everyone around her.

It seemed as if life was repaying my mother for all the sacrifices she had made. Not only was Tom the most loving and caring person she had ever met, but he also made a very good living. Instead of scraping to pay the mortgage on a small home, she and Tom bought their dream home in the suburbs — a beautiful English Tudor with a bedroom for each child and stepchild. They also bought a summer home and some rental real estate. They even had the ability to vacation twice per year and take the children on some of their trips. I bet Mom felt like she was Cinderella and her life was forever changed for the better.

Unfortunately, midnight approached and the ball was ending. Only two years after marriage, Tom was rushed to the hospital with internal bleeding. I was away at college and my mother called me to tell me things were OK and that Tom would be in the hospital for a week or two for some tests. Like any obedient child, I disregarded my mother's wishes and rushed home. When I arrived, I was relieved to find Tom in good spirits and alert. He told me to go back to school and take my exams. He said he'd see me at Christmas.

I returned to school focused to finish my first semester at The University of Rhode Island. On the night before my first exam, I received a phone call. It was my mother. Tom had some complications and had just passed away at the age of 41. Mom said that she would be fine and that I should just stay at school. I left school and drove home immediately. This would be the worst Christmas of our lives.

As you would expect, the emotional healing process took a very long time. Unfortunately, that would not be the only pain. Because Tom had property in numerous states, the probating of his will took almost two years. During that time, my mother was unable to sell the properties to interested buyers and had to use the modest insurance proceeds to pay bills and the 11% interest rate mortgage on their dream house. This was because Tom's co-investors were neither interested in selling nor capable of buying out my mother and there was no buy-sell agreement in place to protect the surviving family (my mother) in the event of a premature death or disability (like Tom's). To make matters even worse, Tom and Dot were in the process of buying more life insurance when he went into the hospital. The papers were on the dining room table to be signed when Tom went into the hospital.

To make a long story short, because of their failure to plan for the worst, within 5 years of Tom's death, the high mortgage payments on all the property and the subsequent real estate downturn destroyed Mom. She couldn't make the payments anymore and couldn't find a buyer either. The impact of the recession on New England in the late 80's was severe. Even though interest rates were then approximately 30% less than what she was paying, the banks denied her refinancing because she did not "qualify" for that loan amount based on her income.

In the end, Mom lost her house and all of her property and was forced to file for bankruptcy. This meant she had to leave her dream home, move to an apartment, and ask her boss to cosign on the rental agreement. Now, her pride, as well as her heart and pocketbook, had been damaged by the tragic loss of her husband.

Even though Tom was a successful attorney who had an estate planning attorney in his own law firm, he hadn't done the necessary planning. Why? He didn't think he would die and probably hadn't thought about the financial repercussions of the worst-case scenario. Though there is nothing we could have done to prevent Tom's passing, a few basic planning ideas could have saved Mom's pocketbook and pride.

David's Story

My Uncle Steve is very close to my immediate family. Uncle Steve made it a point to participate in the lives of all his children and nephews. In fact, I can't remember any of my basketball games or water polo matches when he wasn't in the stands cheering.

Steve is a physician who also was a real estate investor. Back in the late 1980's, he was involved with a residential condominium project outside of Hartford, Connecticut. As part of the deal with the primary bank, Steve had to personally guarantee a $2.5 million loan. $2.5 million was more than twice Steve's entire net worth and he had never signed that large of a guarantee before. Nevertheless, Steve, like many physicians and entrepreneurs, had supreme confidence that his project would sell quickly and that the loan would be paid on time without a problem.

Despite his confidence, my Aunt Karen had reservations from the outset. While Steve slept soundly, Karen always fretted about the debt. In her mind, it hung like a dark cloud over their financial security.

Unfortunately for Karen, her worst fears came to reality. It seemed that just when the construction crew broke ground on Steve's project, the economy began to sour in New England. By the time the construction was complete and the condos were to be sold, the local real estate market was dead. Buyers were few and far between. Even though Steve and his team had brought the project in on time and within budget, the turn in the economy was too powerful to overcome. Sales were much too slow to cover the loan payments to the bank, so with every additional week, the debt continued to build. By the time the last condo was sold, the loan had been called. Steve owed over $1 million personally to the bank. It looked as though the same problem that devastated Chris' family was about to hurt mine.

By this time, the stress on Karen was taking its toll. She had trouble thinking of anything but their financial problems. She grew depressed and even developed a nervous habit with her hands as a result of the stress. Our family tried to be positive and comforting, but there was little we could really do. Even Steve, the eternal optimist, couldn't imagine a positive solution. As close family members, we saw the fighting and increasing marital stress. We also knew their ultimate fear: that they might lose everything in bankruptcy.

Fortunately, my family's story ended more positively than Chris's. Before moving forward with any negotiation with the bank or with the bankruptcy process, Karen and Steve went to see an asset protection attorney. Incidentally, this is the same attorney with whom Chris and I have worked on many cases.

The attorney advised them to follow a detailed plan which involved, among other tactics: 1) paying the loan sporadically with small payments in an effort to buy time, 2) establishing and funding a pension for Steve and the two employees of his company, and 3) moving to Florida where they would eventually file for bankruptcy protection (the move, by the way, wasn't so dramatic in their case, as they were spending much of the winter in Florida anyway).

Karen and Steve followed the advisor's plan to a "T." While enduring the bank's pressure to pay was certainly stressful and moving to Florida was a sacrifice, their plan proved to be successful. When their bankruptcy hearing took place some two years later, the bank in Connecticut did not even participate. The bank had written off the loan and taken it off their books. In fact, Steve's particular loan officer was no longer with the bank.

Following their Wealth Protection advisor's plan, Karen and Steve were able to shield the lion's share of their savings, paying out only $30,000 to creditors and protecting nearly $1 million. Most importantly, Karen and Steve were able to put this one major wealth threat behind them and preserve what they had worked so hard to build. I can happily report that their family finances and marriage are now more secure than ever, although the lingering effects of their ordeal is still evident to those who know and love them.

From our two different stories, you should have learned two things: 1) Wealth Protection solutions can turn a potentially devastating bankruptcy into a minor loss; and 2) Lack of advanced planning can cause unnecessary financial and emotional stress. Why did Dorothy lose so much more than Karen and Steve? The tragedy of Tom's death was an event that could neither be reversed nor delayed while strategies could be put into place for Dorothy. Karen and Steve were luckier, as their debt problems could be prolonged while their planning took hold. The ability to do some Wealth Protection Planning was truly the difference.

Even though Karen and Steve kept their wealth, their situation took its toll on them emotionally. If they had implemented Wealth Protection Planning in advance, however, they would have been reassured that their wealth would be safe despite the bank loan. This would have significantly reduced the stress on Karen and her marriage. How much do you think Karen would have paid to have avoided those three long years of stress?

Is Your Family Like Ours?

Do our stories seem familiar to you? Could you see the lack of prior-planning hurting your family like it did Dorothy? Would you know where to turn to if you were in a situation like Karen and Steve's? These are the two situations that affected our families directly. In our law and financial planning practices, we have helped literally thousands of clients avoid many different "wealth threats." If you can't identify with Dorothy, Karen or Steve, maybe you can identify better with one of these people:

- Dr. Bill loses what he thought was a frivolous lawsuit and had to come up with $2,000,000 in damages.

- A sexual harassment lawsuit against one of Tim's partners costs the practice its equipment, real estate and accounts receivable (over $1 million).

- Larry and Wendy pay over $100,000 per YEAR in income taxes that could be avoided with conservative planning.

- Dave fell off a ladder painting his house, hurt his back and couldn't work for over three years. As a result, Dave and his wife had to sell their newly-painted dream house because $10,000 per month of disability income insurance wouldn't support them and their sizeable house payment.

- Sunil does all the right things and happily retires at the age of 56. Two years later, his mother in law develops advanced Alzheimer's, does not have long term care insurance, and has to come live with his family.

- Jim runs a successful practice but lives frugally while he sees owners of similar practices enjoying much better lifestyles.

- Mike and Shelley now have children and have no idea what legal documents or insurance products are right for them.

- Daniel and Andrea's son just got accepted to an Ivy League school but they can't afford to send him.

- Jim and Janine are happy for their daughter with her upcoming wedding, but they don't want their sizable inheritance lost if she ever gets divorced.

If any of these situations are of concern to you, then Wealth Protection Planning (and reading this book) will help you considerably. That's because, in this book, we will show you solutions to all of the scenarios above. You'll learn how Dr. Bill could have shielded his $2 million from that lawsuit. You'll also see how Larry and Wendy can reduce their income tax bill by over $100,000 (or more) per year. From Dave's disability situation to Jim and Janine's divorce concerns, comprehensive Wealth Protection Planning addresses them all.

PART ONE

UNDERSTANDING WHAT THIS BOOK CAN DO FOR YOU

1

WHY THIS BOOK SHOULD COST $10,000

*This book allows you access to top advisors' secrets and strategies —
and have them tailored to **your situation***

Imagine for a moment that you are not reading this book. Instead, you are opening the door of a ritzy professional office in an impressive New York City corporate center. When you open the door, you are greeted by a receptionist who asks you to sit in the waiting area while she offers you a morning cup of coffee and explains what will happen today.

First, you will meet with asset protection, tax and estate planning attorneys from the top-rated law firms. They graduated from the nation's best schools, have written four books on areas of their practice, and have lectured to fellow attorneys and accountants in professional seminars.

In your meeting with the attorneys, they will take over an hour to ask you questions about your goals in the areas of asset protection, tax, and estate planning. They will also ask you about the planning you have already done with other attorneys or accountants. Once the questions are answered, they will give you an overview of the types of strategies and tools which might make sense in your legal plan. They will even give you articles and executive summaries on these solutions, so you can review them later.

Next, you will break for 15 minutes and enter another office where, for another two hours, a leading financial planner will evaluate your investments, insurance, retirement plan, educational funding and other financial issues. This financial planner, with an M.B.A. from a leading university and author of over 100 articles in his field, has just flown in from Los Angeles to meet with you.

In your two-hour meeting with the financial planner, he will ask you questions about your present financial situation. Your answers will help him provide you with recommendations for:

1. Structuring your practice for maximum efficiency and minimum liability,

2. Saving for retirement,

3. Reducing income taxes,

4. Protecting your family from premature death or disability,

5. Saving for college education costs,

6. Saving for long term care costs for you and for your parents,

7. Using charitable gifts to benefit your family, and

8. Maximizing the estate you leave your heirs.

These recommendations will be appropriate if you are starting practice or if you are already ten years into your retirement. Like your meeting with the attorneys, the financial planner will give you materials to read so you can review them later and discuss them with your family members or advisors.

After this meeting, you will break for lunch. Meanwhile, the attorneys and financial planner will be discussing your case, coordinating their evaluations and recommendations into one cohesive Wealth Protection Plan.

When you return from lunch, you will meet with all four advisors who will not only explain their coordinated Wealth Protection Plan for you but they will also provide you this plan in the form of a clear, comprehensive write-up which you can then evaluate at your leisure.

What would you expect to pay for this kind of tailored Wealth Protection advice from leading professionals? It's a good bet that the figure you would choose would be much closer to $10,000 than to the $50 that you paid for this book. Yet, the detailed tailored analysis of your plan from a coordinated legal-financial perspective is precisely what this book will provide you if you complete the Risk Factor Analysis (RFA) and follow its results (we'll discuss this more in the next chapter).

This Book Will Transport You to Our Offices

Through this book, we have attempted to deliver to you the entire process described above, without the lunch break or morning coffee. In fact, our goal is to make you feel like you are sitting right in our offices where we ask you the same questions and give you the same detailed advice that we will in these chapters.

As we explained in our introduction, we feel strongly that families and individuals need to protect their wealth in order to avoid the problems our own families experienced. That is exactly what we do every day in our professional practices, in situations like what we have just described — meeting with clients, analyzing their risks, and presenting a coordinated Wealth Protection Plan to be executed.

When we set out to write this book, we wanted to re-create to as great a degree as possible the advisory experience we have with our clients in our own offices. This has been a challenging, but successful, task. It is only because we have worked so closely together on so many clients (spending thousands of hours coordinating our planning) and written so many pieces together (over 250 published articles) that we have been able to accomplish this. The result of our hard work is a book that can serve as a theoretical educational tool AND as a practical guide to helping you create YOUR Wealth Protection Plan.

Of course, we welcome new clients in our practices and would like to meet with you to help you achieve your Wealth Protection goals. However, this is not always possible. This book can serve as a substitute for meeting with us personally, at least initially. Also, you can use the book to help you to interact with the local Wealth Protection Alliance advisor in your area. As we noted in the Preface, we worked with a series of advisors from the Wealth Protection Alliance (WPA) in creating this book. The Alliance is a national network of top financial advisors to physicians. These advisors not only have their own successful practices in 50 cities throughout the U.S., but they have also been trained by us in the areas of asset protection, tax planning, and advanced business issues that specifically relate to medical practices. When working with the local advisor — either in conjunction with us or exclusively — you will be able to use this book as a common reference guide while creating your Wealth Protection Plan.

You Need Wealth Protection Planning

As you read the last few paragraphs, you may have thought, "Sure, this book sounds like a good deal...but I don't think I need this type of planning. In my case, I don't think I'd get much out of the meeting with the local WPA advisor anyway."

In our practices, we have assisted clients as varied as our entire population — from extremely wealthy families to individuals just starting their careers; from physicians and business owners to employees of Fortune 1000 companies, from high profile celebrities to anonymous farmers. Moreover, our practices address goals from estate planning (like Dorothy and Tom whom we discussed in the Introduction) and asset protection (Karen & Steve also from the Introduction) to tax reduction, from retirement planning to benefits packaging and more. From this vast and varying experience, we can make this bold statement:

> **There is not a single doctor in the United States — regardless of age, particular circumstance, specialty or level of wealth — who would not benefit from additional Wealth Protection Planning.**

Why can we make such a bold and sweeping statement? How can we be so certain that you need Wealth Protection Planning when we haven't had the opportunity to meet with you in our offices? We can be so bold because of the one principle we have each learned in our practices:

Every doctor wants to build greater wealth, preserve existing wealth — or both!

Does this axiom apply to you? Don't you want to build more wealth than you have today so you can enjoy it retirement, leave it your family, or give it to a worthy cause? If not, don't you at least want to preserve what you have already built so it isn't eroded by taxes, investment downturns or lawsuits? If either of these goals seems worthy, then Wealth Protection Planning should appeal to you.

Perhaps you think you've already done this planning, that your advisors have already put you in the right position in terms of Wealth Protection.

We think this is highly unlikely. Let's discuss why.

Your Advisors Have Not Done Enough

Again, this is a bold statement we are making about your present advisors...and we haven't even met them (or you) yet. "What is our basis for making this statement?" We will give you three reasons.

1. Most people's advisors do a poor job and they don't even know it.

You may feel that your present advisors are very competent, if not excellent. How can you tell? By their education? The size of their firm? Their reputation? Certainly, these are good places to begin screening an advisor, but they really don't tell you how he is doing for you once he is hired. How can you tell whether or not that trust you purchased will achieve the tax benefits it was designed to deliver? How can you evaluate whether this insurance product was really the best one for your situation? How can you tell if you paid too much in taxes this year because you neglected possible tax-saving strategies in your business? Often, there is no way for the client to truly evaluate any of these issues effectively. A new client of David and Celia's law firm recently discovered this costly lesson, although the ending was a happy one.

> **CASE STUDY:** *David's Client: Real Estate Developer*
>
> A few years ago, David's law firm was retained to perform a self-imposed tax audit on a client. The client, an extremely successful businessman and real estate developer, was concerned when one of his business colleagues was found liable for back taxes and penalties because of mistakes by his accounting firm. Nervous that he might become an IRS target soon, David's client hired his law firm to do an audit of his income taxes for the past 5 years, both personally and for his various businesses. What David and his tax partners found was shocking.
>
> Even though this client had used 4 different accounting firms for his various returns (including a well-known national 500+ person firm), the taxes he had paid were far from what he owed. Luckily for him, it was an overpayment. While, at the time this goes to press, we do not know what the final numbers will be, we can write confidently that this client will deserve a refund of AT LEAST $5 million.

> That is correct. Because of the self-imposed audit which David's law firm oversaw, the client will file for a seven-figure refund from the IRS and state tax agency. Lucky for the client, he was concerned enough about poor tax advice to spend the money to hire David's firm to perform the audit. He did so only because he was concerned that the IRS would find a substantial underpayment. Never did he think his returns, prepared by a team of prestigious accounting firms, would prove to be putting millions of dollars in the IRS' pockets unnecessarily. That is, however, exactly what had been happening for the past 5 years.

The key question from this case is the following one: "How many of us would spend thousands of dollars (or hundreds of thousands in this case) in a self-imposed audit, just to see if our advisors had missed something?" Not many. Yet, if we aren't willing to have our professional's work reviewed by third parties, how can we ever know how well our interests are being served?

2. Even our society's wealthiest, most prominent families get poor advice.

If our society's leaders and prominent families can be caught in the trap of poor planning, can't any of us? Let's examine one startling example:

> **CASE STUDY:** *Elvis' family lost over $8 million because of poor legal advice*
> Elvis Presley, one of the most famous celebrities of the 20th century, was a person whom you would think would have top legal talent advising his family on estate planning. The Presleys lost over two-thirds of their net worth to estate taxes and probate fees when Elvis died. All costs could have been avoided with the proper planning. In this way, poor planning cost Elvis' family over 65% of their net worth. If this doesn't have Elvis singing blues from his grave, then we don't know what would.

3. Even with top professionals, advice is rarely coordinated into one plan.

In the next chapter, you'll learn why proper Wealth Protection Planning must be implemented by professionals from different disciplines — from law, tax, finance, insurance, and others. You will also be exposed to a key diagnostic question which always shows how well an individual or family has their planning coordinated. The question is this: "Do your accountant, lawyer, insurance advisor, broker, and financial planner all meet together at least once annually to review your particular situation?"

If you answer "no" to this question, then our first two points are moot. In other words, even if your existing advisors are excellent in their own fields, your disjointed plan is still lacking. If this is so, you need Wealth Protection Planning, if for no other reason than to coordinate your existing planning and fill in the gaps where the lack of coordination has left holes.

Throughout the introduction and this chapter, we have used the term "Wealth Protection Planning." From our own family stories in the introduction and the various references here, you may have a sense of what we mean by this term. However, if you are going to get the maximum benefit from this book, it is important that you have a specific knowledge of what Wealth Protection really means. Let's examine this in the next chapter.

2

WHAT IS "WEALTH PROTECTION PLANNING"?

Key Concepts Essential To Understanding Your Plan

Before we begin addressing your Wealth Protection Planning needs, it is crucial that you understand exactly what Wealth Protection Planning is. Without a complete understanding of the field of Wealth Protection Planning, it is nearly impossible to oversee your own wealth in an effective way for the long term. We have put together a working definition that will serve you throughout the book and in your personal planning:

> **Wealth Protection Planning is a multi-disciplinary process of shielding your wealth from all internal and external threats.**

While we have a fairly short definition, there is more here than meets the eye. In fact, there are five distinct concepts in this definition that are important for you to grasp before continuing the book or beginning your individual Wealth Protection Planning. After you truly understanding what WPP is, you will have a greater appreciation for the value of this book to your overall financial situation.

Concept #1: Multi-Disciplinary

Building and protecting your "wealth health" is like maintaining your physical health — you need to draw upon the knowledge of many specialists with the oversight of a generalist. Even though you are a physician, you are still a patient at times. During your lifetime, you will undoubtedly spend more time with your primary physician than with any other doctor. However, the average person interacts directly with at least five other specialists and possibly indirectly with dozens more.

As a young child, you may have developed allergies and saw an allergist, broken a bone and saw an orthopedic specialist or become concerned with your acne and consulted a dermatologist. You may have needed to "see" an opthalmologist (pardon the pun). You may have had your tonsils or appendix removed and had experience with a general surgeon and anesthesiologist. Females will eventually consult a gynecologist and, perhaps, an obstetrician. As most of us get older, we will unfortunately have reason to consult a urologist, cardiologist, oncologist, or other specialist.

Different challenges require distinct expertise and you will likely do the best you can to get the advice you need. In this way, your physical health demands a multi-disciplinary approach. This doesn't make us hypochondriacs — it makes us smart! We just want the best services available to us.

The same principle of using a multi-disciplinary approach should also apply to your financial "wealth health." Unfortunately, most of us are not as adamant about using this approach in our financial planning as we are for our healthcare. Believe us when we tell you that very few clients have addressed their "wealth health" with a combined legal-financial approach. Most prospective clients show the symptoms of a Wealth Protection Plan that lacks a multi-disciplinary interaction. Does yours? How would you answer these questions?

- Do you write a check for any of your life insurance policies?
- Do you have separate firms handling different portions of your investments (pensions, IRAs, brokerage accounts, cash value life insurance)?
- Did you have a lawyer friend (not a specialist) draft your will or any of your more complex estate planning or tax documents?
- Have you put off funding any of your trusts or other legal entities?
- Is there a chance that your accountant, lawyer, insurance advisor, broker and financial planner don't meet together at least once annually to review your particular situation?

If the answer to any of these questions is "YES," then you are a prime candidate for WPP and you will benefit greatly from this book.

One of the reasons we have been so successful in our practices is that we coordinate the legal planning (David, Glenn, Celia and their firms), the financial/insurance planning (Chris and his firm), and the accounting functions (typically, our contacts or the client's existing advisor) so that the client's plan works seamlessly. As an example, let's start with the first bullet point above.

If a client of ours needs life insurance, Chris will search among hundreds of products to find the right policy for the client. Meanwhile, Glenn or Celia will draft the irrevocable life insurance trust (ILIT) to make sure that it complies with the client's goals and David will review the language to make sure the family is afforded the maximum asset protection allowable. Then, Chris will make sure the trust purchases the policy to keep the proceeds out of the client's taxable estate and to avoid the IRS' 3-year "look back" restriction (discussed in Chapter 66). Finally, we will make sure the client's accountant is up to speed on what the tax filing responsibilities are. The benefit to the client from this simple transaction could be as much as $960,000 on a $2,00,000 insurance policy. Multi-disciplinary, experienced, and coordinated — that is the way superior Wealth Protection Planning should be conducted. Moreover, this is how the 50+ WPA firms and their local attorney and CPA affiliates serve the client.

Concept #2: Process

Wealth Protection Planning is not a one-time event. Rather, it is a process — one that continues from the beginning of one's earning years until at least one year after death. Just as life brings a constant flow of change, so is the challenge of Wealth Protection Planning a continuous one. Why is this so?

One important reason WPP is a continuous process is that your priorities will change during your lifetime. In the early stages of your career, before you have a family, wealth building may be the only focus of your plan. When you're only supporting yourself, you have little regard for an estate plan or insurance planning (life, long term care, etc). In the middle stages of your career, as a family enters the picture, a greater focus is shifted to providing for your family. At that time, creating a basic estate and insurance plan becomes important.

As your income increases and you build greater wealth, you begin to focus more on asset protection planning and tax reduction. Retirement planning will also be important. During retirement, most clients begin to focus on their estate planning — though you'll start earlier after reading this book.

WPP must continuously change in response to the dramatic events that always seem to invite themselves into our lives. A client once told us: "Life is what happens when you are making other plans." A birth of a child, a divorce, a windfall investment, a premature death of a spouse, a large inheritance, a failing business, a disabling disease or injury — these are just a few of a thousand events which will require a significant modification to a family's Wealth Protection Plan. In many cases, like the case of Tom's death, the events cannot be anticipated. However, advanced planning can reduce the potential loss and subsequent modifications to the plan can help put us "back on track" to reaching our goals. The case studies throughout the book will help illustrate this fact.

Concept #3: Shielding

The basic concept of "shielding" is simple — protecting what's yours. In this book, we will discuss how to protect your wealth from various risks. There are chapters dedicated to showing you how to "shield" assets from lawsuits, protect your income from disability and death and protect savings against the devastating costs of nursing home care. In these examples, "shielding" means protecting.

On the other hand, you may also think of "shielding" as "minimizing" or "reducing." When we discuss shielding investments from market risks or shielding income and wealth from taxes, "shielding" means reduction.

From our experiences, we have found that clients neglect the areas of tax reduction and investment downturns more than any other. Often, otherwise bright and capable advisors have no idea what options exist to help reduce taxes. While over 99% of the people we poll at our seminars would like to reduce their tax burden, fewer than 1% have heard of opportunities such as defined benefit plans, deducting long term care insurance premiums through your practice, financed insurance, private placement life insurance, or captive insurance companies. This book will fill that gap and introduce you to a whole new set of options to "shield" your wealth from unnecessary income and estate taxes.

Concept #4: Your Wealth

You have the best handle on your wealth, right? Not necessarily. We have had many clients walk into our offices with significant misconceptions about their wealth. Fortunately, in most cases, they vastly undervalue what they are really worth. When completing our asset questionnaire (in the appendix), clients often leave out certain bank accounts, fail to include a timeshare condo ("because it isn't worth anything yet"), or simply forget about various life insurance policies that were purchased years ago.

If we were to discuss your wealth in our offices, we would need to know about ALL of your assets. We would go down an exhaustive checklist to make sure we do not overlook anything. This is akin to your asking for a patient's medical history and lab work. Without this information, it's hard for you to do your job properly. We would also ask you to give us the present and projected values of your assets and liabilities. Why? Because your wealth may be increased or diminished by foreseeable events...and we will need to consider this in our planning. For example, your wealth may increase by a future inheritance from an elderly relative or decrease by a future debt that will come due. If so, it must be weighed in the plan. Further, you may have contingent assets, which may or may not come to fruition (like an option to purchase land if the value increases). Again, this must be considered.

When you complete the risk factor analysis (the RFA) in Chapter 5, you will see how exhaustive our list of questions is. We do not want you to leave out, forget, or ignore any asset, regardless of how small it may seem. If a Wealth Protection Plan is to be comprehensive, it must deal with ALL of your wealth.

Another important point we must make here regards the concept of "wealth." We know many of you, like thousands of people we speak to in seminars every year, may be turned off by the word "wealth." In fact, the same is true for many new clients we meet in our offices. Whether they be young or old, single or married, a certain percentage of people will say the same thing to us when we bring up the concept of Wealth Protection Planning: "Wealth?" they say, "Who's wealthy? We're got some assets, but we're not *wealthy*."

> **Wealth Protection Planning Mistake #1 — Assuming you are not "wealthy enough" for Wealth Protection Planning.**

Wealth Protection Planning is not just for the admittedly wealthy. This misconception couldn't be further from the truth. From the 24 year-old just beginning her career to the multigenerational family with hundreds of millions in assets, the variation among our clients is astounding. Nonetheless, each, in his or her own way, needs some degree of Wealth Protection Planning. Whether it means developing a better risk/reward ratio in an investment portfolio, saving for college costs, reducing income taxes, protecting assets from creditors, or simply creating an efficient estate plan, WPP impacts us all. Whether you are truly wealthy or just starting out, in a high income tax bracket or a low one, an individual or the head of a family, WPP in general — and this book in particular — has much to offer you. Do not get stuck in the "I am not wealthy enough" trap. It is the first financial landmine you must avoid.

Concept #5: All Internal & External Threats

The final concept in our definition of Wealth Protection Planning may be its most important. That is because you will only value the importance of planning if you truly understand what we are planning against...those internal and external wealth threats. Before you opened this book, or read its cover, you likely had in mind certain "concerns" about your wealth (you may not have verbalized them as "threats"). If you are like most of our clients, income taxes or investment downturns may have been "top of mind." Perhaps you had others, like estate planning or college funding, as well.

Regardless of what your specific "top of mind" threats were, it is imperative that you go beyond this initial gut feeling and realize ALL of the threats that could seriously jeopardize your wealth. It may turn out, in fact, that the threat that eventually does the most damage to your wealth is one that now seems insignificant. This is all the more reason why this factor is so crucial — *systematically recognizing all of the threats to your wealth is actually the first step in protecting it*. In the arena of Wealth Protection Planning, ignorance is not bliss. It is foolish.

> **Wealth Protection Planning Mistake #2 — Ignoring Your Wealth Threats.**

While it will take time and money to learn about and protect against the threats that make your wealth vulnerable, this investment will reap great rewards. You've taken an important first step by buying this book...now take the time to read it, complete the RFA and implement the planning where you need it most. You and your family will truly benefit.

You may already be convinced that you need to dig deeper and investigate where your current plan is vulnerable. How do you know which wealth threats are lurking in your present plan? The answer to this question will depend on your job, family situation, level of wealth and a host of other factors. When you take the RFA and review the results, you will get a thorough sketch of the key threats that make your particular situation vulnerable. That is still a few short chapters away, though. Let's make sure you thoroughly understand the types of threats that exist before you continue.

In our analysis of a client's situation, we differentiate between "internal" and "external" wealth threats. The difference, essentially, is the source of the threat. Internal threats come from your own situation or that of your family, while external threats are created by outside forces. Let's examine a list of common internal and external threats now (we will generalize grossly here, as the RFA will elicit specific threats particular to your situation):

Internal Threats:

- Premature death or disability
- Need for nursing home care
- Divorce
- Mismanagement of investment funds (poor allocation, speculation, etc.)
- Lack of professional guidance
- Poor choice of advisors

External Threats:

- Downturns in the investment markets
- All types of taxes
- All types of lawsuits and claims
- College and other educational expenses
- Estate costs and administration fees
- Divorce, disability or death of a business partner/key financial source

Conclusion

Wealth Protection Planning involves a number of important concepts. While our simple definition required only two lines, it took us over five pages to give you more depth to the basic definition. At this point, you have developed an understanding of what WPP is, what our goals are for all Wealth Protection Plans, what information we need to analyze your risks, what types of expertise are required to create a plan, and what potential traps you may need to avoid. Armed with such knowledge, you are well-equipped to continue the book and move toward the diagnosis and analysis phase.

3

FINDING YOUR
PERSONAL ECONOMY

*To preserve and build wealth, you must
focus on **Your** Personal Economy*

It's *Your* Economy That Counts

As a result of the bull market of the 1990s, Americans became obsessed with the stock market and the nation's economic performance. CNBC, market updates, and "fed-watchers" have become a ubiquitous presence in our lives. Tracking the "health of the economy" is a daily soap opera and the "experts" on talk radio and TV are household names. According to experts, the ups and downs of the market create a "wealth effect" on how positively or negatively we feel about our own economic status. If the market is up, we feel wealthy (as in 1999). If the market is down (as in 2000), we feel poor. Are you susceptible to this phenomenon?

Here's a quick test: Assume CNBC is reporting the following stories:

1. Experts fear the Economy is sliding into a recession;

2. The DOW dropped by 20%;

3. The NASDAQ closed down 300 points;

4. Alan Greenspan appeared on Capitol Hill and announced another change in the "prime" rate.

At the same time:

1. A little-known change in the tax law eliminates a large deduction your business had been taking;

2. Your mother was just diagnosed with Alzheimer's and there is little savings and no long term care coverage to pay future medical bills;

3. Your accountant has informed you that you failed to heed his advice about taxes on retirement plan distributions;

4. A successful lawsuit against a partner or employee exceeds coverage limits and your practice loses its equipment, real estate, or entire accounts receivable!

Which events are REALLY more important to your personal financial situation?

Of course, the second set of events is significantly more important to your overall "wealth health" than the first set. While this may seem obvious, you would be amazed by the number of clients who disregard this simple realization. Millions of us, in fact, behave as if the overall market news is a greater factor in our personal finances than details of our own lives! Many of us succumb to the uneasiness surrounding the volatility of the market, which, in turn, makes us feel powerless to change our own Wealth Protection situation. This can become a vicious cycle where all planning is avoided.

We have now come to…

> **Wealth Protection Planning Mistake #3: Focusing on the macro-economy of the nation rather paying proper attention to your personal economy.**

The Concept of the Personal Economy

To grasp the concept of your Personal Economy, it might help to think of your Personal Economy like you think of your body. You should realize that the choices you make have some impact, or potential impact, on your body. If you cross the street and don't look in both directions, you could severely hurt yourself. If you eat fast food for every meal, your body will look and feel terrible. If you exercise regularly, your body will respond in a positive manner. In general, you try to make decisions that will have a positive impact on your body — you are trying to maximize your physical health. We can't advise you to switch specialty, open a new practice, get married or have children. These are some of the most personal decisions you will make in your life. However, regardless of what choices you do make, you will still be left with the challenge of building and protecting your wealth — in other words, maximizing your Personal Economy. Continuing with this book is the next step in accomplishing this.

PART TWO

CUSTOMIZING THIS BOOK FOR
YOUR PRACTICE AND
YOUR FAMILY

4

THE RISK FACTOR ANALYSIS
Personalizing This Book to YOUR Situation

In Chapter 3, we explained the concept of *"Your Personal Economy."* You may be delighted to know that, along with this book, you also now have a *personal economy*. The $64,000 question is "How will this book help me protect and stimulate *my personal economy*?" This is what the next three chapters will do.

We have created a relatively brief questionnaire (50 questions) for you to complete. Now, once you write down your answers to these questions, you can proceed to the next chapter. We recommend writing down your answers on a separate piece of paper, not in the book, for three reasons:

1. You will want to use that piece of paper to write down the chapters we recommend you read as part of your *customized* book;

2. You will probably want to revise your customized Wealth Protection Plan in the future and your answers may change; and

3. You may let a friend borrow the book and you probably want to keep your answers private.

Every person who completes the RFA will receive a different set of recommendations and will be directed to read different chapters. Also, each time you complete the RFA (assuming your life has changed at least a little), you will be directed to different chapters and will hopefully learn something new. This is how this book differs from every other book on the market. Though we cover over 50 topics in 8 distinct sections (asset protection, practice, taxes, retirement, investments, insurance, estate planning and implementation of your plan), each person may only have to read about 20 to 30 topics to understand what changes need to be made to his/her plan.

Of course, if the RFA recommends that you read 35 to 40 sections, it doesn't mean that you were bad and the teacher has assigned you more homework. Rather, it means that you either have more assets to protect or have more facets of your complete Wealth Protection Plan to address. It may mean that you have been more successful and therefore need to understand more chapters if you intend to keep what you have acquired.

Please take a few minutes to complete this test and feel free to read the other chapters at your leisure. Also, feel free to go to **www.jarvisandmandell.com** for updated and more comprehensive information that we couldn't have possibly fit into one book. We hope you find the remainder of the book very informative and helpful.

5

RISK FACTOR ANALYSIS
The Questions

Please find a sheet of paper and a pen or a pencil. Then, read each question and write your answer on the sheet of paper. After you complete the analysis, we will help you self-grade it and determine which chapters of the book will be the most helpful to you in protecting your own personal wealth and stimulating your personal economy.

ASSET PROTECTION

1. Do you own any assets in your own name, jointly with your spouse or family members?

2. Do you think that your assets are protected in your state?

3. Do you think that your malpractice, homeowners, and other insurance policies will adequately protect you?

4. Do you own over $100,000 of cash values in life insurance or in combined account values of variable annuities, stocks, bonds and mutual funds?

5. Have you ever wondered what family limited partnerships (FLP) or limited liability companies (LLC) were and how they work?

6. Do you own any rental real estate?

7. Would you like to protect the assets you leave to your children and grandchildren from lawsuits and divorce?

8. Do you think that your living trust, family trust or A-B trust protect assets?

9. Are you or will you ever be married?

10. Do you have any interest in international planning, offshore planning? Do you own more than $500,000 in brokerage accounts and other non-real estate investments?

21

11. Would you like to protect more than $50,000 of equity in your home from lawsuits?

12. Would you like to know what a typical doctor's personal asset protection plan might look like or how the strategies in chapters 11 to 19 work?

PRACTICE PLANNING

13. Would you like to avoid employment headaches and reduce your overhead in the process?

14. Does your practice have accounts receivable, real estate or valuable equipment?

15. Does your practice have over $3,000,000 in gross revenue?

16. Are you or your partners concerned about Medicare fraud, HIPAA violations, billing or coding mistakes or employee lawsuits?

17. Is your practice looking to retain some of its medical malpractice risk?

18. Do the partners in your practice earn over $300,000 each?

19. Do you want to protect your personal assets from practice risks and practice assets from personal risks?

20. Would you like to know how every practice should be structured for maximum assest protection, tax efficiency, and corporate flexibility?

TAX PLANNING

21. Are you comfortable with the amount of taxes you pay?

22. Do you have a retirement plan or would you like to implement a retirement plan for yourself, your practice, or your group?

23. Do you have children or grandchildren or do you (or would you like to) provide financial support for anyone else's children or grandchildren?

24. Would you like to get the government to pay for part of your long term care costs and reduce your current tax liability at the same time?

25. Do you make over $1,000,000 per year or do many of the partners in your group make over $500,000 per year?

26. Are you worried that you might get audited, fined, or put in jail for implementing faulty tax-reduction schemes, scams and poorly designed plans?

RETIREMENT PLANNING

27. Do you like paying taxes on gains in investment accounts you plan to use for retirement?

28. Do you think that your pension will adequately support you in retirement?

29. Would you like some principal protection for your investments?

30. Do you own life insurance?

31. Are you concerned about running out of money in retirement or want guaranteed income in retirement for you, your parents, or your in-laws?

32. Are you about to retire?

33. Are you, your parents or your in-laws living off the interest of bonds or dividends from stocks in retirement?

34. Have you factored in spending up to $300 per DAY for you, your wife, each of your parents and each of your in-laws into your retirement plan?

35. Did you know that retirement plans can be taxed at 70% when you die?

INVESTMENT PLANNING

36. Have you taken money out of the market and want to know when and how to get back into the market?

37. Are you tired of paying taxes on your investments?

38. Do you have more than $500,000 to invest in the market?

INSURANCE PLANNING

39. Do you own life insurance?

40. Do you want to know what options you have to your existing medical malpractice insurance policy?

41. Would your family be able to get by if the breadwinner stopped making money?

42. Are you comfortable relying on your children to support you or having your entire estate decimated by long term care costs?

ESTATE PLANNING

43. Do you own any assets jointly OR do you have children from a previous marriage?

44. Do you own life insurance you want to leave to your children or want to protect your children from divorce or other lawsuit risks?

45. Do you expect your individual estate to someday be worth more than $2 million?

46. Do you have a pension or IRA you want to leave to your heirs?

47. Do you have an estate worth over $2 million but have little liquidity to pay for your estate plan?

48. Do you want to maximize your retirement and the inheritance you leave to your heirs?

49. Do you have a charitable inclination or would you consider leaving something to a charity if it helped reduce your taxes and helped your family?

Implementing Your Wealth Protection Plan

50. Do you want to take action and implement Wealth Protection Planning for your family?

6

RISK FACTOR ANALYSIS
Interpretation Of Your Answers

Over the next few pages, we will go over each of the risk factor analysis (RFA) questions from Chapter 5 and, based on your answers, recommend which parts of the book and which specific chapters may best help you reach your goals. Of course, you can go ahead and read the entire book, but your answers to the RFA will help customize this book for you!

You may have purchased this book because you wanted to learn about a few specific tools or strategies. After you read the recommended chapters, feel free to look in the table of contents for your areas of interest and peruse those chapters as well.

The recommendations in this section are generic and can never replace meetings with qualified experts in the areas of financial planning, asset protection, and tax, retirement, investment, and estate planning. We suggest meeting with a member of our national Wealth Protection Alliance to supplement the reading of the book and to help you more thoroughly analyze your particular situation and implement the necessary strategies.

As a first step, you should continue reading as the RFA is the most comprehensive financial planning tool you will find in any book on the market.

Enjoy!

ASSET PROTECTION

As doctors, you must be concerned with asset protection. The Preface and Introduction illustrated the problems of being a physician during the existing malpractice crisis. Do not develop a false sense of security because you have malpractice insurance or other insurances or because your state has recently enacted tort reform. In California, for example, there has been a cap on non-economic malpractice awards for almost 30 years and there are still regular jury awards of two, three and four million dollars. Because you likely only have $1,000,000 per incident coverage (and there are a number of risks that are NOT covered by insurance), you have to pay particular attention to this area of the book.

To begin, every doctor should begin by reading Chapters 7, 8, 9 and 10.

1. Do you own any assets in your own name, jointly with your spouse or family members?

If Yes, then you must read Chapter 11 to learn why these ownership forms are lawsuit traps.

2. Do you think that your assets are protected in your state?

If Yes, read Chapters 12 to learn what assets are, and are not, protected. You should also read Chapter 14.

3. Do you think that your malpractice, homeowners, and other insurance policies will adequately protect you?

If Yes, then you must read Chapter 13 to learn what insurance does and does not protect.

4. Do you own over $100,000 of cash values in life insurance or in combined account values of variable annuities, stocks, bonds and mutual funds?

If Yes, then read Chapters 14 and 15 to learn what alternatives you have to owning investments in your own name or jointly with a spouse, family member or friend.

5. Have you ever wondered what family limited partnerships (FLP) or limited liability companies (LLC) were and how they work?

If Yes, please read Chapter 15 to give yourself a better understanding of these very important asset protection tools.

6. Do you own any rental real estate?

If Yes, then please read Chapters 7, 15, 17, and 18.

7. Would you like to protect the assets you leave to your children and grandchildren from lawsuits and divorce?

If Yes, read Chapters 16, 19, and 73.

8. Do you think that your living trust, family trust or A-B trust protect assets?

If Yes, please read Chapters 16, 63, 64 and 65

9. Are you or will you ever be married?

If Yes or Maybe, read Chapters 19 and 73.

10. Do you have any interest in international planning, offshore planning, or do you own more than $500,000 in brokerage accounts and other non-real estate investments?

If Yes, then read Chapter 17 to learn what you can and cannot expect from legitimate international planning.

11. Would you like to protect more than $50,000 of equity in your home from lawsuits?

If Yes, please read Chapters 12 and 14 on exempt assets to understand state exemptions and then read Chapter 18 to learn how to protect your home.

12. Would you like to know what a typical doctor's personal asset protection plan might look like or how the strategies in Chapters 11 to 19 work?

If Yes, then Chapter 20 might give you a good summary of what most physicians do to successfully protect their personal assets.

PRACTICE PLANNING

If you are working as an employee of a hospital and expect to remain an employee (and not a partner or owner) of a practice for the rest of your career, you may not find the chapters associated with this Part of the book all that applicable to your situation.

If you run your own practice or want to run to run your own practice in the future, these may be some of the most important chapters you read.

We encourage every physician to read every chapter of Part IV Practice Planning. However, we provided a few questions to help direct those of you who are short on time and can't afford to read the nine short chapters.

To begin, every doctor should read Chapters 21, 22 and 23.

13. Would you like to avoid employment headaches and reduce your overhead in the process?

If Yes, read Chapter 24 on Professional Employer Organizations (PEOs) and how they can help medical practices substantially.

14. Does your practice have accounts receivable, real estate or valuable equipment?

If Yes, please read Chapters 25 and 26.

15. Does your practice have over $3,000,000 in gross revenue?

16. Are you or your partners concerned about Medicare fraud, HIPAA violations, billing or coding mistakes or employee lawsuits?

17. Is your practice looking to retain some of its medical malpractice risk?

18. Do the partners in your practice earn over $300,000 each?

If Yes to any of these four questions, you should familiarize yourself with Chapters 27 and 39.

19. Do you want to protect your personal assets from practice risks and practice assets from personal risks?

If Yes, you should read Chapter 28.

20. Would you like to know how every practice should be structured for maximum asst protection, tax efficiency, and corporate flexibility?

If Yes, please read Chapter 29.

TAX PLANNING

No matter what your specialty, you learned general medicine to give yourself a good base for your professional training. You were then forced to do rotations in every major specialty to give yourself a well rounded experience before your specialty training. Understanding your personal economy and embracing the idea of comprehensive Wealth Protection Planning should be analogous to general medicine training. Of your rotations, you should consider asset protection and tax planning the single most important foci for you. We encourage you to read all the chapters in this Part of the book (Chapters 30–40) as taxes impact every part of your practice and can claim 35% to 70% of your wealth. The following questions may help you prioritize the chapters for your situation.

Everyone needs to read Chapters 30, 31 and 32 to understand tax basics before moving forward.

21. Are you comfortable with the amount of taxes you pay?

No, this is not part of a psychiatric exam. If you are not, then you should really understand taxes and the strategies that may help legitimately reduce tax liabilities. Start with Chapters 30–32 then move on to Chapters 33–40.

22. Do you have a retirement plan or would you like to implement a retirement plan for yourself, your practice, or your group?

If Yes, then read Chapter 33 for a basic overview. Then, read Part VI (Chapters 41 to 48 to learn more about specific retirement plans and retirement plan alternatives. You should also read Chapter 38 so you understand the 70% tax trap on the back end of retirement plans. This is also covered in much greater detail in Chapters 68 and 69.

23. Do you have children or grandchildren or do you (or would you like to) provide financial support for anyone else's children or grandchildren?

If Yes, you should read Chapter 34 to see how you may be able to legally "borrow" their lower tax brackets. You should also read Chapter 37 to learn how to save for your children's college costs in the most tax efficient manner. You should read Chapters 19 and 73 to make sure your children don't lose their inheritance to a divorce.

24. Would you like to get the government to pay for part of your long term care costs and reduce your current tax liability at the same time?

If Yes, read Chapter 35 (and then read Chapters 48, 60, and 71 on long term care insurance).

25. Do you make over $1,000,000 per year or do all the partners in your group make over $500,000 per year?

If Yes, you might be able to reduce taxes by self-insuring some of the risks to your practice. Read Chapters 27 and 39 on captive insurance companies (CICs).

26. Are you worried that you might get audited, fined, or put in jail for implementing faulty tax-reduction schemes, scams and poorly designed plans?

You should be! We see dozens of new plans every year and many of them have very sizeable potholes. Please read Chapter 40 for a list of some of the more common strategies to avoid. This is by no means an exhaustive list as you should always consult tax professionals who are unaffiliated with a strategy or promoter before embarking on any endeavor that may have a tax consequence.

RETIREMENT PLANNING

Do you work to live or live to work? Most Americans work to live and have their eyes on the prize at the end of the rainbow — retirement! Despite this typically common goal, we see a great fluctuation in our clients' abilities to retire. Even among clients with the same income, their ability to retire early or with as much money as they had hoped is usually a function of the quality of their retirement plan. If you want to retire early, or retire wealthy, or retire happy, take the time to read these questions and the recommended chapters.

Everyone must read Chapters 41, 42 and 43.

27. Do you like paying taxes on gains in investment accounts you plan to use for retirement?

You should read Chapters 44, 45, 53 and 54.

28. Do you think that your pension will adequately support you in retirement?

If No, you should read Chapters 44, 45, 53 and 54.

29. Would you like some principal protection for your investments?

If Yes to either question above, you should read Chapters 44 and 53 to learn about variable annuities.

30. Do you own life insurance?

If Yes, you should read Chapter 54, 56, 57, and 66.

31. Are you concerned about running out of money in retirement or want guaranteed income in retirement for you, your parents, or your in-laws?

32. Are you about to retire?

33. Are you, your parents or your in-laws living off the interest of bonds or dividends from stocks in retirement?

If Yes to any of the three questions above, you should read Chapter 46.

34. Have you factored in spending up to $300 per DAY for you, your wife, each of your parents and each of your in-laws into your retirement plan?

If No, you need to read Chapters 35, 48, 60 and 71.

35. Did you know that retirement plans can be taxed at 70% when you die?

If No, you should read Chapter 47, 68 and 69.

INVESTMENT PLANNING

Most investors get into trouble because they get greedy, take too much risk, or just don't understand what options they have. Your answers to these questions will help us customize a reading list that will help you achieve your investing goals.

First of all, everyone should read Chapters 49, 50 and 51.

The required reading will explain what investment options exist, identify some pitfalls, and explain how taxes and inflation are commonly overlooked by investors.

36. Have you taken money out of the market and want to know when and how to get back into the market?

If Yes, please read Chapter 52 to learn how.

37. Are you tired of paying taxes on your investments?

If Yes, please read Chapters 44, 45, 53 and 54.

38. Do you have more than $500,000 to invest in the market?

If Yes, please read Chapters 54 and 55 to see alternatives to mutual funds.

INSURANCE PLANNING

This section requires few questions, as almost everyone needs to read the majority of Part VII, Insurance Planning, for three reasons:

1. You will die someday.

2. Either you or your spouse may become disabled at some point.

3. There is a good chance that you, your spouse, your parents, or your in-laws will need long-term care at some time.

For these reasons, everyone must read Chapters 56 through 60.

39. Do you own life insurance?

If Yes, read Chapters 54, 56 and 57 to better understand what you own.

40. Do you want to know what options you have to your existing medical malpractice insurance policy?

If Yes, please read Chapter 58.

41. Would your family be able to get by if the breadwinner stopped making money?

If No, read Chapter 59 on disability insurance.

42. Are you comfortable relying on your children to support you or having your entire estate decimated by long term care costs?

If No, read Chapters 35, 60 and 71.

ESTATE PLANNING

Every year billions, if not trillions, of dollars are paid unnecessarily in the form of estate taxes and probate fees. Don't let oversights, bad planning, or procrastination ruin your life or the lives of your heirs.

Everyone must read Chapters 61, 62, 63 and 64.

43. Do you own any assets jointly OR do you have children from a previous marriage?

If Yes, read Chapters 61 and 65.

44. Do you own life insurance you want to leave to your children or want to protect your children from divorce or other lawsuit risks?

If Yes, you should read Chapters 66 and 73.

45. Do you expect your individual estate to someday be worth more than $2 million?

If Yes, please read Chapters 67, 70 and 71.

46. Do you have a pension or IRA you want to leave to your heirs?

If Yes, please read Chapters 68 and 69 or pay up to 70% in taxes.

47. Do you have an estate worth over $2 million but have little liquidity to pay for your estate plan?

If Yes, please reach Chapter 70 on using other people's money to fund your estate plan.

48. Do you want to maximize your retirement and the inheritance you leave your heirs?

If Yes, please read Chapters 71, 72 and 73.

49. Do you have a charitable inclination or would you consider leaving something to a charity if it helped reduce your taxes and helped your family?

If Yes, please read Chapter 72.

Implementing Your Wealth Protection Plan

50. Do you want to take action and implement Wealth Protection Planning for your family?

If Yes, please read Chapters 74 and 75.

PART THREE

ASSET PROTECTION

7

WHY ASSET PROTECTION IS SO IMPORTANT TODAY

In past generations, physicians might have asked "Why do I need to shield myself against potential lawsuits? It doesn't seem important." We hope that by now, after seeing the explosion of litigation in this country, you won't take this view — especially because you were sent to this section by the RFA due to your asset protection risk. Nevertheless, in case you are still skeptical about the need for asset protection in your Wealth Protection plan, we want to introduce this section of the book by answering one key question:

"Why is asset protection so important to you?"

More Lawsuits than Ever Before

The number of civil lawsuits in this country has skyrocketed in the past few decades, with no sign of slowing. Tort filings rose 20% from 1987 to 2001 (source: Tillinghast). According to Jury Verdict Research, the likelihood of a verdict over $5 million grew from 2% in 1995 to 5% in 2001.

Your Odds of Becoming a Lawsuit Victim

If you believe one estimate, the odds are 1 in 4 that you will be sued this year. Statistically, *you have nearly a 100 percent chance of being hit with a lawsuit within the next four years.* Are you under 40? Expect at least 4 lawsuits against you in your career.

According to *Current Award Trends in Personal Injury*, the median jury award was an astonishing $6,246,000! They also reported that 42% of jury awards were for the plantiffs and 52% of jury awards from 1999 to 2002 were over the traditional $1 million policy limit. How can you afford not to protect yourself?

You Are More Likely to Be Sued Than to...

Be Injured in a Car Accident

Almost 20 million new lawsuits will be filed this year; yet, only 5.7 million injuries and deaths will result from car accidents. Thus, you are nearly four times as likely to be sued as to be injured or killed in a car accident. If you think going without car insurance is foolish, you are four times as foolish to ignore lawsuit protection.

Lose Your Home to Fire

The number of new civil lawsuits filed this year will be nearly 80 times the number of residential fires nationwide. You surely have insurance to protect your home against fire loss and even floods, but have you taken the simple steps to safeguard your home from lawsuits and creditors? We hope that after reading this book, you will.

Our point: Being sued is more likely than many of the losses we typically protect ourselves against. Protecting our valuable savings and possessions from lawsuits and other creditor problems is possible. More importantly, it need not be overly expensive, especially when the protection is established sooner rather than later. In most cases, lifetime asset protection planning fees are considerably less than annual insurance costs.

The Lawsuit Has Become a "Get Rich Quick" Scheme

Why are there so many more lawsuits today? It is because today a *lawsuit is a way to "get rich quick"* and not necessarily a method to achieve justice. We now believe that whenever something goes wrong, someone should pay. Unfortunately, juries routinely adopt this idea and often disregard the facts of the case or the laws controlling the case. Through emotion and bias, they give away large sums of money in the process...whether or not the defendant was at fault.

You read about these cases in your daily newspaper. A woman receives $2.6 million because her coffee was too hot; a homeowner pays thousands of dollars to a trespasser injured while burglarizing the homeowner's property. People see these same awards and ask, "Why not me?" They want to win the lawsuit lottery. Their first step is to spot a target and manufacture a reason to sue. It is only a matter of time until that target is you.

> **FACT: One Chicago law firm proudly announced to its many clients and prospects that it obtained the LARGEST VERDICT EVER FOR AN ARM AMPUTATION: $7.8 MILLION. [*U.S. News and World Report*, January 30, 1995].**

People Abuse the Legal System

Another factor adds to the lawsuit explosion: many people simply abuse the legal system for their own personal gain. This trend is so severe in California that the legislature passed the *Vexatious Litigant Act*, a law establishing a list of people who routinely abuse the legal system by filing too many frivolous lawsuits. Of course, these same individuals cannot be denied their "constitutional right" to sue. However they cannot file suits without attorneys or a judge's permission. This list is available to every lawyer in the state.

Who is on this list? The people on this list are those who, in the court's opinion, have repeatedly filed lawsuits lacking merit or have engaged in other frivolous and abusive tactics. Two awful examples:

1. One Los Angeles claimant filed over 200 lawsuits in seven years. Very few were successful.

2. A court clerk recommended certain individuals for this list. These individuals made the clerk a lawsuit target and the clerk was then sued 11 times in two years — unsuccessfully. The clerk's reaction: "I do not exaggerate when I say I am extremely frightened by these people." (*The Sacramento Bee*, November 26, 1995)

Enormous Awards for Negligible Damages

- An auditor wins over $2.5 million when fired from a $52,000 a year job after employed by the company for 2½ months.

- A college student is awarded $75,000 for a broken arm suffered at a friend's house.

- A physician practice gets sued for $2,000,000 for a sexual harassment suit between two employees and the doctor gets stuck with the bill!

- A mugger shot by the police wins $4.5 million from New York City claiming excessive force.

Such awards were once the exception but are now commonplace. Juries today routinely dole out millions of dollars — frequently even more than the plaintiff demands.

> **FACT:** In a study of over 23,000 Illinois jury trials, the Institute for Civil Justice found that the average punitive damages award increased, in inflation-adjusted dollars from $43,000 in 1965–1969 to $729,000 in 1980–1984. Those figures are even higher today!

The Ground Rules of Asset Protection: Fraudulent Transfer Laws

Now that you have seen why asset protection is so important today, you must understand the basic ground rules under which asset protection operates. Essentially, you must protect assets before any lawsuit or creditor claim arises. That is because, once a claim has arisen, the person suing you can always ask the court to undo any transfers you make to hinder his collection of the debt. The court can do this under what are called "fraudulent transfer" or "fraudulent conveyance" laws.

Think of asset protection planning as a vaccine, not a cure. Once a lawsuit or claim is threatened, many protective strategies can no longer be used — just as a vaccine is not effective once you are afflicted with a disease. Proper asset protection is always preventative planning. For more on fraudulent transfer laws, and how proper asset protection complies with these laws, see the Appendix.

Conclusion

At this point, we hope you realize a cold hard fact: in our litigious society, asset protection planning is an integral part of any Wealth Protection Plan. Welcome to life in the 21st Century America. In the following chapters, you'll learn the various tools and techniques you can implement to shield your wealth from lawsuits and other claims. However, before you learn how to protect your assets, we need to first dispel the myths about asset protection in the next chapter.

8

MYTHS ABOUT ASSET PROTECTION

One of the most important reasons we wrote this book is to dispel the myths that surround the field of asset protection. Every day, we speak to physicians who, because of poor advice or lack of counsel, harbor significant misconceptions of what asset protection means and how they can achieve the protection they desire.

Below is a list of common misconceptions harbored by most physicians. These common myths are dangerous because they seduce the doctor into a false sense of security so he fails to implement pro-active planning. Then, when a significant claim emerges, he is vulnerable in significant and dangerous ways.

Myth #1 — "My Corporation Protects Me"

Do not think that because you have a professional corporation or something similar (PA, PLLC), you are protected! This is what your corporation can and cannot do for you:

- Professional corporations will **NOT** protect you from malpractice. Physicians are always liable for their actions. There is no way to remove the personal liability you may have from your negligent actions as a doctor.

- Professional corporations will **NOT** protect you from the acts or omissions of anyone you supervise. The same risks and liability mentioned above exist here. All risks associated with medical care are potential liabilities for the associated physician(s). If you are on call or if you are a physician who supervises others, you may have much more liability than you realize. This is explained in great detail in *Risk Management for the Practicing Physician*© CME Monograph (6.25 hours of Category I CME Credit) and is available from Guardian Publishing at (800) 554-7233.

- Professional corporations will **NOT** protect your corporation's assets (accounts receivable, equipment, etc.) from other types of claims that arise from acts in the ordinary course of business. Unfortunately, negligence on the part of any physician, a claim for sexual harassment or wrongful termination, or even slip and falls at the place of business can all threaten the practice's assets themselves even when you are incorporated. As for personal assets, the P.C. will only protect the personal assets of the doctors who are not involved with the claim in any way. The P.C. will not protect personal assets from malpractice or sexual harassment actions.

Myth #2 — "My Assets Are Owned Jointly with My Spouse, So I'm OK"

Chances are that you are vulnerable. Most physicians own homes and other property in joint ownership, but this provides little asset protection. In community property states, if the asset is a community asset, it will be exposed to "community debts" regardless of how the asset is titled. This includes any debt that arose during marriage as a result of an act that helped the community. Certainly any claims out of the medical practice would be included, as well as car accidents and the like.

Even in non-community property states, joint property is typically at least 50% vulnerable to the claims against either spouse. Thus, in most states, at least 50% of such property will be vulnerable while all the other problems associated with joint property remain (see Chapter 11).

Myth #3 — "My Spouse Isn't a Doctor, So I'm OK"

One of the most common misconceptions about asset protection is that assets in your spouse's name can't be touched. We can't tell you how many people have come to us with their assets in the name of the non-physician spouse and assumed those assets were protected. The transfer is often reversible by the creditor because they can trace the proceeds from the debtor to the spouse. Ask yourself:

- Whose income was used to purchase the asset?
- Has the doctor used the asset at any time?
- Does the doctor have any control over the asset?
- Has the doctor benefited from "the spouse's assets" in any way?

If the answer is "yes" to any of these, then the doctor's creditor can be paid from these assets.

If you think holding assets in your spouse's or child's name will protect those assets, you are wrong. Please consider implementing the strategies discussed later (if you want to see which assets are protected by your state and federal statutes, please refer to Chapter 12).

Myth #4 — "I Am Insured, So I'm Covered"

While we strongly advocate insurance as your first line of defense, an insurance policy is 50 pages long for a reason. There are a variety of exclusions that most doctors never take the time to read, let alone understand. Even if you do have insurance and the policy does cover the risk in question, there are still risks of underinsurance, strict liability, and bankruptcy of the insurance company. In any of these cases, you could be left with the sole responsiblity for the loss. Insurer bankruptcy used to be a minor risk, but this is a growing concern for most physicians. Lastly, with losses that are covered within coverage limits, you still may see your future premiums skyrocket!

Myth #5 — "I Can Just Give it Away if I Get into Trouble"

Another common misconception is that you can just give away or transfer your assets if you ever get sued. If this were the case, you could just go about hiding assets when necessary. You wouldn't need an asset protection specialist; you would only need a shovel and some good map-making skills so you can find your buried treasure later.

There are laws against fraudulent transfers (or fraudulent conveyances). In a nutshell, if you make a transfer after the incident took place (whether you knew about it or not), the judge has the ability to rule it a fraudulent conveyance and order the asset to be returned to the transferor. The details of fraudulent transfer statutes are discussed further in the Appendix.

> NOTE: Though asset protection is most effective and least expensive when implemented before a claim arises, there are things you can do to protect yourself after a claim is made. If you have a problem and fear that you may lose a sizeable judgment, then we recommend you implement some type of planning ASAP. Typically, these last minute strategies are riskier (for success) and may be much more expensive than the highly successful strategies that can be implemented when there are no creditors lurking.

Myth #6 — "My Living Trust (or Family Trust) Provides Asset Protection"

There have been countless instances where clients have come to us with the impression that their revocable living trust provides asset protection. While you are alive, this is simply not true. Revocable trust assets are fully attachable by any creditor. In Chapters 16 and 66, you will read about Irrevocable Trusts and how they provide varying levels of asset protection for you and your heirs in addition to the estate planning benefits (Chapters 64 and 73). A living trust does provide asset protection when the first spouse dies with respect to the deceased spouse's share of the assets in the trust; it provides complete protection upon the death of both spouses so long as the trust assets are not distributed and remain in the trust. However, no matter how much your attorney charges, dying seems to be (in our opinion) too big a price to pay for asset protection planning.

Myth #7 — "Offshore Trusts Provide Income Tax Savings"

If you are a U.S. resident, you must disclose your worldwide income however and wherever situated. Even if the country in which your assets are located does not report to (or even like) the Internal Revenue Service, and even if the institution holding your assets does not send you a 'form' disclosing to you what you earned, you must disclose your taxable income to the IRS each year, no matter where it is earned, or where it is situated. See Chapter 17 for more on this.

Conclusion

Don't be concerned or alarmed if you believed any of these myths. Don't be disappointed if your perceived protection has just been proved inadequate. With these myths dispelled, you can now embark on "doing the right thing" and implementing legal and affordable asset protection. The next twelve chapters should be very helpful.

9

ASET PROTECTION
IS A SLIDING SCALE

The most common misconception that physicians have regarding asset protection — beyond those described in Chapter 8 — is that one's assets are either "protected" or "not protected." This "black or white" analysis is no more accurate in the field of asset protection than it is in the field of medicine. In fact, asset protection attorneys are very similar to physicians in how they approach any client/patient.

Like physicians, asset protection professionals will first try to get a client to avoid "bad habits." For a medical patient, bad habits might mean smoking, drinking too much or eating poorly. For a client of ours, bad habits might include owning property in his own name, owning it jointly with a spouse, or operating any medical practice with assets of the practice exposed (see Part IV of this book).

In fact, like a physician who judges the severity of a client's illness, asset protection specialists use a rating system to determine the protection or vulnerability of a client's particular asset. The scale runs from (-5) (totally vulnerable) to (+5) (superior protection).

Negative Numbers for "Non–Planning" or "Adverse Planning"

When most clients initially come to see us, their asset planning generally scores negatively. For personal assets, they typically own them jointly (-3) or in their individual name (-5). Both of these ownership forms provide little, if any, protection from outside lawsuits. Owning assets in many ways may have negative tax and estate planning consequences as well. As you learned in the previous chapter, these forms of ownership or having the spouse own the asset outright are not effective.

In terms of business assets, the worst way to operate a practice or business or to hold any assets would be in a general partnership (-5). Although using a professional corporation or other legal entity may provide some protection, it never protects against malpractice. Thus, owning business assets in the P.C. is extremely unwise (-3).

Before we implement any sophisticated asset protection planning, we want to move the client from a (-5) or (-3) to at least a neutral number. This means eliminating any of the "bad habits" named earlier. If you see yourself as a physician who has business assets exposed and owns personal assets in your name or jointly with a spouse, you should talk to an asset protection advisor immediately. You don't want to linger too long in the (-3) or worse category, as it is only a matter of time until you get "sick."

Basic Asset Protection

Using the sick patient analogy, if you see a patient with a particular condition or disease, you try to treat it. For us, we try to treat physicians to cure their lawsuit vulnerability. In this regard, we use particular structures to protect a physician's assets.

Keeping with the analogy, you would not recommend surgery for a patient if the patient were not sick enough to warrant surgery. As this relates to asset protection, an asset protection advisor may not recommend the most protective structure for a client who didn't need it. Perhaps, given that client's net worth and income, the cost of the most advanced structures may not be justified. In those instances, we may recommend the next best strategy — a slightly inferior but cost-effective alternative.

If you want solid asset protection but do not want to pay more for advanced tools, then we would recommend exempt assets — those automatically shielded under state or federal law (Chapters 12 and 18 explain in greater detail). Next, we might recommend debt shields where the proceeds of the loans are invested in exempt assets. With these two simple strategies, you can achieve +4 or +5 protection without incurring expensive legal bills. Beyond these strategies basic asset protection tools like family limited partnerships (FLPs) and limited liability companies (LLCs) should be used. Essentially, these tools will provide good asset protection against future lawsuits, allow you to maintain control of your assets, and may provide income and estate tax benefits in certain situations.

In essence, FLPs/LLCs will provide adequate asset protection and give you an asset protection score of (+2). Obviously, your asset protection plan is reliant upon proper drafting of the requisite documents, proper maintenance and respect for formalities, and proper ownership arrangements. If all these are in place, the physician can enjoy basic asset protection for a relatively low cost.

Ultimate Asset Protection: Advanced Strategies

For many physicians, a basic asset protection plan, which has some potential vulnerability, is not good enough. A (+2) asset protection score is not enough to give them the psychological comfort they want. Other clients may feel the extra expense of an advanced structure is worth it, especially when significant tax benefits may be achieved as well. For this reason, these clients use advanced structures to put themselves at a (+4) or (+5), the ultimate asset protection score. Like a physician giving the ultimate medicine or most effective surgical procedure, asset protection consultants rely on a number of tools to provide ultimate asset protection. As you'll learn in upcoming chapters, these advanced tools include:

Funding of Exempt Assets

Each state law has assets that are absolutely exempt from creditor claims. Federal law also exempts certain assets. We always recommend exempt assets as the preferred asset protection tool because excellent protection is achieved without legal expense or hassle. Because these assets are inherently protected by law, they enjoy (+4) to (+5) protection. A good example of how state laws can protect assets can be found in Texas and Florida where the homestead exemptions are unlimited for personal residences and the cash value in life insurance policies and annuities are completely protected. At the federal level, the law affords unlimited protection for ERISA-Qualified retirement plans that include at least one employee that is neither an owner nor a natural heir of an owner.

Enhanced Debt Shields

These strategies are ideal for protecting equity in real estate, especially the personal residence — where they would achieve a +4 or +5 rating. When structured properly, after-tax wealth can be built while protecting the real estate equity in a superior way. Typically, we use the debt shield in conjunction with an exempt asset. Chapters 18 and 26 offer some further explanation of debt shields.

International Limited Liability Companies

If implemented in the right jurisdictions, properly structured, and their assets are held offshore, foreign LLCs can be a (+4). US-based creditors will have so many procedural hurdles and expenses to overcome before they can institute proceedings in certain foreign jurisdictions, they often settle for pennies on the dollar in out-of-court settlements. See Chapter 17.

International Asset Protection Trusts

These are the elite tools of asset protection legal structures — the ultimate (+5). When created in jurisdictions where US judgments are not respected, and where procedural hurdles are toughest, these structures typically intimidate most US creditors. Most creditors and attorneys will give up rather than even try to attack these structures. (Both international strategies are discussed in Chapter 17.)

Captive Insurance Companies

Structured offshore or domestically, these tools can also reach the (+5) status. Such companies can provide superior asset protection for a medical practice and are extremely beneficial for tax planning as well. Chapter 27 is a good place to start. Chapter 39 adds helpful tax information.

What Kind of Patient Are You?

The most difficult question that arises in asset protection planning appears to be distinguishing those situations where asset protection is appropriate from those where it is not. Although this question may seem abstract in nature, the answer to this question appears to have compelling practical effects. The moral implications of creating an asset protection plan, including *who you are* and *what you have done*, may determine whether the plan ultimately succeeds or fails.

It must be understood that any judge or jury is likely to be influenced by moral considerations when determining whether or not to allow an asset protection structure to shield assets from a creditor. Much has been made recently of cases where the courts have ordered judgment debtors to assign assets over to their creditors in order to satisfy an outstanding judgment. Assignment can occur in a variety of ways, ranging from the partition of limited partnership interests to a forced sale of corporate assets. In one case, the judgment debtors were ordered to send their offshore assets back to the United States to satisfy a judgment. When the debtor refused to do so, the court held them in contempt and sent them to jail until they complied with the order to return the assets.

If there is one pattern or principle that can be gleaned from the line of decisions in this area, it may be this: "the worse the conduct resulting in the debt or judgment, the more aggressively the courts will try to undo your asset protection plan and assign or partition your ownership interests or assets." Hence, a person that has frauduently separated elderly people from their money is more likely to have his plan penetrated than is a person who lost a slip and fall case. Applied to physicians, this principle would render a physician who committed Medicare fraud far more vulnerable than one who had a malpractice judgment. Without question, who you are and what you have done are factors to consider when creating an asset protection plan.

Conclusion

Asset protection planning, like any sophisticated multi-disciplinary effort, is measured in degrees. Nothing in life is 100% certain (except perhaps death and taxes — both of which are discussed in other chapters). For asset protection planning, this adage holds true. In your asset protection plan, make sure you understand the cost and benefits of the various tools you employ as well as the type of asset protection client you are. It will not only help you protect the wealth you have already built, but it may assist you in building greater after-tax wealth for your retirement and beyond.

10

ANATOMY OF A LAWSUIT

The lawsuit is the most serious and common threat to your financial security. Now, you will learn about the extraordinary rights other people have to find out about your wealth and to seize it through a lawsuit. You will see how frustrating it is to defend against a lawsuit-spending so much time and money on lawyers that even if you win, you lose because of the emotional strain on you and your family and the lost income as a result of time spent out of the office.

Key Litigation Terms

Before reading on, you must review and understand some basic terms.

Civil Lawsuit: A lawsuit between private parties, *plaintiff* and *defendant*, usually for monetary compensation.

Award: The sum the plaintiff is entitled to from the defendant because of the lawsuit. Also called *recovery*.

Judgment: A court finding that determines the outcome of a civil lawsuit, usually declaring that a sum of money (the *award*) is owed.

Judgment Creditor: The person that is owed the money, the amount of which has been decided in court in the form of a judgment. This person "won" the lawsuit.

Judgment Debtor: The person who owes the judgment creditor the money. This person "lost" the lawsuit.

Economic Control: "Are You Worth Suing?"

Before anyone sues you, he and his attorney will make an economic analysis of their case against you. This analysis weighs the costs of suing you against the likelihood of success against you and the amount of probable recovery. In short, no one will sue you unless it is "worth it."

In order to determine whether or not you are worth suing, the plaintiff's counsel will make a thorough financial investigation of your assets and income. This is especially important for *contingency fee* lawyers in personal injury suits. Contingency fee lawyers dislike working on a case against a defendant who cannot pay a judgment. If the defendant cannot pay, the lawyer receives no fee.

How will the plaintiff's attorney investigate your ability to pay? By hiring private investigators to do an asset check and determine if you have sufficient assets to satisfy the desired recovery amount. With a social security number and a current telephone number or address, these private investigators can quickly and easily discover much of what you own and earn. Consider the following:

- Investigators check the county records for real estate you own. This information is a matter of public record and easily obtainable, especially in computerized record-keeping systems. They can learn the date of purchase, its value at that time, and the amount of loans and mortgages on the property. The investigator thus knows how much *equity* you have in your home, as well as any other real estate you have in that county.

- Your credit reports will also be examined. Through credit reporting agencies, investigators gain access to your reports and their valuable information, including your payment history and possibly the name of your bank. It may even include a financial statement revealing your assets and liabilities, if you have filled one out for the credit agency. Investigators can also trace your bank accounts, brokerage accounts, and just about any other type of account that bears your social security number.

From the investigator's findings, the plaintiff and his lawyer decide whether or not it makes economic sense to sue you. If you have the ability to pay a judgment, the lawyer will push forward. You will be served a summons and the lawsuit nightmare will begin…again!

CASE STUDY: *Rick's assets are found*

Rick, a dermatologist, was sued by a former medical assistant. He had been forced to discharge the assistant because his revenues were down after a competitor opened a clinic down the street. The former assistant brought an age discrimination claim against Rick, alleging that she was fired because of her age.

The medical assistant's lawyer hired an investigator. Within one week, the investigation revealed that Rick had about $500,000 of equity in his home, an investment property with another $250,000 of equity, and a money market account of $210,000. It is little wonder the lawyer decided to sue Rick.

The Lawsuit Process

Once a lawsuit is filed against you, your options are to settle (and pay) or defend. Defending a lawsuit is time-consuming, expensive, and emotionally draining. Defending a lawsuit will also subject you to the following burdens:

Pre-Judgment Remedies

Depending on the specific case and the laws of your state, a party suing you may be able to place a lien on your real estate, attach your personal property, or even seize your property before proving the case at trial! While these remedies are not widely known, lawyers throughout the country commonly use devices such as an Attachment, Injunction, Lis Pendens, Replevin, Mechanic's Lien, and Receivership.

Attachment: Allows the plaintiff to get the court to direct the sheriff to seize your property, whether in your or someone else's possession. While the plaintiff must show that she can expect to win the suit at trial, under state law, the plaintiff may ask for such a seizure without notice to you. New York, for example, allows attachments in certain cases and it can be granted before you even know you are being sued.

Injunction: A court order which directs action or prevents action. Again, although the plaintiff must comply with specific requirements, the preliminary injunction is often available before you are given notice of the lawsuit.

Lis Pendens: Also called a *notice of pendency*, it is a lien the plaintiff can file against real estate which you own in the county where the lawsuit occurs. This notice informs potential buyers or lenders that a lien may be coming as a result of a lawsuit. This makes the property virtually unmarketable.

A plaintiff can usually file the lien before you even realize you are being sued and the plaintiff need not ask the court for permission.

Replevin: This is available for a plaintiff suing to recover possession of an asset. Similar to attachment, the plaintiff asks the court to direct the sheriff to seize the property in dispute. Like the other remedies, there are specific requirements that the plaintiff must fulfill to use this remedy.

Receivership: A receiver is appointed by the court to manage property or money during a lawsuit. A plaintiff can ask the court to appoint a receiver to take over your savings or property and manage it while she sues you. Again, the court requires the plaintiff to show good cause before it makes such an appointment. In New York, this is one remedy which cannot be granted until you are served with a summons (notified that you are being sued). Other states have similar laws which allow others to tie up your property and possessions before they have actually won in court.

Mechanic's Liens: Typically, this remedy is afforded only to building contractors (including electrical and plumbing contractors). If a dispute arises over the payment owed a contractor, the contractor can simply file a lien on the real property where the services were performed. Moreover, this lien may be filed without notice or warning and, perhaps worse, places the contractor in a position to request judicial foreclosure on your property.

Discovery

With the lawsuit started, the discovery phase begins. Discovery is the process by which each side probes the other side for information which may be helpful to them at trial. Discovery usually takes the form of depositions (oral questioning under oath), interrogatories (written questions answered under oath), requests for production of documents or other "things," and requests for admission which will require you to admit or deny under oath whether you have an ownership interest in a particular asset.

A large percentage of the time and cost of a typical lawsuit involves discovery. Why? Because the more powerful party often tries to intimidate the opposition by piling on the discovery requests. While the official rules of discovery prohibit using discovery as a tactical weapon, lawyers do violate the rule.

> **FACT: A recent survey of a bar association disclosed that 77% of litigators had used discovery as an economic weapon against their opponents.**

Discovery becomes so expensive because appearing at each deposition or answering each interrogatory involves hiring lawyers to guide you through the process and defend against unwarranted questions. Even worse are requests for documents, which are easily made. The cost of responding involves the time to find and produce the materials, attorney's fees for reviewing the materials, and the physical copying and recording costs.

> **FACT: In one antitrust case, the discovery process lasted almost a decade! The plaintiffs final pre-trial statement, over 100,000 pages long, referred to approximately 250,000 pages of documents, all produced through discovery. Imagine what this cost the defendant in legal fees, and the trial still had not started!**

Trial

The trial may take years, and you will have spent many thousands of dollars. Also, no matter how strong your case, you may still lose a large judgment at trial because the jury often disregards the facts or the law and votes with emotion. This is called *jury nullification*. Any observer of today's trial environment knows it is foolish to risk trial and play the "legal lottery." Consider these actual cases and judgments. Then, ask yourself, "How can I defend myself when juries are making these decisions?"

- A Philadelphia jury awarded a soothsayer $700,000 after she allegedly lost her psychic powers following a CAT scan.

- A Roanoke, Virginia jury gave a former railroad brakeman $2.6 million because the noise of the trains left him with a hearing problem that supposedly drove him crazy.

- A San Francisco cab driver rescued a 24-year-old Japanese woman who was being mugged. After he saw the perpetrator take her purse and shove her to the ground, he set off in pursuit and pinned the assailant against the wall until the police arrived. The perpetrator was convicted of a felony and sentenced to 10 years in prison, but the cabbie was not treated as a hero. Instead, the mugger sued the cabbie and won over $24,000 for use of excessive force.

One point we make repeatedly throughout this book is that you should always try to avoid the need to defend a lawsuit. Lawyers, law school professors, and even judges recognize this. Now, you understand why. *Protect your assets. It is less likely that you will be sued if your assets are protected and more likely that you will settle before a trial even begins.*

Expect Hefty Legal Fees

Whether you win a case at trial or lose, you can expect a large legal bill. The U.S., in fact, is one of the few countries in which a successful defendant must pay his own legal fees and costs. In England and other countries with similar legal systems, the losing party pays the victor's legal fees. In the United States, each party pays his own fees and costs unless a contract between the parties expressed otherwise. *You may "win," yet still owe tens of thousands of dollars in legal fees and costs. Not much of a victory!*

Legal fees will likely be significant. Furthermore, the practice of overbilling is now alarmingly rampant. An auditor who investigates attorney bills reported to us that 90% of the cases he examined contained overcharges between 25% to 50%. While the auditor only works on already suspicious bills, consider some outrageous examples:

- A bankruptcy firm charged its bankrupt client over $177,000, simply to prepare their bill.

- An attorney drafted one legal motion which applied to thousands of separate cases that his insurance company client faced in asbestos litigation. The attorney billed the client 3,000 separate times for the same 12 minutes spent on the motion.

- A lawyer billed 62 hours in a single day.

Bill-padding is no laughing matter, especially when you must pay the bill. Nonetheless, it reminded us of this joke: A lawyer appeared at the gates of heaven and loudly protested that he was only 42 and much too young to die. "That's funny," St. Peter replied. "According to the hours you've billed clients, we figured you were 93."

You May Own More than Just the Judgment

If you lose the lawsuit and become a judgment debtor, you may owe more than the amount the judge or jury awards the plaintiff. You will also owe interest on the award, which starts from when the lawsuit was filed with the court. In many civil cases, the trial begins 2–3 years after the lawsuit was filed, and in larger cities, 4–5 years! You will then likely owe between 2 and 5 years of interest on the award plus the award amount. What is the interest rate? It depends on the state, but ranges between 5% and 18% annually.

> EXAMPLE: If you are in a state with a 12% interest rate (about average) and found liable for a $50,000 award and live where there is a five year backlog of cases, you will owe $38,117.07 in interest for a total loss of over $88,000! Check with a local attorney for the statutory interest rate in your state.

The "Joint & Several Liability" Trap

The doctrine of Joint and Several Liability applies when two or more parties jointly cause injuries or damage to the victim. The victim can then sue any one of the defendants for the full damages, even if the defendant was only partially at fault. Consider this example:

> Valerie Victim was injured when Driver Dave, Driver Dan, and you were all involved in a car accident. The jury finds that Valerie's injuries warranted $100,000 in damages. The jury also finds that Dave was 45% at fault, Dan was 35% at fault, and you were 20% at fault. Even though you were only 20% at fault, joint and several liability allows Valerie to sue you for the full $100,000. Of course, you can then sue Dave and Dan for reimbursement. This costs time and money.

While each state has different limitations on when Joint and Several Liability applies, it is available in many types of cases. For example, partners of a general partnership always have joint and several liability for the debts and liabilities of the partnership. The key point to realize is that you may have to pay for negligent acts.

Between expensive legal fees, outrageous awards, severe interest, and joint and several liability, you can see how any lawsuit can become a financial disaster.

The Post-Judgment Search for Your Assets

A plaintiff who wins a judgment against you becomes a judgment creditor. The judgment creditor can then commence a thorough investigation of your assets and income by way of a *debtors' examination* (You may appeal the judgment before the debtor's exam, but this may involve posting a bond, paying more legal fees and costs, and it is as risky as the trial).

In the debtor's examination, the judgment creditor and his attorney have the authority of the court behind them. They can use depositions, interrogatories, requests for production of documents, subpoenas, and possibly even in-court questioning to force you to reveal information regarding your finances. In most states, your spouse can also be compelled to reveal financial information. The creditor may use all these tools or any combination thereof. You and your spouse must make good faith, reasonable efforts to respond truthfully to such requests.

Your judgment creditor will minimally want to know:

- Your/your spouse's current employment and full compensation, if any

- Your/your spouse's part-time employment, if any

- Any other sources of income

- Occupations or business interests held by you/your spouse during the last five years

- Bank accounts, savings accounts, checking accounts, CDs, and securities in your/your spouse's name

- Safe deposit boxes in your/your spouse's name

- Real estate owned in your/your spouse's name

- Whether or not you/your spouse own any life insurance with cash values, or any annuities

- Whether or not you/your spouse own any automobiles, boats, RV s, trucks, etc., and what the equity in such items may be

- Whether or not you/your spouse own any jewelry, collectibles, antiques, and what the equity of such items is

- Whether or not you/your spouse own any patents, trademarks, or copyrights, and whether or not any rights to them are assigned

- Whether or not you/your spouse has transferred any property within the last five years

- Whether or not you/your spouse made any gifts of property within the last five years

- The extent to which you/your spouse has other liabilities

- Whether or not you have filed for bankruptcy

- Whether or not there is anyone holding property on your behalf

Remember, answers to the judgment creditor's questions and requests are under oath. A false response to these questions is the same as lying on the witness stand. It is perjury; a felony punishable by imprisonment. If you ignore a creditor's requests to appear in court or at a deposition, or fail to respond to interrogatories or requests for production, the creditor can obtain a court order to compel you to comply. Failure to respond to a court order will put you in contempt of court, which can result in fines and incarceration.

> **TIP #1: Answer questions at depositions, in-court examinations, or interrogatories directly and briefly without offering additional information. In daily conversation, we often feel the need to explain our responses. Do not do so here. Make the creditor's job as difficult as possible by answering the question and offering no more. But remember, never lie under oath.**

> **TIP #2: Dress down when attending any examination or deposition. The appearance of wealth only makes your opponent more determined to take your assets.**

How Judgment Creditors Seize Assets

Once a judgment is entered against you, the judgment creditor can seize your assets or execute on a judgment. Although the process varies by state, typically:

- For real property, the creditor must file a summary of judgment with the county recorder where your real property is located. This "liens" the property for the amount of the judgment. This lien is valid against any real property you own in that county at the time, as well as future real estate you acquire. Once a lien is placed, you cannot sell or refinance the property(ies) without satisfying the judgment. This effectively ties up your real estate until the judgment is paid!

- Personal property is seized through a levy. The sheriff or marshall who enforces the levy can physically take property named in the levy. He can seize property directly from you or someone else. This can include money in a bank account, items in a safe deposit box, automobiles, jewelry, antiques, collectibles, equipment and other unprotected physical assets. If the item seized is not cash, the sheriff will convert the property into cash through a *sheriff's sale* at public auction.

- Wages are also seized by levy or *garnishments*. The creditor, through a levy, can order your employer to send your pay, except for legally protected amounts, to the creditor.

- If you are self-employed, revenues can be seized by court-appointed "sitters," who literally sit in your place of business and are empowered to seize cash or checks paid to your business as they are received. This method of judgment enforcement is perhaps the most humiliating to the judgment debtor.

How to Stop Seizure of Your Assets

If a creditor is in the process of taking your assets or garnishing your wages, there are three possible steps to protect yourself:

- File a claim of exemption to protect exempt assets. Each state lists assets which a creditor cannot take. Generally, this includes tools of the trade, household items and a specified amount of other personal property. Federal law provides further exemptions. Often, you must file a claim of exemption to properly shield your property; protection is not automatic. We will more fully discuss state and federal exemptions in Chapter 12.

- Offer to pay the judgment amount voluntarily, perhaps over time. Negotiating payment saves the creditor the hassles of foreclosure and allows you to keep your property.

- File for bankruptcy under Chapter 7, 11, or 13 before the auction sale. While filing bankruptcy has serious consequences, it stops any forced sale of your assets. If you plan bankruptcy anyway, do so before seizure and sale, thereby saving your assets.

Summary

- Potential plaintiffs and their lawyers can, and will, discover what you own before deciding whether or not to sue you.

- Defending a lawsuit is time-consuming, extremely expensive, and an emotionally draining experience.

- Plaintiffs can possibly get at your assets before they even begin their lawsuit against you through pre-judgment remedies.

- Even when you supposedly "win" a lawsuit, you lose.

- To defend against a lawsuit at trial, you play a "legal lottery" where the payouts come out of your pockets.

- Through joint and several liability, you can be forced to pay damages you did not cause.

- If you lose a lawsuit, expect a thorough investigation of all your income and assets. The plaintiff has powerful legal tools to find and take your property, possessions, and even your income.

- Avoid lawsuits by protecting your savings, possessions, and property. In so doing, you discourage lawsuits and make it possible to negotiate from a position of strength when your assets are protected.

Conclusion: Avoid Lawsuits

This is obvious. You probably tried this before you bought this book. However, now you know exactly how expensive, time-consuming, stressful, and risky defending a lawsuit can be. So, how will you avoid a lawsuit?

We could tell you to always act reasonably, foresee behavior that might get you in trouble, pay debts when due, pay your taxes, avoid marriage, and never start a business. This would be ridiculous. We do not want you to surrender to the threat of a lawsuit — we want you to insulate yourself from the threat!

The key to avoiding lawsuits is to protect against them. Your property, possessions, and savings must all be shielded from the lawsuit. Only when you are properly protected can you partake in all of life's various activities and not worry about being sued and losing what you have worked so hard to build.

11

OWNERSHIP FORMS YOU MUST AVOID

Your Own Name, Joint Ownership, and General Partnerships

A comprehensive Wealth Protection Plan should not only protect your assets from outside threats but it should also steer you away from the many dangerous liability traps that exist. If you have been directed to this chapter by the RFA, it means that these traps are lurking in your plan right now. That is why we decided to warn you of these potential dangers before getting into the various tools you can use to protect assets. If you can avoid these dangerous ownership forms, you will have done better than most to shield your wealth before you even consider advanced wealth-building strategies discussed later in the section. Let's see what these dangers are and why they are so perilous.

Do Not Hold Assets in Your Own Name

If you hold property in your name, you have absolutely no asset protection against your creditors unless the asset is exempt under state or federal law (see Chapter 12), an asset held in your name is wide-open for attack. While owning assets in your own name does provide you with maximum flexibility, such flexibility is too minor an advantage to justify exposing your wealth to all of the lawsuit and creditor risks facing physicians today. This is especially true because many tools provide you with flexibility while also protecting your assets.

Why Joint Ownership Is So Dangerous

Joint ownership is the most popular form of ownership in the United States for stocks, bonds, real estate, and bank accounts. In most states, when one joint owner dies, property owned in joint ownership automatically passes to the surviving joint owner(s). This is called "joint ownership with right of survivorship." In this common interpretation, jointly owned property passes outside of a will and avoids the expense of probate (see Chapters 61 and 63 for more on the pitfalls of probate). Because jointly held property avoids probate, many financial and legal advisors recommend joint ownership. What these advisors do not tell you, however, is how owning assets in joint ownership can burn you — especially in terms of asset protection.

Here we will examine the two major asset protection risks of joint ownership. Later, in the estate planning section, you will learn how joint ownership can ruin your intended estate plan as well.

Joint Ownership Creates Lawsuit and Creditor Risks

If you own property (personal property or real estate) jointly, you face even more lawsuit and creditor risks than if you owned the property in your own name. Let's examine these risks through the following case study:

> **CASE STUDY:** *The Building You and Frank Own*
>
> You and your friend Frank are joint owners of a residential apartment building. Each of you can sell, give away, or mortgage your 1/2 share of the building without the consent of the other. You are partners in the business of renting the apartments, collecting the rents, maintaining the premises, etc. You plan to use the building to provide you both with supplemental income. You both agree that, given the right market conditions, you should sell the building for a hefty profit.
>
> If Frank is ever sued for a reason unrelated to the building, Frank's creditors can only come after his half of the building. Your half is safe from Frank's creditors. While this arrangement may seem like an asset protection advantage because you are the *safe* joint owner, it actually is not. This is because Frank's *creditor can ask the court to sell the entire property, including your share, to satisfy the outstanding debt.* This is called *forced liquidation* or a *forced sale*. Here, the court can sell the entire property on the open market. You will lose your share of the property, but you get to keep your share of the proceeds.

Returning to the above example, Frank's financial problems could cause any number of problems for you, even though you are supposedly *safe*. Consider these:

- Frank's creditors force a sale of the entire building during a terrible market for sellers. They know even a rock bottom price will pay off their debt, so they do not care. Because you cannot come up with the cash to buy Frank's share, the building is sold well below its fair market value. Frank's creditors are paid, and you get half of the proceeds. However, you lose a building which provided you a steady cash flow, and which you know is worth much more than its selling price.

- Suppose Frank's creditors like the apartment building. They decide they would rather keep the building than sell it. Now, you have a new partner — someone (or likely something, like a bank or credit union) you do not know, trust, or understand. Not an ideal partner for a business venture.

- Frank's creditors like the apartment building. They take Frank's half share. When the market turns into a strong seller's market you want to sell the building and make your profit. However, your new partners, Frank's creditors, disagree. You end up selling your half, which gets much less on the market than half of the whole building would yield. Why? Because it turns out that few others also want to accept Frank's creditors as their partners.

Joint Ownership Creates a "Winner Takes All" Game

In addition, joint ownership puts you in a "winner takes all" waiting game, where you are gambling that you survive longer than your fellow joint owners. Jointly owned property automatically passes to the surviving joint owners(s) at death, if the safe owner dies before the debtor owner, the whole property becomes the debtor's and it can be taken by the debtor's creditors. Returning to the previous example, if you and Frank owned the building in joint ownership and you died before Frank, Frank would own the building outright. Frank's creditors could then seize the entire building and your heirs would have no rights whatsoever.

The other outcome of the "winner takes all" game is that the safe co-owner (assume that is you for now) survives longer than the debtor co-owner (assume that is Frank). Does this mean that you take the building free and clear of Frank's creditor problems? In most cases, the answer is yes. This is the one asset protection aspect of joint ownership — winning the "winner takes all" game. This victory, however, is not absolute. In the following situations, even if you survive and take the entire building, Frank's one-half share may still be vulnerable.

Situation 1: Frank owed federal or state taxes.

Situation 2: Frank declared bankruptcy — the bankruptcy trustee can sell any property Frank owned, even if he is now dead. You must then claim a share of the sale proceeds.

Situation 3: The property is situated in one of the limited number of states that allow a the deceased joint owner's creditors to come after the surviving joint owner's property.

Joint Ownership Provides Little Protection

If you are a physician and your spouse is not, you may think that jointly-held property is immune to lawsuits against you alone. You would be wrong! At least 50% of joint property will be vulnerable to a claim against you. If you are the only breadwinner, 100% could be exposed. Do not rely on joint ownership to protect you — it is a (-3) on the sliding scale.

General Partnerships: a Liability Nightmare for Businesses

In a general partnership, two or more people join together to run a business or venture for profit without registering the business as a corporation, limited partnership, or other legal entity. The law assumes that any business involving more than one person is a general partnership unless the partners prove otherwise. Similarly, the law assumes that a business run by one person is a proprietorship unless proven otherwise. A proprietorship provides no asset protection whatsoever as the person is, for all intents and purposes, the business.

Like the proprietorship, general partners have the right to manage partnership affairs and are personally liable for the debts and liabilities of the partnership. The general partnership is even more of a liability trap than the proprietorship, because general partners can incur liability because of their own acts, the acts of their employees and the acts of their fellow partners.

Three Reasons Not to Operate Any Business as a General Partnership

The headline should make this clear but we will repeat it anyway: *Never* operate any business or practice as a general partnership! A general partnership is a creditor or plaintiff's dream and a partner's liability nightmare. It should not be part of anyone's asset protection strategy. Why is a general partnership so dangerous? Consider these three hidden dangers of a general partnership:

Partners Have Unlimited Liability for Partnership Debts

This tragic fact goes unrealized by many business people, professionals, and other entrepreneurs when involved in general partnerships. They, in effect, personally guarantee every partnership debt and personally assume the risk for malpractice, accidents, and other liability sources of the entire partnership. They fail to realize that their liability as a partner is "joint and several" with other partners This means that a plaintiff who successfully sues the partnership can collect the *full judgment* from any one partner. An example:

> **CASE STUDY:** *Jane and Ted's Real Estate Venture*
> Jane and Ted were friends who decided to go into a real estate venture together to refurbish old three-family homes and sell them as condominiums. Events went well for a while, but the local real estate market went sour and they defaulted on a $650,000 bank loan. Jane was much wealthier than Ted, so the bank pursued Jane for the full amount, completely ignoring Ted. Jane ended up having to pay over

$600,000 to the bank. Of course, she could sue Ted for his share of the debt but Ted didn't have the money anyway, so Jane didn't see the point.

Partners Have Unlimited Liability for Their Partners Acts

As a partner in a general partnership, you assume all the risk that another partner may cause. When the lawsuit arises from one partner's act or omission in the ordinary course of business, every other partner is personally liable. The dreaded "joint and several liability" doctrine applies! If one of your partners gets into trouble, you can be personally liable for the entire amount — even if you were neither involved in the alleged incident nor aware of it.

Think of the many ways a partner could get you into trouble: he commits malpractice, gets into a car accident while on partnership business, defrauds someone through the business, sexually harasses an employee, wrongfully fires an employee, etc. Multiply this risk times the number of partners in your partnership and you have a lawsuit liability nightmare! A real-world example:

CASE STUDY: *Michael Gets Burned By His Partner*

Michael was the founding partner in a successful three-partner software development firm near Portland, Oregon. One of firm's customers sued the firm when a program malfunctioned, causing a loss of valuable data. The lawsuit alleged breach of contract, product liability, and even punitive damages.

Settlement negotiations were unsuccessful and the trial jury awarded an extremely large verdict against the partnership, exceeding its liability policy limit. Because Michael was the wealthiest of the partners, the plaintiff's lawyer pursued him first and forced Michael to pay the entire $250,000 amount (above the insurance policy limit) from his personal savings. Although Michael had less contact with this customer than his partners, he learned the risks of a general partnership the hard way.

You May Be an "Unaware" General Partner

Unlike a limited partnership, a general partnership does not require a formal written agreement. You can verbally agree to start a venture with another person and create a general partnership with all of its liability problems. Think about this whenever you start a new business venture with someone.

Even if you make no agreement to partner with another person, the law may impose general partnership liability on you if the general public reasonably perceives you as partners. Hence, you may already be part of a liability-ridden general partnership and not even know it. To illustrate, we submit the following:

> **CASE STUDY:** *Roger Inadvertently Has Partners*
>
> Roger was one of four physicians who used a common office arrangement. They each had their own patients, which they did not share. They did, however, share a common waiting area, support staff, and accounting. Each professional had his own practice methods, set his own hours, and was not otherwise accountable to the others.
>
> When a client sued one of the doctors for medical malpractice, Roger and the two others had a rude awakening. Although only the suing patient's physician was negligent, all four were defendants in the lawsuit. The court found that the client could reasonably conclude the four professionals were partners together because of their office set-up and common support staff. Therefore, the court allowed the plaintiff to proceed with the suit against all four — as a general partnership with each jointly and severally liable for the plaintiff's losses.

How to Protect Yourself in a General Partnership

We repeat our warning: *Do not run any business as a general partnership!* It is too risky. Rather, convert the business into a limited partnership, a corporation, or a limited liability company. Despite our warnings, many professionals and businesspersons will continue their general partnerships or set-up new ones because they do not want to change. One suggestion of how to set-up a general partnership for maximum asset protection purposes is therefore essential.

If you do use a general partnership for any type of business venture, each partner should set up corporations or limited liability companies (LLCs) and the corporations or LLCs should become the partners in the general partnership. This advice is followed by many medical professionals and attorneys using professional corporations (PCs). Each doctor or lawyer sets up a PC and the PC, not the individual professional, is the official partner in the partnership. Structuring the partnership this way, the underlying corporate owner's personal assets remain protected from claims against the partnership. However, as with any corporation, the corporate formalities must be followed to achieve the asset protection.

Conclusion

The first step in any asset protection plan is to avoid dangerous ownership forms to the maximum extent possible. Once this is accomplished, we can move to the next stage of planning: using insurance and legal tools to proactively shield assets going forward.

12

—————◆—————

USING EXISTING LAWS
TO PROTECT ASSETS
Your State Law Is Often the Key

As we noted in Chapter 9, exempt assets are the preferred tools in most physician's Wealth Protection Plans. This is true for a number of reasons, including:

1. They enjoy a +4 / +5 on the sliding scale of asset protection.

2. They all enjoy tax-deferred growth.

3. Most of them enjoy tax-favored liquidation.

4. You can own them in your name and control them without losing any of the asset protection benefits.

While such assets are obviously very attractive to most clients, not everyone can take advantage of them. That is because — aside from federally-exempt pensions — exempt assets are controlled by state law. Each state has statutes that establish which assets are exempt and to what extent. Even more, there are numerous cases interpreting the statutes — further defining what is and is not exempt.

For this reason, it is crucial that you work with an advisor well-versed on your state's exemption law. In fact, this is one of the many reasons that Wealth Protection Alliance (WPA) has been so successful — by matching potential clients with educated, experienced local advisors. If this is of interest to you, contact the WPA at (800) 554-7233.

13

USING INSURANCE AS
AN ASSET-PROTECTOR
A Mixed Blessing

As licensed insurance professionals, we strongly believe that various types of insurance are required components of every Wealth Protection Plan. Certainly, property and casualty (P&C) insurance is one of these tools.

What P&C Insurance Is

To begin with, there are two "categories" of insurance — life & health (L&H) and property and casualty (P&C). L&H includes all life insurance and health insurance as well as disability and long term care, among others. P&C insurance is designed to protect against property and casualty losses. Often P&C is referred to as "property and liability" insurance because it protects people from all types of liabilities. Examples of P&C coverages are: automobile, homeowners & renters, umbrella liability, professional liability, medical malpractice, general liability, flood, earthquake, premises liability, errors & omissions, products liability, and others.

P&C insurance is designed to "indemnify" the insured. The insurance industry's definition of "indemnify" is to "make whole" or restore the status quo. If you suffer a loss and have the proper coverage, you should be "put back" in the same financial place you were before the loss (minus any applicable deductibles or co-payments). P&C coverage also covers your legal bills and other loss adjustment expenses, as well as the actual loss. This may include the costs of adjusters, estimates, expert testimony, or other associated costs.

This is very important because, as you know from earlier chapters, the nuisance lawsuit is more popular than ever. As long as there is one ambulance-chasing attorney who is willing to take the case, there is no out of pocket cost (or deterrent) to the plaintiff. If you didn't have insurance, but still won your case, you still might have tens, if not hundreds, of thousands of dollars in legal fees and related expenses. It is usually worth buying insurance to avoid these costs and the potential judgment or loss.

Best Uses of P&C Insurance

As we mentioned, there are various types of insurance that fall under the P&C category. The most common of these are homeowners (or renters) and automobile insurance. You probably have coverage for these because you have a mortgage on your home or because you have a loan or a lease on your car. In a way, you do not own your home or car yet — the bank or credit department does. They require, as collateral, that you insure their asset while you are paying for it. Once you pay off your home or car, you no longer are required to have insurance. Of course, we would NEVER recommend dropping the insurance on your home. The odds are very slim that you will suffer a house fire or burglary, but if you do, you will be very upset that you lost so much and could have avoided that loss by paying a few hundred or few thousand dollars.

Another common P&C insurance is the umbrella liability policy. For a very reasonable premium, you can get an additional one to two million dollars of excess liability insurance on top of the liability protection you may have from your homeowners or auto policies. If you are a high net worth individual or are in a high liability profession, you should seriously consider an umbrella policy.

Other popular P&C coverages are for professional liability and premises and products liability. Depending on your occupation, you may have medical or legal malpractice insurance. If you own your place of business, you should have premises liability insurance. If your business makes a product (toy, part, widget, etc.), then you should have product liability insurance. This will protect you from claims when a product you place into the "stream of commerce" malfunctions and causes bodily injury and damages.

Five Limitations of P&C Insurance

While some P&C insurance always makes sense as part of a Wealth Protection Plan, there are significant limitations to this tool. That is why we typically recommend using the strategies asset protection tools we describe in this section, in addition to any insurance. Let's examine these limitations individually:

1. Policy exclusions

Often we find that clients are completely unaware of the "fine print" exclusions and policy limitations. Of course, they often become aware of such exclusions after it is too late. For example, many clients fail to realize that "umbrella" policies only pay if certain underlying insurance coverage amounts are in effect. If your liability limits on your homeowner's policy or auto policy are too low, then you'll have to pay out of pocket before the umbrella coverage is in effect. Recommendation: Know Your Policy.

> **CASE STUDY:** *Alan's daughter's car accident*
>
> Alan was sued for over $150,000 when his teenage daughter was involved in a car accident, using his car. Alan was certain that his insurance policy covered his daughter. Only then did his insurance agent tell Alan that the policy no longer covered his daughter. There was an exclusion of coverage for child drivers if they did not reside in the same residence as the parents. Now, Alan alone faced a lawsuit which eventually cost him over $150,000.

2. Inadequate policy limits

Even if your insurance policy does cover you on a particular lawsuit, the policy coverage may be well below what a jury will award. You must pay any excess above the coverage out of your own pocket. Juries routinely hand out awards in excess of the coverage limits of traditional auto, medical malpractice, employee harassment and other common P&C insurances. If you were hit by a large judgment, would your policy cover you completely? Recommendations: Don't skimp on coverage, consider an umbrella policy and utilize other asset protection tools.

3. Your insurer no longer exists

There is no guarantee that your insurance company will exist when you finally get sued. Insurance companies are not invincible. Like other businesses, insurance carriers go bankrupt or out of business for other reasons and leave you without coverage when you most need it. This is exactly what happened to a large physician-owned malpractice carrier in California. Now, the physicians are being forced to pay the outstanding debts of their former insurer. Recommendation: Use Top-Rated Carriers.

4. Insurance forces you to lose control of the defense

Even if your insurance policy covers against a specific claim, you must consider the consequences. You have lost negotiating power because your insurance company will dictate when the case is settled and for how much. While this may not matter with a personal injury car accident lawsuit, a case against you professionally is another matter. Here you may not want to admit liability and settle, while your insurance company does.

On the other hand, if the claim involves your professional reputation, you may want to settle the case out of court and away from the public view. There is no guarantee that your insurer will see things the same way. In these situations, if you rely solely on insurance, you lose all ability to negotiate effectively.

5. Claims bring ever-higher premiums

An additional consequence of relying solely on insurance to protect you from lawsuits is that once you make claims on the policy, your premiums rise. Given the dismal statistics, you will probably endure a number of lawsuits over your life and your cost of insurance will rise with every claim, even if you are not at fault. Consider the following solution for a construction company owner who, before protecting his assets, relied solely on insurance. After his insurance company defended four unsuccessful lawsuits against him, three of which went through trial, his insurance premiums rose to over $100,000 per year. Insurance cost him more over the next five years than any one lawsuit. This is not an extreme example. The point is clear: even if you successfully defend against claims and lawsuits, there is a significant price to pay.

Conclusion

P&C insurance should be a part of everyone's Wealth Protection Plan. Certain types of coverage, such as homeowner's, auto, umbrella and medical malpractice for physicians are compulsory. Beyond this, however, more must be done to adequately shield assets and discourage claims from the outset. In the next chapters, you'll learn about powerful legal tools you can use to protect all assets and enjoy significant tax benefits.

14

USING
EXEMPT ASSETS
How To Achieve Maximum Protection
With Minimum Expense

When given a choice between two equally effective drugs, patients request the less expensive generic prescription. When given a choice, patients choose to have prescriptions called into pharmacies that are conveniently located to save them time and aggravation. Wealth Protection has a number of similarities to healthcare. Certain assets are given special creditor protection by law. The question thus becomes: if you have a choice between using complex legal structures that require maintenance, separate tax returns and other formalities, or using simple assets you can own and control without any additional cost or inconvenience, why would you chose to make your plan more complicated and more expensive? Obviously, the wise choice is to make use of the exempt asset. Let's see how this works.

Federal Law Generally Does Not Shield Assets

In general, federal law does not protect particular investments from creditors. However, it is important to know that federal law does shield certain pensions, profit-sharing plans, 401(k)s and other plans from creditors under its ERISA rules. For more on these types of "qualified retirement plans," see Chapters 33, 42 and 43.

State Law Does Protect Certain Assets

Every state has laws that shield certain assets from creditors. These are called "exempt assets" as they are exempt from seizure in a lawsuit or in bankruptcy. What types of assets are afforded this protection? The most common are an IRA, a home, life insurance or annuities.

As far as the IRA goes, many states protect the entire amount in the IRA while others protect only "the amount reasonably necessary for support" leaving it up to a judge to decide how much should be shielded in any particular case. To see what the level of IRA protection is in your state, speak with an asset protection specialist or member of the Wealth

Protection Alliance in your area who is familiar with your state's statutes and case law.

As for the homestead exemption, there is tremendous variation among the states in terms of what and how much is protected under homestead laws. Some states shield an unlimited value (Florida) while others protect $0 (New Jersey). Most protect around $30,000 — not much in today's real estate market. For this reason, few clients can rely on homestead to shield their home. Instead, they rely on tactics described in Chapter 18.

Life Insurance: Protected Almost Everywhere

Unlike homestead, 50 states have laws protecting life insurance to differing amounts. Some general trends:

- Many states shield the entire policy proceeds from the creditors of the policyholder. Some also protect against the beneficiary's creditors.

- States that do not protect the entire policy proceeds set amounts above which the creditor can attach proceeds. For example, Arizona exempts the first $20,000 of proceeds.

- Many states protect the policy proceeds only if the policy beneficiaries are the policyholder's spouse, children, or other dependents.

- Most states also exempt term and group life policies.

- Some states protect a policy's cash surrender value in addition to the policy proceeds. If this is so in your state, you have tremendous opportunity to create wealth while you protect it.

- No state can protect a life insurance policy from the IRS — the IRS can take your insurance proceeds and cash value if you owe them money.

If you are fortunate to live in a state like New York, Florida, Texas or Tennessee where cash values in life insurance policies are protected, you have an opportunity to create a very flexible Wealth Protection Plan at very small expense and with very little maintenance or inconvenience.

Annuities Are Shielded In Many States

As you will learn in the retirement section, there are two types of annuities — variable annuities and life annuities. Variable annuities are insurance contracts that invest the contributions on a tax-deferred basis (these are covered in Chapter 44). A life annuity is an insurance contract where the investor pays a certain amount of money to an insurance company up-front and the insurance company then pays the investor back a fixed payment every month, quarter or year for as long as the investor (or spouse) is alive. See Chapter 46 for more on life annuities.

Although rare, some states protect annuities from creditor claims. In the states that do exempt them, annuities are an ideal tool to safeguard wealth. Let's see how this works:

> **CASE STUDY:** *Sam chooses between mutual funds and a variable annuity*
>
> Sam is a physician who is concerned that a future lawsuit may threaten his personal wealth. He has $50,000 to invest and he lives in a state where variable annuities are protected (like New York). His financial planner had recommended two potential investment vehicles — mutual funds and variable annuities. In the investment section, you will learn that annuities have higher charges than mutual funds. However, for that higher expense, you receive some life insurance, the value of tax deferral and, for Sam, asset protection. Let's assume that the difference in charges is about 1.5% annually. Is it worth it for Sam to use the annuity when it is protected from creditors and grows tax-deferred rather than the mutual fund which offers no creditor protection and no tax deferral? We can't say for sure without knowing more about Sam's goals and portfolio, but the asset protection concern can only be alleviated by purchasing the annuity or by owning the mutual funds in a legal entity he must pay to create and maintain.

Turning Non-Exempt Assets into Exempt Wealth

After learning that exempt assets enjoy +4 / +5 protection and can be owned in your own name without any legal or government fees, you should strive to maximize your use of such assets. Though this goal is easily achieved when you are dealing with cash and other liquid assets, you may wonder about assets that cannot easily be converted into protected homestead, life insurance cash value or a protected annuity. Real estate and business assets can still be "turned into" an exempt asset through the use of a debt shield. Let's look at one case study.

> **CASE STUDY:** *Dr. Jim Turns Real Estate into Exempt Assets*
>
> Dr. Jim lives in New York, where there is no exemption for real estate (even homestead is only shielded to $10,000). There is, however, an unlimited exemption for cash value life insurance. A recent NY supreme court case even confirmed this protection for insurance cash values. Jim sought to turn his $1 million (debt free) rental property into a protected exempt asset while maintaining his ownership and control of the property.
>
> The NY WPA member worked with Jim to secure a 4.5% fixed loan of $800,000 against the real estate. Now, any future lawsuit could not get to the $800,000 of value protected by the mortgage. The debt created a "shield" against Jim. As for the loan, most of the interest was deductible as a business expense. This meant the

net cost of the loan to Jim was about 2.5%. Jim used the loan proceeds to purchase a cash value life insurance policy that guaranteed a minimum return of 4% — a guarantee backed up by a AAA-rated $100 billion insurance company.

In this way, Jim is building wealth at 4% to 7% (minus mortality and administrative expenses) while borrowing the funds at 2.5% — a nice arbitrage. When Jim wants to pay the loan principal back, he will have the protected cash value to use.

By using a "debt shield," Jim was able to covert $800,000 of exposed equity into $800,000 of exempt cash value. Further, he was able to do it in a way that increase his wealth. Moreover, it allowed him to keep the property (and policy) in his own name. Finally, he enjoyed the death protection of the life insurance for his family to boot!

Conclusion

To determine which assets are given protection your state, it is important to look beyond the statutes. The statutes in your state are a good place to start, but the courts do not always follow the statutes. There are many instances where assets have been protected by statute but the courts have not upheld those protections. To make sure you do not rely on inadequate law, consult with a member of the Wealth Protection Alliance or another asset protection specialist in your area. Once you know the scope of protection afforded these investments in your state, you can better evaluate the role they may play in your Wealth Protection Plan.

15

FAMILY LIMITED PARTNERSHIPS AND LIMITED LIABILITY COMPANIES

If exempt assets are not available to you or if you want to bolster them with legal structures, you must read this chapter. This is because the legal tools we use most are family limited partnerships (FLPs) and family limited liability companies (LLCs). Of course, having family members play a role in these tools is common — that's why we use the word "family" in front of the LP or LLC. However, using family members in this way is NOT required. Whether you use family members or non-family members, these entities can provide solid asset protection.

We have combined these two tools in this chapter because they are so similar. You can think of them as closely related, like brothers or sisters, as they share many of their best characteristics. In fact, unless we make the point otherwise, we will use these tools interchangeably. If a case study refers to a FLP, you can assume that an LLC could have been used and *vice versa*.

Similarities Between the FLP and the LLC

1. They both are legal entities certified under state law

Both tools are legal entities governed by the state law in the state where the entity is formed. Many of these laws are identical as they are modeled after the Uniform Limited Partnership and Limited Liability Company Acts that have been adopted at least partially by every state. As state-certified legal entities, state fees must be paid each year to keep an FLP or LLC active.

2. They have two levels of ownership

Both entities allow for two levels of ownership. We'll call one ownership level "active ownership." The active owners have 100% control of the entity and its assets. In the FLP, the active owners are called "general partners" and with the LLC the active owners are called "managing members." As you may have already guessed, the second ownership level is passive ownership. The passive owners have little control of the entity and only limited rights. The passive owners are called "limited partners" in the FLP and "members" in the LLC. This bi-level structure allows a host of planning possibilities because clients can then use FLPs and LLCs to share ownership with family members without having to give away any practical control of the assets inside the structures. Why is it optimal to be able to give away ownership but still maintain control? The asset protection reasons will be discussed in great detail in this chapter and the estate planning benefits will be explained in Chapter 67. For now, you need only understand that these benefits will be of enormous benefit and continue your reading.

3. They both have beneficial tax treatment

In terms of income taxes, both tools can elect for "pass through" taxation — meaning neither the FLP nor the LLC is liable for income taxes. Rather, the tax liability for any and all income or capital gains on FLP/LLC assets "passes through" to the owners (partners or members). Also, as discussed in the income tax and estate planning sections, both entities allow the participants to take advantage of "income sharing" and "discounting" techniques in the same ways. See chapters 34 and 67 for more on these strategies.

> **NOTE:** Each state has different fees and taxation for each type of entity. There is no consistency between states so make sure you know the annual fees, franchise tax fees and other tax ramifications of each entity in your state before moving forward with either the FLP or LLC.

4. They both have the beneficial 'charging order' asset protection benefit

While state laws do vary slightly, those based on the Uniform Acts provide "charging order" protection to FLP and LLC owners. The "charging order" will be discussed in greater detail later in this chapter.

5. The legal costs associated with each entity are roughly the same

To create a basic FLP or LLC, design how the entity will work in a client's plan, draft the operating or partnership agreement and minutes, prepare tax forms and assignments, and handle the other formalities, experienced attorneys in the field will charge between $2,500 and $25,000. Of course, the complexity of the ownership, the size and complexity of the assets owned by the entity and the purpose of the LLC or FLP are significant factors in determining the cost of the planning.

Two Big Differences Between the FLP and LLC

The two significant differences between the FLP and LLC are:

1. Only the LLC can be used for a single owner

Most states now allow single-member (owner) LLCs, while a limited partnership in every state must have at least two owners. Thus, for single clients, the LLC is often the only option. So, if we are considering having an FLP or LLC protect an asset other than the home, then the single member LLC is one alternative. See chapter 18 for further discussion on the protection of one's home (also called "primary residence").

2. The FLP's general partner has liability for the FLP

While a general partner has personal liability for the acts and debts of the FLP, a managing member has no such liability for his/her LLC. For this reason alone, asset protection experts always recommend using an LLC rather than an FLP when the entity will own "dangerous" assets.

Dangerous assets are those which have a relatively high likelihood of creating liability. Common dangerous assets include real estate (especially rental real estate), cars, RVs, trucks, boats, airplanes, interests in closely-held businesses, and others.

Safe assets, conversely, are those which are unlikely to lead to lawsuits. Common safe assets include cash, stocks, bonds, mutual funds, CDs, life insurance policies, checking or savings accounts, antiques, artwork, jewelry, licenses, copyrights, trademarks, and patents, among others.

Because FLP general partners have liability exposure and LLC managing members do not, it usually makes sense to use an LLC rather than an FLP to own dangerous assets.

How FLPs / LLCs Protect Assets

FLPs and LLCs are solid asset protectors because the law gives a very specific and limited remedy to creditors coming after assets in either entity. When a personal creditor pursues you and your assets are owned by an FLP or LLC, the creditor cannot seize the assets in the FLP/LLC. Under the Uniform Act provisions, *a creditor of a partner* (or LLC member) *cannot reach into the FLP/LLC and take specific partnership assets.*

If the creditor cannot seize FLP/LLC assets, what can the creditor get? The law normally allows for only one remedy: the "charging order." As previously indicated, assets owned in your name are still vulnerable. However, when assets are owned by an FLP/LLC, the best the creditor will usually be able to do is obtain a charging order (a very weak remedy).

Of course, this discussion assumes that in transferring assets to an FLP or LLC, you do not run afoul of fraudulent transfer laws. We introduced the concept of these laws earlier (for more on fraudulent transfer laws, see the Appendix). It also assumes that one remain in compliance with state laws and not use the FLP/LLC as an alter ego of one's personal business affairs.

The Weaknesses of the Charging Order

The charging order is a court order which instructs the FLP/LLC to pay the debtor's share of distributions to his/her creditor until the creditor's judgment is paid in full. More importantly, the charging order does not:

- Give the creditor FLP/LLC voting rights; or
- Force the FLP general partner or LLC managing member to pay out any distributions to partners/members.

While this may seem like a powerful remedy, consider its limitations:

It Is Only Available After a Successful Lawsuit

First, the charging order is only available after the creditor has successfully sued you and won a judgment. Only then can your creditor ask the court for the charging order. It must be noted that once the threat of a charging order exists and even while a lawsuit is proceeding, FLP/LLC assets are completely untouchable and available for you to use (so long as you avoid fraudulent transfers).

Does Not Afford Voting Rights — So You Stay in Complete Control

If the FLP/LLC is drafted properly and a charging order exists, you remain the general partner of your FLP (or managing member of the LLC). You make all decisions about whether the FLP/LLC buys assets, distributes earnings to its partners or members, shifts ownership interests, and so forth. Your judgment creditor cannot vote you out because he cannot vote your shares. Even after the creditor has a judgment against you, you still make all decisions concerning the FLP/LLC, including the decision to refuse to pay distributions to the owners. Why would you decide to pay distributions when you know that the creditor (not you) will receive them?

Perhaps you want to compensate yourself and your spouse as general partners (or managing members) by paying yourself a salary for running the FLP/LLC. This course of action would be 100% permissible and your creditor still wouldn't receive one red cent! If your creditor wishes to get access to this income, he will have to file to have your wages garnished. If, however, you did not receive a salary before the initial judgment, the creditor would not have had any cause or reason to pursue a wage garnishment against you in the first place. If the creditor decides to file for this remedy, you can then stop paying yourself a salary or pay another family member to perform your duties.

Keep in mind that a charging order may have no impact on most FLP/LLCs. If your FLP/LLC simply owns cars, vacation homes, antiques, or other non income-producing assets, your FLP/LLC would likely have little or no income to distribute.

The Creditor May Pay the Tax Bill

The real "kicker" is how the charging order may backfire on creditors for income tax purposes. Because taxes on FLP/LLC income are passed-through to the parties who are entitled to the income, the FLP/LLC does not pay tax. Each partner/member is responsible for his/her share of the FLP/LLC income. This income is taxable whether or not the income is actually paid out. Because a creditor who gets a charging order against you "steps into your shoes" for income tax purposes with respect to your FLP/LLC interest, your creditor will receive your tax bill and owe income taxes on your share of the FLP/LLC income. This tax liability exists even though the creditor never received the income. (Remember, you and your spouse decide if and when to make distributions and you certainly won't make any when there is a creditor with a charging order). Although a sophisticated tax attorney might be able to argue differently, most plaintiff's attorneys do not know the specifics of such rules. Thus, once the creditor realizes that he will get more money out of a cheap settlement than from an elusive FLP or LLC distribution, he will likely opt to settle cheaply. For this reason, we deem FLPs/LLCs a +2 / +3 on the asset protection scale.

CASE STUDY: *Woody and Marge are protected by their FLP*

Return to the example of spouses Woody and Marge. Assume that Woody is an oncologist. After two years of employment, Woody's assistant, Maribel, sues Woody for sexual harassment and wins an award of $750,000. Woody's general business insurance package does not cover this type of lawsuit. Once Maribel discovers, through a debtor's examination, that Woody and Marge's assets are owned by their FLP, what can she do?

She cannot seize the vacation home, stocks, and cars owned by the FLP. The ULPA provisions prohibit that. She also has no fraudulent transfer claim to cling to in an attempt to undo the FLP because the FLP was created in advance of her claim. She can get a charging order on Woody's 39% share of the FLP, but Woody and Marge would still control the FLP. Maribel would probably not receive any distributed profits, only a tax bill on dividends paid out by the stocks which Woody and Marge never distributed. The charging order will not sound too inviting to Maribel, will it?

Maribel could look only to Woody's assets not owned by the FLP. Because Woody had an incomplete asset protection plan and retained personal ownership of copyrights and business interests in a film company worth about $75,000, Woody settled the judgment for just that — $75,000 cash. Woody and Marge's FLP helped them avoid financial disaster and settle the claim for pennies on the dollar. Moreover, they never lost control of their assets.

You may wonder why we have such protective laws for limited partnerships and limited liability companies. The charging order law, which can be traced back to the *English Partnership Act of 1890*, is aimed at achieving a particular public policy objective which, to wit, is that business activities of a partnership should not be disrupted because of non-partnership related debts of the individual partners. The rationale for this objective is that if non-debtor partners and the partnership were not at fault, why should the entire partnership suffer? American law has adopted this policy for over 100 years, culminating in the charging order law of the Uniform Limited Partnership and Uniform Limited Liability Company Acts.

Two Tactics for Maximizing FLP / LLC Protection

You now understand the basic strategy for using FLPs/LLCs — contributing your assets to the FLP/LLC so they will be protected from your personal creditors. This is basic "outside" asset protection. Assets inside the FLP/LLC are protected against outside threats to you. Beyond this, consider these two basic rules:

1. Don't put all your eggs in one basket

We never know when a court of law is going to make a surprise departure or deviation from the accepted legal norms or precedents. If any asset within a single FLP/LLC causes a lawsuit, all assets owned by that FLP/LLC could still be vulnerable. By using multiple FLP/LLC "baskets," you will better protect each of your eggs. This also makes it more difficult for any creditor to come after your entire wealth. Practically, creditors must conduct more investigations, file more motions with the court and perhaps even travel to different states. The more entities used, the more difficult it will be for your creditors to attack your wealth. The result: creditors agree to settlements that are favorable to you and your family.

2. Segregate the dangerous eggs from the safe ones

Separating safe assets from dangerous assets increases your "inside" asset protection. While "outside" protection focuses on shielding your wealth from claims against you, "inside" protection concerns shielding your total wealth from liability created by one of your own assets. As we explained in the beginning of the chapter, dangerous assets should be owned by an LLC rather than by an FLP because LLCs give better "inside" protection. Continuing with this logic, it makes sense to isolate the dangerous assets from the safe ones...keeping them apart in separate LLCs. We'll see this in the case study discussed below.

Putting it Together: An FLP / LLC Case Study

Let's take a look at a real case utilizing FLPs and LLCs. Harry Gump, a 53-year-old co-owner of a retail company, and his wife Wilma, a day school teacher, have two teen-aged children and have the following assets. They live in a state that offers no significant exemptions.

	ASSEST	EQUITY
Safe Assets	Home (depends on state)	$550,000
	Cash	$50,000
	Mutual Funds	$550,000
	Interest in Business	$600,000
	Antiques	$20,000
	Total Safe Equity	$1,770,000
Dangerous Assets	Rental Condo #1	$275,000
	Rental Condo #2	$255,000
	Cars	$20,000
	Powerboat	$30,000
	Total Dangerous Equity	$,580,000
	TOTAL EQUITY	$2,350,000

To provide the Gump's with maximum financial security using FLPs/LLCs, we use three entities. Let us examine each.

Tool #1: "Gump Safe Asset FLP"

Owns: Cash, mutual funds, business interest and antiques.
Total value = $1,220,000

Interests: Mr. and Mrs. Gump, 2% as general partners
Mr. and Mrs. Gump, 96% as limited partners
Each child 1% limited partner

Strategy: The family home is not included because of the special tax consequences afforded homes in their state. By isolating safe assets from dangerous assets, we ensure their security. Further, because Mr. and Mrs. Gump are general partners, they have 100% control of the FLP and all FLP assets. They are more comfortable with this ownership arrangement.

Result: All $1,220,000 now enjoys +2 protection. The Gumps may decide to gift their interests in the FLP to their children for estate and income tax reduction (see chapters 34 and 67 for further discussion of this strategy).

> ## Tool #2: "Gump Dangerous Asset LLC"
>
> **Owns:** Condo #1 and Condo #2. Total value = $530,000
>
> **Interests:** Mr. Gump 1% owner as managing member; 49% as member
>
> Mrs. Gump 1% owner as managing member; 49% as member
>
> **Strategy:** These assets are dangerous because of the likelihood of lawsuits from tenants, guests, or neighbors. While one LLC owned both condominiums, a strong argument can be made to set up separate LLCs for each condo.
>
> **Result:** Any lawsuit arising from the condos is isolated to the condos. All other wealth is shielded.
>
> ## Tool #3: "Gump Dangerous Asset LLC 2"
>
> **Owns:** Cars and the powerboat. Total value = $50,000
>
> **Interests:** Mr. Gump 1% owner as managing member; 49% as member
>
> Mrs. Gump 1% owner as managing member; 49% as member
>
> **Strategy:** These assets are extremely dagerous, especially because the children drive both cars and the boat regularly. With an LLC, we give some protection to the Gump's personal wealth from liability caused by the cars or boat. Yet, Mr. and Mrs. Gump still completely control the boat and cars.
>
> **Result:** All other wealth is isolated from lawsuits arising from car and powerboat ownership. Also, Mr. and Mrs. Gump achieve personal protection through the LLC/corporation.

Without the FLPs and LLCs, the Gump's family had over $2.3 million exposed to lawsuits. Now, Mr. Gump has better shielded over 75% worth of that wealth...and we haven't even addressed the home yet. Further, they have the tools now to reduce income taxes and perhaps even eliminate estate taxes. Perhaps most importantly, they have not relinquished control over any of their assets in the process.

Conclusion

FLPs and LLCs are the two most utilized and most flexible legal tools we use to protect assets. We would be astounded if you did not use at least one as part of your Wealth Protection Plan. Make sure to read Chapters 34 and 67 on how FLPs and LLCs also can reduce income and estate taxes.

16

USING TRUSTS TO SHIELD WEALTH

This chapter explains what a trust is and what asset protection role a trust can play in your Wealth Protection Plan. A number of different trusts that are used in asset protection planning are covered. We will also refer to other chapters where different trusts are explained more thoroughly.

What Is a Trust?

A trust is a legal entity, often misunderstood by the general public. The following definitions and diagram should help you understand a trust and how it functions.

Definitions

Trust: The trust is essentially a legal arrangement where one person holds property for the benefit of another. The person who holds the property is the *trustee* which can be an individual or an entity. The trustee "holds" the property for the benefit of the *beneficiary(ies)*. A trust is created by a trust document that specifies that the trustee holds property owned by the trust for the benefit of the beneficiary of the trust. The trust document also establishes the terms — how the trust should be administered and how the trust assets should be distributed during the lifetime of the trust as well as after the trust is terminated.

Grantor: The Grantor is the person who establishes the trust. Usually, the grantor is the person who transfers property into the trust. He is also called the *Trustor* or *Settlor.*

Trustee: The trustee(s) are the legal owners of the trust property. The trustee(s) are responsible for administering and carrying out the terms of the trust. They owe a fiduciary duty to the beneficiaries — an utmost duty of care to follow the terms of the trust document and manage the trust property properly. A trustee may be a person, such as a family member or trusted friend. The trustee can also be an institution such as a professional trust company or trust department of a bank. When there is more than one trustee, they are called *co-trustees*. The trustee is the legal owner of any assets owned by the trust and has "legal title" to the assets owned by the trust. For example, assume that Dad wants to create a trust for his children. Dad wants his brother, Uncle, to serve as trustee. If Dad transfers his house into the trust, the title to that house will be with "Uncle, as trustee of the Dad trust."

Beneficiary: The beneficiary (or beneficiaries) is the person for whom the trust was created. While the trustee has legal title to assets owned by the trust, the beneficiary has *equitable title* or the rights to the benefits of the trust property. The beneficiary can sue the trustee if the trustee mismanages the trust property or disobeys specific instructions of the trust. The beneficiary may be the same person as the grantor and can possibly be the same person as the trustee. For asset protection purposes, the trustee, beneficiary, and grantor, cannot all be the same person (unless the trust is created in certain jurisdictions, see Chapter 17).

Funding: Funding the trust means transferring assets to the trust. A trust that is "unfunded" has had no property transferred to it. The unfunded trust is completely ineffective. You must title assets to the trust if you want trust protection. This is consistent with any other legal entity/asset protection tool discussed previously. To transfer title of real estate to the trust, you must execute and record a deed to the property to the trust. Bank and brokerage accounts can be transferred by simply changing the name on the accounts. Registered stocks and bonds are changed by notifying the transfer agent or issuing company and requesting that the certificates be reissued to the trust. Other assets, such as household items, furniture, jewelry and artwork are transferred by a simple legal document called an *Assignment* or *Bill of Sale*. Your asset protection specialist can transfer assets simply and quickly.

Trust Classifications

Trusts follow these classifications:

Revocable: A revocable trust is one that you, the grantor, can revoke or change at any time.

Irrevocable: An irrevocable trust is one that you cannot revoke or change once established.

Inter vivos: An inter vivos trust takes effect during your lifetime.

Testamentary: A testamentary trust takes effect at your death. Testamentary trusts are usually created in wills, living trusts, or other documents taking effect at death. All testamentary trusts are irrevocable: you cannot come back to life to undo the trust! If you can, you will have an even greater interest in estate planning (Part IX) of this book.

Living Trusts: Illusory Asset Protection

Living trusts are excellent devices for avoiding probate. They also effectively sidestep the hidden dangers of joint tenancy. However, *living trusts do not provide asset protection while you are alive!* Are you willing to die to protect your family from lawsuits?

Revocable Trusts Do Not Protect Assets

During your lifetime, living trusts provide absolutely no asset protection because they are revocable. As a revocable trust, the grantor of the living trust can undo the trust at any time during his or her lifetime. This is a great benefit for probate avoidance and estate planning purposes. You, the grantor, can amend the trust whenever you wish to change who receives your assets when you die. This greatly comforts those that create living trusts. However, while revocability is good for estate planning goals, it renders a trust useless for asset protection. Remember this simple rule: *revocable trusts are vulnerable to creditors!*

Creditors Can "Step into Your Shoes" and Revoke the Trust

Revocable trusts are useless for asset protection because revocable trusts allow the grantor to undo the trust. If the grantor's creditors want to seize assets owned by a revocable trust, they need only petition the court to "step into the shoes" of the grantor and revoke the trust themselves. Trust assets will no longer be owned by the trust but by you personally. The creditors then have the right to seize these assets now owned by you.

Other Benefits of Living Trusts

Despite its weakness for asset protection planning, the living trust is still commonly used in asset protection plans. It is the ideal way to own FLP interests, LLC membership interests, or other interests in entities that will provide protection.

While these legal entities are owned by your living trusts rather than in your own name, you later save estate taxes and expensive probate fees. You get the best of both worlds: protecting your assets while alive and saving your family estate taxes and probate fees when you die. For more about living trusts, including how to use them, see Chapter 63.

Irrevocable Trusts: The Asset Protectors

While revocable trusts offer no asset protection, irrevocable trusts are outstanding for asset protection. In fact, the irrevocable trust can be a +4 on the sliding scale of asset protection given the right circumstances. Once you establish an irrevocable trust, however, you forever abandon the ability to undo the trust and reclaim property transferred to the trust. With an irrevocable trust, you lose both control of the trust assets and ownership.

Of course, this discussion assumes that in transferring assets to any irrevocable trust, you do not run afoul of fraudulent transfer laws. We introduced the concept of these laws in the Introduction of this section. For more on fraudulent transfer laws, see the Appendix.

Why Irrevocable Trusts Protect Your Assets

Irrevocable trusts protect assets for the same reason that revocable trusts do not. Revocable living trusts do not provide asset protection because creditors can step into your shoes and undo the trust. The logic here is that if you have the power to undo your trust, so do your creditors.

An irrevocable trust leads to the opposite result. Because an established irrevocable trust cannot be altered or undone, your creditors cannot step into your shoes and undo the trust any more than you can. Assets in an irrevocable trust are immune from creditor attack, lawsuits, and other threats. An irrevocable trust carries a heavy price — you must give up control and ownership of the asset to gain protection. This is why most clients do not opt for the trust and instead prefer to utilize an exempt asset or international planning.

When does the heavy price of an irrevocable trust make sense? When you 1) would inevitably gift the assets to the beneficiaries, and 2) do not foresee needing the assets for your own financial security. When both factors are satisfied, your "price" is not particularly heavy. You do not personally need the assets and the trust will accomplish what you would do yourself — distribute the assets to your beneficiaries (usually children) at some future time.

Three Pitfalls to Avoid with Irrevocable Trusts

Keep three precautionary measures in mind:

1. You cannot reserve any power to revoke, rescind, or amend the trust or retain any right, either directly or indirectly, to reclaim property transferred to the trust. Simply put, there can be no strings attached.

2. Gifts to trusts are given the most scrutiny under fraudulent transfer laws because there is no "for value" exchange as there is with LLCs or FLPs. Often, for asset protection purposes, these tools are superior.

3. You, as the trust's grantor, should not be the trustee. Nor can you appoint a trustee not considered at arm's length. Those who do not qualify for arm's length include your spouse or any close relative. Even appointment of a distant

relative or close personal friend will invite scrutiny and it will be necessary to show that the close personal friend was serving independently and was not subservient to the interests of the Grantor. Courts closely examine the relationship between the grantor and the trustee to determine whether the trustee is only the grantor's "alter ego." If there is such a relationship, courts will ignore the trust and allow creditors to reach the trust assets.

> **TIP: A corporate trustee, such as a bank or a trust company, is much less likely to be judged as an alter ego, thereby giving your trust an added layer of security.**

Three Clauses Your Irrevocable Trust Should Have

An irrevocable trust should have three particular clauses for it to provide rock-solid protection. These clauses are important not necessarily to protect you, the trust creator, but to shield your beneficiaries from their creditors.

Spendthrift Clause

The spendthrift clause allows the trustee to withhold income and principal, which would ordinarily be paid to the beneficiary, if the trustee feels the money could or would be wasted or seized by the beneficiary's creditors. This clause accomplishes two goals. First, it prevents a wasteful beneficiary from spending trust funds or wasting trust assets. This is especially important to many grantors who set up trusts with their children as beneficiaries. If you worry that money in trust for your children would be wasted if not controlled, then use a spendthrift clause. The trustee can then stop payments if your child spends too quickly or unwisely.

Secondly, the spendthrift clause protects trust assets from creditors of the beneficiaries. Beneficiaries may now be young but as adults they will face the same risks we all face: lawsuits, debt problems, divorce, a failing business, etc. The spendthrift clause protects trust assets from your children's creditors by granting the trustee the authority to withhold payments to a beneficiary who has an outstanding creditor. If the beneficiary and trustee are at "arm's length," the creditor has no power to force the trustee to pay the beneficiary. The creditor only has a right to payments actually made by the trustee. He cannot force the trustee to make disbursements.

Anti-Alienation Clause

The anti-alienation clause also protects trust assets from the beneficiary's creditors. Specifically, the anti-alienation clause prohibits the trustee from transferring trust assets to anyone other than the beneficiary. This, of course, includes creditors of the trust beneficiary(ies). Thus, while the spendthrift clause allows the trustee to withhold payments if a creditor lurks, the anti-alienation clause goes one step further — it prohibits the trustee from paying trust income or principal to anyone but the named beneficiaries.

Generation-Skipping Language

Although it is not technically an asset protection provision, generation-skipping language is crucial if the goal of the trust is to provide benefits to two or more generations. Because the IRS imposes a harsh "generation skipping tax" in addition to the estate tax on gifts to grandchildren (or younger generations), this language is necessary to minimize those taxes and make full use of the special exemption value for that tax. For more on generation skipping taxes and "dynasty trusts" that deal with them, speak with a member of the Wealth Protection Alliance or another qualified estate planning professional.

CASE STUDY: *Jerry and His Kids*

Jerry, a successful orthopedic surgeon, had a sizable investment portfolio, including $200,000 in mutual funds that he planned on leaving to his two children, Steve and Stephanie. Jerry knew that he and his wife could live quite comfortably without these mutual funds and he wanted to save estate taxes and provide security to his children. Jerry, however, was concerned that his kids would unwisely spend the funds.

We established an irrevocable trust for Jerry and named his local bank trust department as trustee. Jerry told the trust officer about his concerns for the funds. Jerry's wishes were incorporated into the trust document.

Although Steve and Stephanie were only 12 at the time, Jerry and his wife funded the trust with $20,000 worth of mutual fund interests each year — so the gifts to the trust were completely tax-free. The trust was made irrevocable so that if Jerry or his wife were sued, their creditors could not seize these funds. The trust also had anti-alienation and spendthrift clauses so the funds would be protected from his children's poor spending habits as well as their potential future creditors.

Jerry realized that the trust would eventually be substantial in value. He also recognized the possibility that his children could someday have creditor or divorce problems. With this irrevocable trust, Jerry protected these funds from his creditors, gifted them tax-free to the trust, provided for his children's future (which he intended to do through his will or living trust), and did so in a way that fully protects the funds from his children's creditors as well.

Five Tips for an Ironclad Irrevocable Trust

You can greatly increase the asset protection for your irrevocable trust by using the following five tactics:

Fund the Trust Early

As with any asset protection strategy, avoid fraudulent transfers. Create the trust and fund it before a lawsuit arises. You greatly ensure that your trust cannot be undone by a creditor crying "fraudulent transfer."

Use an Independent Trustee

Do not be the trustee of your own trust. The best trustees are completely independent: a bank or a professional, such as an attorney or accountant, are preferable. Less desirable are close family friends or relatives.

State a Non-Protection Purpose for the Trust

It is usually desirable to state a non-protection reason in the trust document. Courts are less likely to set aside a legal entity, such as a trust, established for estate planning purposes or to provide support for a family member. Often, we write this non-protection purpose in the trust Preamble.

The Beneficiary Should Not Be The Grantor

If the beneficiary is the grantor, courts will disregard the trust and allow the grantor's creditors to seize the trust assets.

Keep Accurate Records

Operate the trust in a businesslike way. Keep accurate records of all transfers to the trust, as well as disbursements of income and principal to beneficiaries. This is another benefit of a corporate trustee. They keep accurate records.

Conclusion

As you have seen, irrevocable trusts play an important role in any Wealth Protection asset protection plan. Please refer to the other chapters in the book that discuss specific types of trusts which might play a role in your plan.

17

USING INTERNATIONAL PLANNING TO PROTECT ASSETS

Whether you were directed to this chapter or to the asset protection section in general, you need to shield your wealth from potential claims and lawsuits. Because international planning, along with domestic exempt assets, qualifies as a +5 on the asset protection scale, this chapter is extremely important to anyone who values asset protection. In this chapter, you'll learn what to do (and what to avoid) in international planning, and about specific tools you can utilize in your plan.

International Planning: A Worldwide Phenomenon

Using foreign jurisdictions to protect wealth has been a popular strategy for estate and family-wealth planning since the early Roman days when emperors attempted to preserve their riches for their descendants. Nevertheless, international planning has never been as popular as it is today. For tens of thousands of Americans each year, international structures become part of their Wealth Protection plan. Certainly there are tremendous benefits to be gained by using opportunities outside of the 50 states…you just have to make sure you do it right.

Would you be surprised to know that there is over $5 trillion U.S. in foreign vehicles? Most of this wealth is held in international financial centers, such as the Bahamas, Bermuda, the British Virgin Islands, the Cayman Islands, the Cook Islands, the Isle of Mann, Jersey & Guernsey, Luxembourg, Nevis, Switzerland, Turks & Caicos, and a host of other nations. Because they have favorable tax, banking, privacy, estate planning, and asset protection laws, these international havens are extremely desirable countries in which to set up a trust or other structure.

Wealthy individuals and families from around the world have established legal entities in these countries for decades. In fact, for much of the world, the United States is an "international financial center" itself, with numerous tax benefits offered to foreigners who want to invest here. Nonetheless, only in the last ten years have middle-income professionals, entrepreneurs, and other savvy U.S. citizens taken advantage of planning outside the United States.

The Three Reasons Americans Go Offshore

Asset Protection

This is the goal which we will focus on in this chapter. Note: Many Americans (and potential clients of ours) may initially indicate that they want to put some of their wealth outside of the U.S. for "privacy" reasons. While there certainly are some high-profile clients who do hold this as a true objective, we have found that when one gets down to the truth of it, these clients almost always use the word "privacy" to mean either asset protection or tax planning. Thus, we will not address "privacy" concerns separately here.

Tax Planning

A common and extremely dangerous misconception about international planning is that by simply going offshore, one can avoid U.S. taxation. Simply put, this is dead wrong. Americans are liable for taxes on income wherever earned. The vast majority of solid international asset protection plans are tax neutral. There may be significant tax advantages by having captive insurance companies or foreign life insurance and annuities, but these tax benefits are allowed under the U.S. tax code.

Investing

Consider that the U.S. market now only represents approximately 35% of the world's capital market (contrast with over 60% circa. 1960) and that market share is declining. This means that if you only invest in the U.S., you are missing out on 2/3 of the world's investment opportunities. You are also making a 100% bet on the stability of the U.S. currency, which has been steadily declining.

Because the Securities and Exchange Commission (SEC) makes it almost impossible for foreign companies to sell their stock in the U.S., many clients use an international entity to purchase foreign securities. This way, the other two-thirds of the world's investments become available.

Two Threats to Your International Plan

The Devil Within & The Devil Without

Almost always, there are one or two common culprits to be found in every case where a client fails to "do it right" offshore. The first is client greed (the devil within) and the second is the inept or ethically-challenged advisor (the devil without).

As you might imagine, in our business we see too many people go international for the wrong reasons and get burned in the process. Often, they are so anxious to avoid taxes, shield assets improperly (as above), or get rich that their reasonable judgment is clouded …and they engage in planning which would never be viable in the U.S. Combine these desires with an unregulated international jurisdiction (i.e., no reporting to the IRS, no SEC or NASD disclosure requirements, no state attorney generals remedying fraud, etc.), and one has a situation ripe with potential abuse. Let's see how most clients get in trouble.

The Devil Within: Why Greed Is Bad

Offshore planning strategies that will not work without committing perjury

As explained in this section, +5 level of asset protection can be achieved in the U.S. through the use of state and federally exempt assets such as ERISA-qualified pensions, cash value life insurance and annuities. Protection at a level of +2 to +4 can be acheived domestically through FLPs, LLCs, and trusts.

In this way, international entities have many of the same asset protection features as domestic counterparts. Thus, the "right" way to protect assets internationally is to combine the same legal structures one would use here in the States with the practical difficulty of having those entities located in foreign nations where American attorneys are unable to practice and thus unfamiliar with the law. This makes a +2 or +3 tool a +5 tool.

Unfortunately, while creating legitimate international asset protection plans is not difficult for experienced advisors, many Americans forego such planning and simply try to "hide" wealth in these international centers. Rather than use an entity like an LLC, they simply set up a bank or brokerage account in countries where there is little reporting. No one is any the wiser, right?

The problem with this "no entity" approach is that in any litigation, whether it is a civil lawsuit, divorce, or even governmental case, there will eventually be some type of formal inquiry of assets. This might occur by way of a "debtor's exam" after a successful lawsuit, a bankruptcy filing, or a list of assets for a divorce settlement, etc. For the "no entity" approach to work, the client would have to omit the international assets or lie about their existence. This amounts to perjury, bankruptcy fraud, or obstruction of justice, depending upon the forum of the case. This type of crime, it should go without saying, is completely unacceptable.

Desiring to Avoid U.S. Taxes Internationally Leads to Tax Evasion

As explained above, Americans are liable for taxes on all income earned offshore. However, it is true that many international banks, mutual funds, and other financial institutions will not report earnings or interest income to the IRS. This is the chasm where many greedy clients — or unscrupulous advisors — operate. This is also where the federal crime of tax evasion is committed.

While the client is required under U.S. law to make the necessary tax reporting on income earned internationally (and his/her advisors should instruct them so), many clients will keep quiet and hope that they are never caught. This "hide the ball" strategy is used not only by knowing clients, but also by shady advisors who concoct ever more sophisticated schemes such as moving money from one trust to another company to a third foundation...and so on.

Although their pitch may seem complex and impressive, you can always ask them the following question: If the income will eventually accrue to my benefit, how come I don't have to report it to the IRS? Unless a licensed U.S. advisor will go on the record (i.e., write an opinion letter) as to the tax treatment of a particular entity, steer clear of these schemes unless you want the cloud of a possible tax evasion indictment hanging over you for years to come.

Desiring to Get Rich Internationally Leads to Scams & Frauds

The type of greediness that leads clients into problems is most pervasive in the investment arena. Here, scam artists and fraudsters abound, poised to take advantage of the next client who wants to "get rich offshore." For an updated list of common traps in the world of offshore, contact your local Wealth Protection Alliance member.

The Devil Without: Why Your Advisor May Be Your Worst Enemy

As common as the situation where a client's own motivations get him in trouble is the scenario where a client with good intentions is "up the creek" because of his/her advisors. Creating a viable international plan requires expertise in international and domestic taxation, conflicts of laws, asset protection, the law of corporations and partnerships, estate planning, and others. The bottom line is that while there are thousands of advisors in the U.S. who promote themselves as experts on international planning, probably only 1 in 50 is truly knowledgeable and experienced.

What are the most common errors advisors make in international planning? The following are always at the top of the list:

The Advisor Is Not Experienced In International Planning...
So Clients Get Caught in "Scams"

A top international advisor should have experience in dealing with international havens and have contacts in many of them. They should keep abreast of up-to-the-minute developments in the field which, for those in the field, is not difficult through informal professional contacts (not to mention professional journals and websites).

Moreover, advisors should have existing relationships with top fiduciary firms in the country where their structures are established — including trust companies or bank officers, insurance managers, actuaries, money managers, attorneys and accountants, among others. These contacts can buttress the advisor's analysis of any international opportunities.

Advisors who are new to the field, or who have not put in the years of due diligence required to be competent in offshore planning, will not have these contacts and resources. Thus, when faced with tough judgment calls regarding whether or not to use a particular trustee firm or local accountant or trust investment, they cannot accurately evaluate the risks and rewards. Too often, these advisors put clients in structures or investments that a more resourceful advisor would have avoided.

The Advisor Is Not An Expert in International Taxation

If you go offshore, you will need to use an attorney or CPA who is an expert in international taxation unless you want to risk committing tax fraud.

This is the most common failing of otherwise competent attorneys involved in offshore planning. They simply don't know *all of the rules* regarding U.S. taxpayers with investments and structures abroad. They may know most of the rules, but unless they are familiar with them all, clients will pay a hefty price — either tax penalties for not reporting correctly or (like our example below) paying too much tax because of a lack of planning.

We see this all the time with clients who have used another advisor and have created an international structure that purchased international mutual funds. Often, these are very stable, recommended mutual funds from large European financial institutions, so there is no "scam" risk. Nonetheless, in 99% of the cases, the client is looking at a tax nightmare, paying income taxes at effective rates ranging from 46% to 84% depending on how long the client holds the investments! Investment returns become almost irrelevant when tax rates are this high.

How many advisors have heard of the PFIC QEF rules regarding the taxation of foreign mutual funds? Not many. These rules allow investors in "Qualifying Elective Funds" to use U.S. income tax rates on their income from the fund, including the most favorable long term capital gains rates. Less than 1% of international funds qualify under these rules, so most clients end up paying the horrid rates of 46% to 84% for no reason other than the incompetence of their advisor. WPA advisors have access to such US-reporting European money managers.

International LLCs & Trusts: The "Dynamic Duo" of International Planning

By using international planning as part of your Wealth Protection plan, you will have the most powerful asset protection tools at your disposal. In this chapter, we continue where the previous chapter left off, concentrating our discussion on two effective international tools — the international limited liability company (LLC) and the international trust.

Of course, the following discussion assumes that in transferring assets to any international entity, you do not run afoul of fraudulent transfer laws. We introduced the concept of these laws in the Introduction of this section. For more on fraudulent transfer laws, see the Appendix.

Nevis: An Important Jurisdiction for LLCs

When Nevis, a small Caribbean nation that is part of a Federation with St. Kitts, began to compete for the multi-billion (US$) asset protection business in the early 1990's, it revised its trust and business entity laws. As part of this process, the lawmakers studied American LLC statutes and improved upon them in terms of providing asset protection for American citizens. Today, Nevis has the oldest and most stable LLC legislation outside of the U.S., specifically modeled after the well-drafted Delaware legislation. The result is a superior asset protection tool used by many attorneys specializing in the field for years: the Nevis LLC.

The Nevis LLC

As we explained in an earlier chapter, domestic LLCs (those in the states) enjoy +2 / +3 protection, because a creditor of yours can only obtain a "charging order" against your LLC interest. This "charging order" entitles the creditor only to your share of any distributions actually made from the LLC (which you, as the manager of the LLC, control). The "charging order" does not allow the creditor to seize your interest in the LLC or vote your interest. In this way, the assets within the LLC are shielded. Only when you decide to make distributions does the creditor get anything of value. This will provide you strong settlement leverage.

The Nevis LLC has the same charging order protection incorporated into its legislation, thus simulating the Delaware LLC law. However, it adds a number of significant benefits that the domestic LLCs cannot provide — the deterrence factors of Nevis Law. These include the following:

No Contingency Fee Attorneys/Local Attorneys Only: This means that any creditor attacking transfers to a Nevis entity (LLC or trust) must hire a lawyer in that country.

Bond Required: Certain havens require a bond to be posted when filing a lawsuit because, in these countries, the losing party pays the prevailing party's legal fees. This is the "British or Commonwealth Rule." The bond is often required to cover tens of thousands of dollars in legal fees, making the prospect of suing even more expensive.

Tough Burden of Proof: In many countries, a plaintiff must prove you fraudulently transferred assets beyond a reasonable doubt. This is an extremely difficult standard. In our legal system, this standard is only for criminal cases. In your offshore haven, however, any civil suit to get at your entity's assets may have to satisfy this difficult burden of proof.

Favorable Statute of Limitations Period: As mentioned in previous chapters, the statute of limitations is the time period within which a lawsuit must be brought. When the time expires, the lawsuit will not be allowed. In certain asset protection international havens, lawsuits against the entity must be commenced in the haven's courts within two years from the time the legal right to sue or cause of action arose.

Other Benefits of the Nevis LLC

Tax Neutral

The Nevis LLC is tax neutral, like a domestic LLC. In terms of estate planning, the LLC can be used as part of a gifting program to move value out of a couple's estate by moving ownership units to children. This can be accomplished while the clients (parents) maintain 100% control.

Easy & Inexpensive to Maintain

Unlike a foreign trust, a Nevis LLC has minimal tax reporting requirements. Moreover, there are no conditions to keep minute books, hold annual director or member meetings, or observe other customary corporate formalities. Costs for maintaining the entity are around $600 per year.

CASE STUDY: *"Protected Howard" settles claims for pennies*

Howard, a geology consultant, and brother of a physician client of ours, is well-respected in his scientific community. While he had never been sued before, Howard recently learned that one of his colleagues lost a judgment for $1 million over coverage limits. This was the result of the colleague's advice on a structure that was heavily damaged in an earthquake. Howard quickly decided to engage in asset protection planning.

Howard set up a Wealth Protection plan, part of which involved transferring his non-pension liquid assets to a Nevis LLC. The LLC then established a bank account, through which he then purchased a high-grade tax-deferred variable annuity from a multi-billion dollar Swiss insurance company.

If Howard is ever threatened with a lawsuit, he won't be worried about losing what he has already earned. Instead, Howard now feels secure, knowing that his most important assets are safe from all creditors and that he is no longer at the mercy of the lawsuit and the legal system.

International Trusts: The Classic International Tool

While many U.S. asset protection experts are using Nevis LLCs in place of international trusts, there are still instances where the trust may be preferable. In the following instances, the international trust (IT) may make sense:

Owning foreign insurance policies

One of the leading international Wealth Protection strategies today is to have a client purchase a permanent (cash value) life insurance policy offshore. In terms of tax planning, if the policy is U.S. tax-compliant, then all of the growth within the policy will accumulate tax-free. Further, the proceeds will be distributed to the beneficiary income tax free and the client can take tax-free loans against the accumulated cash values during his lifetime. This is similar to the benefits of a domestic cash value life insurance policy, which you can read more about in the tax section.

As in the U.S., we would typically advise a client purchasing such a policy to do it in their name if their state exempts cash value life insurance policies. When dealing with a foreign insurance policy, we would use an IT. Often, the foreign insurers must sell their policy to some non-U.S. entity, even if that entity is completely disclosed and compliant with U.S. law. In this situation, we use an IT to purchase the policy with the client as the beneficiary.

Why would a client want to use an international policy, rather than a domestic policy? Aside from the obvious asset protection benefit of having the asset offshore, one reason is that many foreign insurers will allow the selection of a particular U.S.-based money manager in a much smaller policy than U.S. insurers. These policies are called "private placement" policies (PPLI). In this way, the client gets the asset protection value of the international life insurance with the financial stability of U.S. based money managers. It is not surprising that foreign life insurance is one of international planning's fastest-growing strategies.

Multi-generational planning

Let's say your Wealth Protection goal is to create a nest egg for future generations such as grandchildren and beyond. Let's also say it was important to you that the nest egg be asset-protected in an ironclad way. In this circumstance, an international trust would be an ideal tool for you, especially in countries where the law does not limit the duration of trusts pursuant to the "law against perpetuities" found in many of the states. By using an IT, you could literally secure that your family will enjoy the fruits of your gift for hundreds of years as long as other estate planning tax issues were addressed.

Using an International Debt Shield to Protect U.S. Real Estate

In the next chapter, we will review a popular option for protecting your home. It is called a "debt shield." By transferring all of your equity from your real estate to an exempt asset or to an asset that offers substantial protection and some upside potential, your net worth is increased while your home is protected <u>and</u> you still enjoy the upside of the home.

Whether the real estate you are looking to protect is your home, rental property, or other real estate, an international trust debt shield structure created by the WPA can also be ideal. The WPA international debt shield structure essentially involves a European bank, European money manager, and an IT. The strategy's goal is to protect the equity of any of your

U.S. real estate — and do so in a way that you have significant upside as well. In essence, because we cannot move the real estate offshore, we do the second best thing by transferring the equity to a +5 IT through the use of a legitimate mortgage.

As you can see in the diagram below, the strategy is quite simple. The European bank lends their money to your IT — at a commercially reasonable, yet low and fixed, interest rate. The collateral for that loan is the real estate you want to protect. The bank files a mortgage on this property (or properties) — thereby shielding it against any future lawsuits and creditors. Because the European bank will loan to 100% of the real estate value, there is literally nothing for a future creditor to get.

IAPT Debt Shield

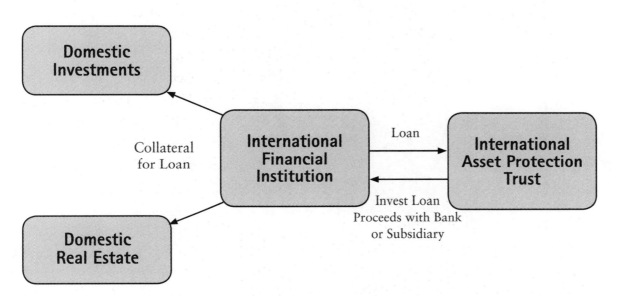

Meanwhile, your IT invests the loan proceeds with the European money manager. This manager is a top firm with over $1 billion US in client funds. Further, they manage accounts with all the necessary US tax reporting noted earlier in the chapter. Finally, they give your trust a number of investment options within the debt shield structure — from protecting conservatively against any loss of capital to investing more aggressively for more upside potential. Your trust will be in control here — for your benefit. Further, according to the loan terms, the IT can payback the loan at any time, putting the trust in control of the structure at all times. This gives you +5 protection of any U.S. real estate through an offshore shield. For more about the IT real estate debt shield, contact your local WPA member.

Find an Expert

As with any area of Wealth Protection planning, using an expert advisor experienced in these matters is paramount. Nowhere is this more important than with international planning.

18

HOW TO PROTECT
YOUR HOME
Turning Your Castle Into A Lawsuit-Proof Fortress

Along with retirement accounts, your home is likely the most valuable asset you have. Even beyond its pure financial value, your home probably has large psychological value as well. In fact, we find that most of our clients who engage in asset protection planning often begin with the question: "How can I protect my home?" That is why we thought it important to dedicate an entire chapter to discussing this asset and how to protect it from outside threats. Before we do, however, consider this short case study:

> **CASE STUDY:** *Victor the Victim of Bad Luck and Poor Planning*
>
> Victor is a physician who recently started a new practice as a general partnership with another doctor with whom he had worked and trained under some years ago. Victor and his wife have a home worth $350,000, with a $100,000 mortgage. Victor also has $100,000 in a SEP-IRA from his earlier practice and he has $150,000 in brokerage accounts. Victor's partner, whom we shall call Unlucky Lou, had the misfortune of a bad outcome. Initially, the family members surviving the patient were hurt but not vindictive. After a few conversations with an attorney, their opinion changed and they sued Lou along with the partnership and the anesthesiologist who was involved.
>
> After a long 18 months of depositions and discovery, the case actually went to trial. The court entered judgment for the plaintiffs in the amount of $3,000,000. Lou's malpractice carrier paid the $1,000,000 coverage limit. The creditor then seized Lou's $400,000 brokerage account. Lou still had $2,000,000 in the profit sharing plan from his old practice. Aware of the federal protection afforded the plan assets, Lou then filed bankruptcy to rid himself of the creditor. He did lose what little equity he had in his home along with his brokerage account, but he was able to save his profit sharing plan and his cash value insurance policies.

The judgment creditors were not happy with partial satisfaction of the judgment. They then pursued the practice and its general partners (Lou) for the remainder. The attorney successfully took the practice accounts receivable ($400,000). Under the premise of joint and several liability with the general partnership, Lou still had to personally come up with the remainder. Victor's attorney could not protect him. Victor couldn't believe this. He asked his attorney if he could declare bankruptcy to save his assets. Victor unfortunately found out the hard way that his SEP-IRA, home, and brokerage accounts could be lost in this lawsuit. In actuality, they were all lost.

Victor hadn't even seen the client, but through the miracles of litigation and the creativity of the suing attorney, Victor lost everything. What could he have done? There are advanced strategies to protect IRAs, the Accounts Receivable of a practice, and brokerage accounts. (These are highlighted in our new special report or on our website **www.jarvisandmandell.com**). The focus of this chapter is to discuss how Lou and Victor could have protected their homes.

While the above case study is extreme, the need to protect the home is an important one. While the precise game plan for you depends on the facts and circumstances of your situation, the most common tools we use to shield a physician's home from potential creditors are set forth below.

State Homestead Law

Every state has some type of homestead protection. In most states, as in New Jersey, New York, and California, the level of protection is very low when compared to what real estate is worth (New Jersey $0, New York $10,000, California up to $75,000). On the other hand in states like Florida and Texas, there is unlimited protection of the home's value aslong as the parcel of land isn't too large. However, even these state laws are now under the gun, as proposed bankruptcy legislation may limit how much homestead value can be protected in any state.

If your state has adequate homestead protection, make sure you work with a local advisor to comply with the state formalities. You don't want to ignore any specific formality and lose all the homestead protection. For example, some states with unlimited homestead protection will not shelter the home if it is owned by a revocable living trust, a tool often recommended to own the home for estate planning purposes. By ignoring this simple but little understood rule, many physicians think their home is protected when in fact it is 100% vulnerable.

If your home equity comes within the homestead amount AND you have complied with all formalities, state homestead law can be a very high level of protection. On our sliding scale that we introduced in Chapter 9, homestead protection can qualify for a +4 or +5 level of protection.

Tenancy by the Entirety

In states like Arizona (and others), you can file to have your home owned by Tenancy by the Entirety (T/E). Theoretically, this means that only a creditor who has a claim against both you and your spouse can take the home if it is titled this way. T/E is not automatic. You have to file to have your home titled this way. Also, there has been a case when a litigant successfully penetrated T/E and took a home from a couple because the couple had at least one joint creditor (it was a credit card with both of their names on it). Because of this case, we hesitate to consider T/E as a very strong protector although we do admit it is much better than simple joint ownership. Another limitation of T/E is that parents are both responsible for actions of their minor children. If a child causes a very serious accident, you can lose a home owned T/E. Again, the key here is to work with a local member of the Wealth Protection Alliance to make sure that the T/E protection in your state is reliable. If the T/E law is absolutely solid in your state, then this ownership form can be a +3 to +4 on the scale.

LLCs and FLPs

Limited Liability Companies (LLCs) and Family Limited Partnerships (FLPs) are very powerful asset protection tools. In most cases, assets held by an LLC or FLP cannot be taken by a creditor (see Chapter 15). As explained earlier, a creditor who has a judgment against someone's interest in an LLC/FLP can generally only get a "charging order" against that person's interest. What this means, very simply, is that the creditor has to wait until the doctor decides to take a distribution. This puts the doctor in a very strong negotiating position on any settlement. The attorney only gets paid when the settlement is paid. The attorney, and client, will generally settle for pennies on the dollar rather than wait 10, 20, or 50 years for the charging order to be fulfilled. Because of this, and the fact that the FLP/LLC is simple, relatively inexpensive, allows one to maintain control and creates no additional tax burden, the FLP/LLC is given a +2 on the asset protection scale.

Drawbacks of LLCs and FLPs for the Home

Unlike other assets, the family home has unique tax attributes — most notably, the deductibility of the mortgage interest and the $250,000/$500,000 capital gain exemption. By owning the home within an LLC or a FLP, these tax benefits may be lost, unless only one spouse owns 100% of the interests in the LLC or FLP. However, in a very recent case, the court set aside the protections of an LLC when only the debtor owned 100% of the interests in the LLC. For these reasons, we no longer recommend single-owner LLCs and FLPs to protect the family home — especially when the enhanced debt shield is available.

Qualified Personal Residence Trusts (QPRTs)

When using a QPRT, you irrevocably transfer ownership of the home to the QPRT. While this is certainly effective for both asset protection and estate planning purposes, it comes with a significant cost you no longer own your home. In fact, when the term of years is up (typically 10 years), you have to pay rent to the trust just to live in the home. Also, homes with mortgages on them (most do) present further tax difficulties as well. For these reasons, while the QPRT is a strong asset protection tool, we typically do not advise using it for most clients whose main concern is asset protection instead of estate planning. Nonetheless, in terms of pure asset protection benefits, QPRT gets a +4 or +5 level of protection if it can be implemented correctly as part of a comprehensive Wealth Protection Planning that addresses asset protection and estate planning.

Debt Shields: Background

The debt shield can be the most effective way to shield the equity of the home or any other real estate. Essentially, using a debt shield means getting a loan against most of the equity in your home. For many clients, this is counter-intuitive because they want to pay down the mortgage as much as possible. While this may have an emotional appeal, for asset protection purposes, it is the exact opposite of what you want to do.

Consider for a minute real estate developers. From your local developer to Donald Trump, their strategy is always the same — build equity in a project and then leverage it as much as possible. Take a loan against that equity in a new project and then take a loan against that. And so on and so on. Why do these savvy investors use debt this way? Put simply, they want to create wealth — by building their assets at a greater rate than the cost of the loan. For example, if Mr. Trump can get a mortgage at 5% after tax, and can invest in a new project that makes 10%, then Mr. Trump has created wealth on "OPM" — other people's money! Further, Mr. Trump still enjoys the upside of Building A. This is the way every real estate developer builds wealth. It's also the way every bank works — take deposits and pay a low interest rate and use those funds to make loans at a much higher rate. Again, OPM.

Now we are not recommending that you leave the practice of medicine and become the next Donald Trump or Wells Fargo Bank. We do, however, strongly recommend that if you want to protect your home, keep it in your name, and build wealth, that you seriously consider the debt shield strategy for your home.

The Enhanced WPA Debt Shield: Build Wealth While Protecting Your Home

Over the past few years, the 50+ WPA members have helped thousands of clients with their asset protection planning. More recently, the WPA itself has developed a proprietary enhanced debt shield strategy that helps clients shield their homes, maintain the upside of the home values, and build additional asset-protected wealth, while protecting their downside. We will illustrate and describe the WPA strategy on the next page.

Debt Shield

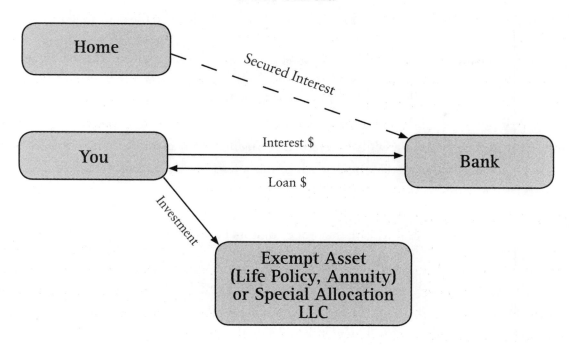

As the diagram above makes clear, the WPA strategy is quite simple. It involves you, your home, and a particular national bank (with which the WPA has negotiated an ideal loan package for the debt shield). Depending on your state, it may either involve a life insurance policy, annuity and/or specially designed LLC. The steps of the debt shield strategy are as follows:

1. Protect the home equity with the mortgage.

Using a re-fi or home equity loan, the WPA bank loans you money and protects the home against future claims via the mortgage. Here, the particular economics of the loan package make the strategy so appealing. Using an interest-only loan, we can typically lock in fixed rates for 5, 7, 10 years. Depending on exactly how we structure the investment of the loan proceeds, the after-tax cost of the loan might be 3–4%, or even less. "Can you do better than 3% after-tax?" We know you can. In fact, we can structure the investment to eliminate downside risk <u>and</u> allow substantial upside. Once again, you have OPM working for you.

2. Invest the loan proceeds in an asset-protected tool.

As with any debt shield, the loan proceeds must be invested in a strong asset protection tool — or there is no "shield" at all. Ideally, you invest in a +5 exempt asset, such as life insurance and annuities in certain states. If your state does not exempt these assets, we need to use a specially-designed LLC to own the investments — to protect them while allowing you tax-favored access to them as well.

3. Why life insurance?

Typically, we use cash value life insurance as the investment vehicle in the debt shield structure — even if it must be owned by an LLC in your state. Why do we recommend life insurance:

- You can enjoy guaranteed returns. Many policies we use guarantee the crediting rate at a level even with (or even greater than) the loan interest. This helps you lock in wealth creation.

- You can enjoy upside while protecting downside. Many clients have used a policy tied to the S&P 500 index which has a floor of 1% and a cap of 17%. Getting between 1–17% tax free when the loan costs 3–4% can be a great way to use OPM. For a free copy of our special report on insurance vs. market investing where we illustrate this policy and its benefits, call the WPA at (800) 554-7233.

- The growth in a life insurance policy is tax-free. No mutual fund enjoys this benefit.

- The funds can be accessed by you completely tax-free — even through the LLC — at any time. Again, such tax benefits only increase the economic return to you.

- If you have any existing life insurance before the debt shield, you could stop paying on these policies, further improving your cash flow and upside of the strategy.

> **CASE STUDY:** *Vance protects his home, his family and saves money*
>
> Vance is a gynecologist in North Carolina. His state is in the midst of a malpractice crisis and many physicians there have been the victims of substantial malpractice judgments. Vance owns a home worth $635,000 with a $351,166 mortgage. His monthly mortgage payment is roughly $2,993 per month. $1,300 of the mortgage payment is interest and he is in a 46% marginal tax bracket (when you factor in state and federal income taxes, payroll taxes, social security, etc.). As a result, there is a tax savings of $598 on his mortgage, leaving him with a net after-tax monthly mortgage payment of $2,395.
>
> He is concerned with protecting his home and investments from lawsuits, reducing his annual expenses, and protecting his family from an unexpected death.
>
> Vance took out an interest only loan for the full $635,000 against his home. This loan was used to repay the existing mortgage. After repaying the bank, he still had $283,834 leftover and he had $0 equity in his home — thus making his home worth nothing to future lawsuits claimants, from his practice or otherwise. The new mortgage payment was $2,858 — all interest, since he now has an interest-only loan.

If you factor in the 46% tax savings (assuming your accountant deems the entire mortgage tax deductible — this depends on your exact circumstances), there will be a tax savings of $1,314 each month on the mortgage. The new after tax monthly mortgage is only $1,544 per month. This is a savings of $851 per month.

Vance had his attorney establish a special-allocation asset protection limited liability company (LLC) to protect his brokerage account and the new $283,834 he has to invest. The LLC then invests the $283,834 into a cash value life insurance policy — in his case, he chose an equity indexed life insurance policy that grows at the same rate as the S&P 500 subject to a 1% minimum and 17% maximum annual return.

Vance's new mortgage payment is $851 per month lower than his previous mortgage($10,212 per year after-tax savings). His home is now protected since he has no exposed equity. The value of the house is growing at the same rate as it was before. Even better, Vance has $283,834 invested in a cash value life insurance policy that projects to have almost $1.2 million of cash value after 15 years of growth (if you assume a rate of return of 9.9%). The policy projects tax-free income of $106,812 per year of tax-free income from age 68 through age 100. This is in addition to the extra $10,212 of spending he has each year!

As you can see, the benefit of this plan is threefold:

1. His home is now protected from creditors — while he still owns in his name and enjoys the capital gains tax exemption for homes.

2. His monthly expenses are reduced by $851.

3. He has an additional $283,834 invested for his future use (possibly generating over $106,812 of tax free retirement income from ages 68 to 100).

In this way, Vance has actually made money by protecting his home. In other words, rather than this asset protection strategy costing him money — this strategy actually made him money. Just like real estate developers, he was able to use financing to build wealth and protect home equity. Why wouldn't every physician at least consider the enhanced debt shield?

Conclusion

For most physician families, there is no more important asset than the home. If you are concerned with protecting your home, you should speak to a WPA member to make sure the barbarians at the gate of your family's castle can do nothing more than make a lot of noise and not disrupt your quality of life. Better yet, why not leverage the equity in your home that is not doing anything for you? You could achieve the same asset protection Vance did and possibly generate millions in additional tax-free income in retirement.

19

PROTECTING WEALTH FROM DIVORCE
How To Keep Family Assets In The Family

Of all the risks to our assets, the most common threat to our financial security is divorce. Over 50% of all marriages in this country end in divorce and that percentage grows to almost 75% for second marriages. Interestingly, our extensive research shows that 100% of divorces began with a marriage. If you, your children or your grandchildren are married or may one day be married, you have to protect against divorce. Undoubtedly an emotionally devastating experience, divorce can be a financially disastrous experience as well.

Divorce planning is not about hiding assets from a soon-to-be ex-spouse. Nor is it about cheating or lying to keep your wealth. Rather, it concerns resolving issues of property ownership and distribution before things go sour. By agreeing in advance what will be yours and what will be your spouse's, you save money, time, and emotional distress in the long-run. In fact, this type of asset protection planning inevitably benefits all parties (except the divorce lawyers, of course).

Divorce planning is also about shielding family assets from the potential divorces of children and grandchildren. Given the statistics enumerated above, it is almost a certainty that either a child or grandchild of yours will get divorced. Thus, for purposes of intergenerational Wealth Protection Planning, this is a crucial topic unless you want to give half of your inheritance to the ex-spouses of your heirs. As you will learn, there are ways to protect your children and grandchildren <u>without</u> making their spouses sign a prenuptial agreement.

Why Divorce Can Be a Financial Nightmare

Most Americans do not have to read newspapers to see how financially devastating a divorce can be. While high-profile divorces involving tens of millions of dollars illustrate the point dramatically, most of us need only look to family or friends to see how a divorce turns into financial upheaval. The prevailing attitude toward divorce comes from a relatively recent movie. In the film, Ivana Trump explains her theory of divorce to three ex-wives, played by Goldie Hawn, Diane Keaton, and Bette Midler. "Don't get even," she says, "get everything!"

Combine this fight-for-everything attitude with the terrible odds of getting a divorce and you have a very serious threat to financial security. In fact, a divorce threatens not only former spouses, but also their families and possibly their business partners as well. To truly understand how a divorce affects the finances of the participants, you must first understand how property is divided when the marriage is dissolved.

Community Property States

Nine states have community property laws: Arizona, California, Idaho, Louisiana, Nevada, New Mexico, Texas, Washington, and Wisconsin. If your divorce occurs in one of these states and there is no valid "pre" or post-marital agreement, the court will equally divide any property acquired during the marriage other than inheritances or gifts to one spouse. Even the appreciation of one spouse's separate property can be divided if the other spouse expended effort on that property during the marriage and the property actually appreciated concurrent or subsequent to the effort so expended. Obviously, how the asset is titled is not the controlling factor. When the asset was acquired and how it was treated are far more important factors in determining how the asset will be treated.

Equitable Distribution States

Non-community property states are called "equitable distribution" states because courts in these states have total discretion to divide the property equitably or fairly. The court will normally consider a number of factors in deciding what is "equitable," including the length of the marriage, the age and conduct of the parties, and the present earnings and future earning potential of each former spouse. The danger of equitable divorces is that courts often distribute both non-marital assets (those acquired before the marriage) as well as marital assets (those acquired during marriage), in order to create a "fair" arrangement. In so doing, the courts often split-up property in ways that the ex-spouses never wanted or expected.

Examples of "Disaster Divorces"

The following are examples to help you consider whether you and your family are adequately prepared for divorce:

> • A couple marries, each party for the second time and each with adult children from their first marriage. Without any pre- or post-martial agreement, they title many of the wife's previously separate income-producing properties (such as her rental apartment units) into the name of the new husband to save income taxes. Within two years of the marriage, they divorce. The husband gets half the rental units (in addition to alimony and other property) even though both spouses understood that the wife intended them to go to her

children. The court simply ignored their understanding, giving half the properties to each spouse.

- A couple marries, each for the first time. Over the next 20 years, the husband acquires more ownership in his family's bakery business. His father, the founder, gradually transferred shares to him. At 42, he is the majority owner. Unfortunately, he and his wife then undergo a bitter divorce with the ex-wife is granted half the husband's bakery business as community property. She then forces 1) high dividends and 2) a sale of the company to a competitor.

- An internal medicine resident gets married. She and her husband discuss her medical education and agree that she should not have to compensate him for his greater financial contribution in the early years of their marriage. However, they file for divorce eight years later. The husband considers the wife's professional degree as marital property, so he claims a share in her earning potential. The court agrees, even though the couple verbally agreed to the contrary.

Can a "Pre-nup" Protect You?

A premarital agreement (or, prenuptial agreement, premarital contract, ante-nuptial agreement, etc.) is the foundation of any protection against a divorce. The premarital agreement is a written contract between the spouses. It specifies the division of property and income upon divorce, including disposition of specific personal property such as family heirlooms. It also states the responsibilities of each party with regard to their children after divorce. Finally, these agreements lay out the respective responsibilities during marriage, such as the financial support each spouse can expect or which religion will be used to raise future children. The agreement cannot limit child support as the right to child support lies with the child and not the parent.

Not Only for the Rich

Premarital agreements are often perceived to be only for the wealthy, but this is not true. The three scenarios above didn't involve rich people, yet all could have benefited from a premarital agreement because these agreements deal with both current and future property. Such agreements also help those who eventually acquire significant property because they protect assets that existed at the time of execution of the agreement as well as those that exist in the future.

A premarital agreement, in fact, can be more important for the less wealthy spouse entering a second marriage. Why? Because that spouse typically gives up a major source of income — alimony from the first marriage. A pre-martial agreement can ensure that, if a divorce occurs, he/she will be at least as well-off as before remarriage.

Court Enforced

A premarital agreement is properly drafted if it makes thorough disclosures and if other state law requirements are met. Courts will then abide by its terms. With a rock-solid premarital agreement, you can limit surprises in divorce. The court will simply order you to split property as you had originally intended. This not only ensures that you retain property but also saves you time, aggravation, and attorneys' fees. It can avoid a difficult process and a nasty fight.

Requirements for a Premarital Agreement

Each state differs slightly on what is required for an enforceable premarital agreement. The following are fairly common requirements:

The agreement must be in writing and signed

Every state requires that a premarital agreement be written and signed. Many also require that it be notarized or witnessed.

> TIP: Notarize your agreement, even if your state does not require it. This adds protection against claims of duress or forgery. Some attorneys even recommend video-taping both sides agreeing to the terms of the agreement.

There must be a fair, accurate and reasonable disclosure of each party's financial condition

> TIP: Attach financial statements to the agreement and have the spouse confirm knowledge of the other's financial condition.

Each party must be advised by a separate attorney

Many states either require separate legal advice explicitly or use it as a factor in determining whether or not the agreement was fair.

> TIP: Hire separate lawyers and allow enough time between the agreement and the wedding date to avoid any appearance of duress. Courts frown on last second premarital agreements.

The agreement must not be unconscionable

Courts will not enforce a one-sided agreement. Also, the contract must not be structured to encourage divorce. For example, by stating that one spouse has no rights to property except upon divorce.

> TIP: Avoid extremely one-sided agreements. It need not be a 50/50 split, but should provide a fair balance.

The couple must follow the agreement during the marriage

Courts disregard premarital agreements when the spouses blatantly disregard it during their marriage, such as when property designated as the husband's separate property is re-titled to the wife.

> TIP: Treat designated separate property as separate. If loans are made from one spouse's separate property to the marital unit, then those funds should not be commingled when repaid.

Special Considerations for Family Business Owners

Divorce commonly causes a major disruption to a family-owned business. Commonly, when a child of the founder of the business gets divorced and the ex-spouse sues for half of that child's interest in the business, it creates a terrible strain on the business.

The ex-spouse's demands can lead to a formal discovery process where information intended to be private becomes accessible (such as salaries for family members, benefits, contracts, etc.) Dealing with this process often injures the family and the business.

This is why family business owners are increasingly using lawyers to protect them from divorce before it occurs. What is the preferred tool to prevent such disaster? The premarital agreement, of course. The *Wall Street Journal* recently reported that *"the number of premarital agreements drafted for members of family-owned businesses has skyrocketed in recent years."* One New York attorney now drafts close to 300 agreements per year. Fifteen years ago it was closer to 20.

Protect your business from the destruction that can result from a bitter divorce. Have every owner of your family business create an agreement (premarital or post-marital) which prevents the in-law from claiming a stake in the business upon divorce. Specify a cash settlement instead. Should a divorce then occur, the ex-spouse will still be fairly treated while your business remains undisrupted and in the family.

Irrevocable Spendthrift Trusts: Ideal Tools to Keep Assets "In the Family"

Irrevocable trusts are very effective asset protection tools because you no longer own the assets owned by the trust. You have transferred the property with no strings attached. Because you neither own nor control the property, your creditors, including an ex-spouse, cannot claim the property.

Moreover, you can make children, grandchildren, and even future great grandchildren beneficiaries of an irrevocable trust. However, even though they can benefit from trust assets, the trust can be drafted so that their creditors, including ex-spouses, cannot get to trust assets. As we explained in Chapter 16, these trusts have special "spendthrift" provisions.

Nonetheless, using an irrevocable trust should not be taken lightly. It means giving away those assets forever with no strings attached. This is a serious consequence when protecting against divorce, lawsuits, or other threats. When would such a strategy make sense? Under circumstances where you would have inevitably given the assets to certain beneficiaries anyway. For example, the trust might be used for assets which 1) you will leave to your children or grandchildren when you die, and 2) you do not need for your financial security. Consider this case:

CASE STUDY: *Irving's Trust Protects His Summer Home*

Irving, a gastroenterologist, bought a summer home on Cape Cod. He and his first wife had three small children. Unfortunately, they divorced about six years later. In the settlement, he received the summer home.

Fifteen years later, Irving was ready to marry again, now in Santa Fe. Both he and his prospective spouse had been married previously and understood divorce. Irving considered a premarital agreement to keep the summer home as his separate property. He had planned to give it to his three children and wondered whether working on the home would jeopardize this plan if he later divorced.

After speaking with Irving, we noted three important points: 1) his handiwork on the home might make it marital property; 2) his children and their families used the home throughout the year; and 3) Irving had a lawsuit from a failed real estate venture. It was clear that the best strategy for Irving was to have an irrevocable trust own the summer home, giving beneficial interests to use the home to all three children equally (which was already the case).

By using an irrevocable trust to own the summer home, Irving protected the home against possible future divorce and also shielded it from other creditors and lawsuits. By including spendthrift provisions, Irving protected the home from his children's creditors, as well. This will insure that the Cape house stays in the family for generations.

Protect Your Children From Divorce

When your children or grandchildren come to you, giddy with exciting new news about their recent engagements, the last thing they want to hear you ask is "are you going to sign a prenuptial agreement?" In fact, if you weren't paying for the wedding, you might lose your invitation for making such a statement.

As you learned earlier, the key to protecting assets from divorce is keeping the assets "separate property" and not commingling them with community or marital property. You can't trust your children to do this, so you are going to do it for them without needing the consent of your child or their spouse.

By leaving assets to your children's irrevocable trusts with the appropriate spendthrift provisions rather than to them personally, you can achieve this goal. Of course, if the children take money out of the trust and use it to buy a home or other property, that property will be subject to the rules of their state. Let's look at an example:

> **CASE STUDY:** *Rob and Janelle — college sweethearts*
>
> Rob and Janelle got married right out of college. Their romance quickly turned sour within a few years and Rob could no longer handle the physical and emotional abuse. However, during their three-year marriage, Janelle received a sizeable inheritance and used it to pay off the couple's home. When they filed for divorce, Rob's attorney successfully argued that his time and labor on the house and the fact that he lived in it (except when Janelle occasionally kicked him out and he had to stay at his mother's) made half of the equity in the home (or $100,000) Rob's fair share. Although Rob and all of his friends will argue the $100,000 was a small consolation for what he endured, Janelle's grandparents certainly didn't intend for Rob to receive their inheritance.

What could Janelle have done? Her grandparents could have left her the inheritance through an irrevocable trust that only allowed her to take out so much per year. In that case, she would have used the interest from the inheritance to pay the mortgage down each month and the corpus of the inheritance would have remained separate property and would not have been part of the divorce settlement. In the short three years of their marriage, they would have had next to no equity in their home and Rob would have left the divorce with what he brought into the marriage and his wounded pride but he would have none of Janelle's grandparent's life savings. It is left to the reader to determine what is equitable — we aren't marriage counselors. We are only trying to help you reach your desired objectives.

In a nutshell, a little planning can go a long way to making sure that a divorce doesn't completely disrupt a family's financial situation.

Conclusion

Whether you are single person considering marriage or already have a family and are concerned about losing family assets to the divorces of younger generations, divorce protection planning is essential. It is to be an integral part of your family's Wealth Protection Plan.

20

HOW PERSONAL ASSETS SHOULD BE OWNED

We hope you have learned from this asset protection section that you have a number of choices of owning for your personal assets. Ideally, you should maximize your use of exempt assets — whether they be homestead, life insurance, annuities, or ERISA-qualified plans.

For other assets, we would first recommend a "debt shield-into-exempt asset" strategy to protect the equity in these other assets. If this is not available, then an international debt shield might make sense.

Next, we would examine domestic and international FLPs and LLCs. In addition, irrevocable trusts (here and abroad) also should be considered.

If you work with a local WPA advisor and follow the guidelines above for each of your assets, you will be well on your way to implementing a solid Wealth Protection Plan that adequately protects family wealth from creditors.

PART FOUR

PRACTICE PLANNING

21

AVOIDING THE FINANCIAL MISTAKES OF THE TYPICAL PHYSICIAN PRACTICE

Do you run your own practice or hope to run your own practice? If your answer is "yes," then you will want to get the most (financially-speaking) out of your practice. You will have to do more than the typical cookie-cutter planning that many CPAs and attorneys will suggest. In this part of the book, we will discuss the importance of buy-sell agreements, the ideal corporate structure for asset protection and tax efficiency, strategies for protecting accounts receivable, and captive insurance companies. Before we show you what you should do with your practice, we have to show you what NOT to do with your practice.

Would you believe us if we told you that most doctors who call us have practices that are structured with four things in common:

- Maximum Lawsuit Exposure

- Minimum Tax Saving Potential

- Maximum Bureaucracy

- Minimum Flexibility

If you think we are kidding, let's take a little quiz and see how you fare:

1. Are your equipment, real estate or accounts receivables owned by the practice or by the doctors personally?

2. Do you have one group entity (P.C., P.A., P.L.L.C) that employs all of the doctors in your group?

3. Do you need to get any one else (or a majority of the group) to agree before you can make a financial decision in your practice?

If you said YES to any of those three questions, then you probably have those four problems.

The Worst Corporate Structure

The following diagram illustrates how nearly all medical practices are arranged in the United States. Perhaps yours is organized this way. In this arrangement, there is one legal entity that operates the practice and owns all of the key assets of the business — the accounts receivable (AR), the real estate (RE), and any valuable equipment.

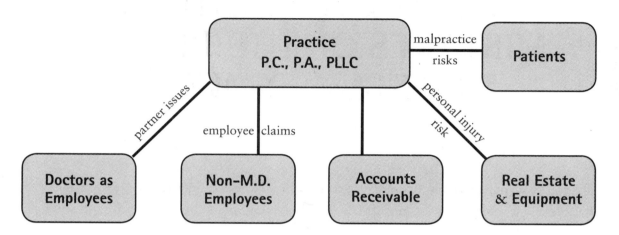

First, all of the assets of the practice are at risk to claims against any of the doctors or the practice employees. This is an unacceptable and unnecessary risk.

Second, financial decisions have to be made at the corporate level through whatever decision-making process you have implemented in your practice. Undoubtedly, this is not simply your vote — unless you are a sole practitioner. When was the last time your group made a major financial decision? How long did it take? How painful was it to be part of that process?

If your practice looks anything like this, then you will benefit greatly from this book. From an asset protection standpoint, we can help you structure your practice and personal assets (Chapters 7–29). From a tax standpoint, we can help you with the use of strategies discussed in Chapters 30 to 42 (once you have implemented the perfect corporate structure discussed in Chapter 29).

Take good notes as you read through the next few chapters on Practice Planning and keep in mind all the strategies you learn throughout the book. You are well on your way to restructuring your practice to better serve you.

While we are able to outline a few of the strategies we employ for many of our physician clients here, this area of planning is the most fact-sensitive part of our practice. In other words, there are few tools or strategies that work well for all practices. Often, the same tools may be used differently in distinct cases. For these reasons, much of what we can do for our clients is not specifically discussed in these pages. For more information on these areas of planning, we encourage you to contact the local member of the Wealth Protection Alliance (call 800-554-7233).

22

USING CORPORATIONS IN AN IDEAL MEDICAL PRACTICE STRUCTURE

Why Corporations Should Be Used Only For Medical Practices

As you learned in Chapter 15, limited liability companies (LLCs) are the tools of choice for almost every business situation. This is because the ownership interests of the LLC are given "charging order" protections in all states. Corporations, on the other hand, offer absolutely no protection whatsoever against a creditor of a shareholder. In other words, if you own shares in a corporation and we successfully sue you, we can take those shares.

In the case of professional corporations (PCs) for medical practices, corporations do have some practical barriers to a creditor taking the stock of a PC as non-physicians cannot own a medical practice.

Professional Corporation Basics

Most physicians, dentists, accountants, lawyers, architects, and other professionals use professional corporations (PCs) or professional associations (PAs) to structure their practices. Some use professional limited liability companies (PLLCs) in the states that allow them (and they are generally recommended). Although PCs are not as beneficial as the PLLC, PCs may be the best option in your state. Let's explore what asset protection characteristics exist for a PC. The most important are:

Professional corporations cannot protect the professional from his acts of negligence. If you as a doctor negligently mistreat a patient, you cannot avoid personal liability in a malpractice action.

Professional corporations can protect the professional from the acts or omissions of subordinates and associates. A doctor can protect him or herself from the acts or omissions of nurses or other doctors, as can other professionals.

To take advantage of this type of protection, professionals often combine a PC with a partnership entity. The various professionals working together each set up a PC. These PCs then become the partners in the partnership. In this way, the professional can protect personal assets from the lawsuits caused by anyone but themselves, and still get the benefit of working as a partnership. See below for more on this.

> ***Professional corporations can protect the professional's personal assets from other types of claims which do not involve the act or omission of the professional*** These potential risks may include car accidents using the corporate car, slip and falls at the place of business, and harassment of one employee by another employee.

> ***The stock of a professional corporation — because it is a corporation — is not shielded from claims of creditors.*** Corporate stock is not protected from claims against the corporate owner. Theoretically, a lawsuit claimant could take a physician's stock in his professional medical corporation. However, most states have laws that prohibit a non-physician from owning a medical professional corporation's stock. In this way, unless a physician is suing another physician, the vulnerability of a medical practice stock is not high. Practically, shares of a medical practice would be essentially worthless if the owner were not a physician providing services to patients.

PCs in a Medical Group

The authors and the advisors of the Wealth Protection Alliance meet with thousands of physicians each year who are part of medical groups. In the typical situation, the younger members of the group are very motivated to reduce their income taxes, and the older doctors are disinterested in making significant changes. Either they are already so close to retirement that don't need extra retirement planning or they are simply set in their ways and don't want to change anything — the old "if it ain't broke, don't fix it" mindset. The result: planning gridlock.

Unfortunately for the younger physicians, the long-term costs of such gridlock are significant — as they will have to work more years to reach the same retirement goals as their older partners. Gone are the "golden days" of medicine...and these new times demand more creative planning. Nonetheless, each year we meet with hundreds of motivated doctors who cannot implement the planning we recommend because the "powers that be" in their group won't allow it. If you see yourself in this situation, please do not hesitate to contact us. Our advice in this area is the following:

Bring in an expert

In conjunction with Wealth Protection Alliance advisors, we speak to over 1,000 physicians each year, many of whom experience this planning gridlock. Most, in fact, find no solution to this dilemma. The only ones that are able to navigate past the gridlock have help — typically in the form of outside advisors or consultants who convince the group to implement creative planning (including the solutions below). These experts in the field of tax, benefits planning, or corporate law have the credibility and expertise to convince your partners to "see the light" in a way that fellow physicians cannot. Often, we are asked to play such a role. But whether it be us or another advisor or firm, strongly consider bringing in an expert to speak to your group in order to get productive discussions started.

Use non-traditional plans

You should also consider using non-traditional plans, in addition to your typical qualified pension or profit-sharing plan. That is because, while tax and ERISA-qualified plans require the participation of virtually all employees, non-qualified deferred compensation plans (NQPs) can be offered to select employees. In this context, this means that only certain physicians need participate — even if it means only one or two out of a large group. Applying this to the common scenario described above, the younger physicians could participate in such a plan and let the older uninterested doctors opt out.

Furthermore, when compared with qualified plans, NQPs are typically much easier and less expensive to implement. In this way, even if a few physicians decide to implement a NQP for their practice, they could personally cover all plan expenses themselves so their partners truly have no out-of-pocket costs. One would think that this fact alone would eliminate any gridlock.

Still, NQPs do not win automatic approval. Because they are at least partially deductible to the practice, they must usually be formally adopted by the corporation or limited liability company (LLC). This requires the proper legal paperwork. Further, compensation accounting may need to be adjusted to make sure that each doctor not participating is in the same position he or she was in before the plan was in place. Nevertheless, these adjustments are easy for the attorney and/or accountant to implement... if they are pushed hard enough by you, the client. After all, if Fortune 500 companies can adopt such plans for their executives, the corporate inertia from a relatively tiny medical group should not be insurmountable.

In the end, NQP adoption typically succeeds or fails depending upon the effort by the motivated physicians. When hundreds of thousands, if not millions, of retirement dollars are at stake, this extra effort will be handsomely rewarded.

Employ a more flexible corporate structure

Despite the availability of NQPs, we still see medical groups stuck in planning gridlock. Another way to solve this problem is to alter the practice's legal structure so that it allows individual physicians their own planning flexibility.

In the typical medical group structure, there is one legal entity — whether it be a PC, PLLC, or PA. Physicians are either owners of the entity (informally referring to themselves as "partners") or non-owner employees. In all such cases, the physicians have no ability to separate themselves from the central legal entity. If the central entity does not adopt a planning strategy, no individual doctor has any flexibility to adopt it on his own.

If this is the case in your practice, you might consider a superior structure where the central entity is not owned by, nor employs, the doctors directly. Rather, we recommend physicians be employed by their own PCs or PAs. In this way, the group is paid by the insurers. The group, in turn, pays the physicians' PCs — best through 1099 independent contractor income. The PCs pay the doctors.

Tax-wise, there is no downside to the central entity or to the doctors who are not motivated to engage in any additional planning. However, for the physicians who want to implement advanced strategies, they may do so through their individual PCs. Their strategies will be implemented at the PC level, leaving the central entity unchanged.

While this again may seem simple, it is not. Experienced corporate counsel is required to navigate issues such as the state rules on the ownership of medical practices, Medicare billing rules, ERISA and Department of Labor rules on affiliated service groups, and a host of other issues.

Conclusion

If you are personally grappling with financial gridlock in a group practice or would like to explore advanced planning options, be advised that your partners may be an important hurdle to overcome. This chapter lays out some of the ways to deal with such a roadblock. However, nothing substitutes for working with a professional experienced in these areas. Often, advice from an outside advisor is met with less resistance than if the same suggestion were made by someone who may appear "too close" to the situation to be impartial.

23

BUY/SELL AGREEMENTS
The One Contract Every Business Must Have

Why the Buy/Sell Agreement Is So Crucial

As owner of a private business, professional practice or other venture, you likely spend ten hours per day and countless nights and weekends on call to get your practice to the point where it can provide a measure of security for your family. We know because we have been there ourselves with our professional practices. Nonetheless, if you ignore one fundamental legal contract, all of your work may be in jeopardy. That contract, a key to your business Wealth Protection Plan, is the buy/sell agreement. Succinctly put, the buy/sell agreement is a must for any partner or shareholder in any private company — especially medical practices.

If, in the odd chance you haven't considered the following questions, now is a good time to think about them:

- What happens if and when any of my partners die? How will the family survive? Do I want them as new partners? How will I buy them out at that time?

- What happens to my share of the business or practice if I decide I want out of the business or practice or eventually retire?

- What happens if any of my partners become disabled or get into messy divorces? Will I have to take on their ex-spouses as partners?

- What happens to my family if I die or become disabled? How will I know they get a fair amount for their share of the business?

- Since nonphysicians cannot own medical practices, your family may get $0 from your partners in return for your interest in the practice if you die without a buy/sell agreement. Would you be happy to know your partners received additional equity in the practice at no cost while your family received no benefit from your hard work at a time when they need money most?

Let's look at a quick case study involving only one of the many areas where a buy/sell agreement has great utility. As you'll see, it is a pretty typical case:

> **CASE STUDY:** *When a Surgery Center Loses A Partner*
>
> Fred and Bob are owners of a $10 million (annual revenues) surgery center. Fred has the business acumen and Bob is a physician with the medical expertise and contacts. Their overall profitability is due to their joint efforts. If Fred were to die prematurely, Bob would have to hire a new employee to fill Fred's position — or promote someone and fill the position. With the new hire, it's unlikely that the person could duplicate Fred's results.
>
> At the same time, Fred's widow would want to continue to take the same money out of the business that Fred had received. In fact, if Fred's widow is raising a young family or has children in college, she may have to force a sale of the business at distressed prices just to meet her needs. Maybe Fred's son fancies himself an entrepreneur and has his own ideas on how things should be run. Perhaps Fred's spouse wants to see Fred's son take over his father's place....it doesn't matter that he is incompetent. Can you see how many problems can arise? Needless to say, it may be impossible for Bob to continue a profitable business under such circumstances.

Only by planning ahead can you and your partners answer these questions in a a way where all parties are satisfied and the business is maintained. The best tool for solving these problems is the buy/sell agreement in its various forms.

Buy/Sell Basics

There are various types of buy/sell agreements that we will discuss. Nonetheless, there are some basics regarding all buy/sell agreements that can apply to any type of business — specifically the benefit different stakeholders can gain when one is in place. Buy/sells can be used for corporations ("S" and "C"), partnerships, limited partnerships, limited liability companies ("LLC") and other forms. For these discussions, we will use the words "business owner" generically to mean any type of business owner (i.e., shareholder in a corporation, partner in a partnership, member in a LLC, etc.).

Benefits to the business and remaining owners

From the standpoint of the business and remaining partners, a properly planned buy/sell agreement will provide orderly continuation of the ownership and control of the business upon the death, disability, divorce, or bankruptcy of any owner. It can even be crafted to accomodate the desire of any owner to sell his/her ownership share.

The buy/sell can prevent unwanted outsiders from becoming owners and can eliminate the need for negotiation with surviving spouses and/or children. The agreement may also perform the role of a succession plan, providing for continuity or orderly succession of business management. Further, as discussed below, the buy/sell agreement is often used in conjunction with life and disability insurance policies to effectively provide liquidity for the business to purchase outstanding ownership interests.

This planning guarantees that the remaining owners will continue to control the business — and be able to participate in the future growth of the business while also preventing a competitor from purchasing ownership interests from a retired, disabled or deceased owner, or surviving family members. This guarantees continuity of management in the business, which makes the business more attractive to customers, creditors, and employees.

Benefits to each owner

From the standpoint of a living business owner, the agreement can provide the individual partner with an opportunity to negotiate and obtain the fairest or best price for his/her share of the business. Further, in the case of retirement or disability, the agreement can be an additional source of funds for each owner.

Benefits to family members

For a deceased owner's family, the existence of the properly funded buy/sell can assure the family or estate a liquid asset rather than an interest — often a minority interest at that — in a private business, which is extremely difficult to sell. This can be extremely important as the family may be burdened with estate tax payments. Further, the agreement itself may provide an estate tax valuation of their business interest, saving the heirs the headache and expense of fighting the IRS on valuation. The importance of the buy/sell cannot be overstated in the case of a physician practice. Without a buy/sell, your heirs will forfeit their shares and receive $0 when they need money most.

In the event that an owner becomes disabled, the buy/sell guarantees that the disabled owner's family does not have to become involved in the business in order to protect the total family's interest. Further, it frees the disabled owner and his family from the risk of future business losses and creates funds which may be used to pay medical bills and living costs of his own family, thus protecting the rest of the family's estate. This, in turn, creates peace of mind as the disabled owner can rest in comfort knowing that he has retrieved his investment in the business organization and does not have to continue to worry about its future.

Funding the Agreement

Where the agreement contemplates a buy/sell transaction at the time of an owner's death or disability, insurance policies are generally recommended to fund the transaction. There are many reasons for this, including the following:

- Insurance policies pay a pre-determined amount, with proceeds available at exactly the time when they are needed (no liquidity concerns).

- Proceeds will be available regardless of the financial state of the business at that point (so long as premiums have been paid and the policy performed as illustrated).

- The business "leverages" the cost of premiums to create the proceeds. It costs the business less to buy insurance than it would cost to save money in a special buy-out fund.

- The economic risks of early death or premature disability of any owner are shifted to the insurer.

- Insurance proceeds are paid to the owner/owner's family income-tax free.

If the payment contemplated under the agreement is not a lump sum cash payment at closing or is a periodic payment other than through a disability insurance policy, it is important to consider some type of security arrangement for the departing owner. This might include personal guarantees from remaining owners, mortgages or security interests in real estate, a bank standby letter of credit, or even collaterally assigned life insurance. The key here, of course, is what is negotiated upfront between the various owners — ideally, before there is an idea of who may die/become disabled/retire/divorce first. This way, each owner will be unprejudiced in determining what a fair buy-out price should be.

The Need for a Coordinated Team

Creating a buy/sell arrangement that fits a particular business requires expertise and experience. Expertise in areas of corporate and business law, tax law, insurance products, and valuation are all absolute requirements. Just as important is the experience in dealing with different owners and being able to negotiate and draft an agreement that meets the needs of all parties involved.

Too often we business owners make one of two key mistakes in deciding who should oversee the creation of a buy/sell arrangement: 1) Some chose their lawyer friend to create the strategy and draft the document...rather than an expert in the area; and 2) Some do not have a coordinated team implement the plan.

Ideally, a coordinated buy/sell team would involve an attorney experienced in creating these arrangements, a life or disability insurance professional who has worked on these issues before (especially with first to die life insurance), and a business appraisal firm, whose expertise may be needed continually in the future for annual business valuations.

Conclusion: Plan Early

As with any legal or insurance planning, the early bird is richly rewarded. No place is this more true than in buy/sell planning. The reason here is both economic and political. The younger and healthier you are, the less expensive any insurance used to "fund" the buy/sell will be. If this planning is done before an owner is close to disability, divorce, retirement death, etc., all owners are in the same relative position. That makes the negotiation of a standard deal for all owners a much easier and smoother process. Planning early for a buy/sell will truly benefit you, your family and your business. Consider it an essential part of your Wealth Protection Planning.

24

—————◆—————

REMOVING HEADACHES
WITH PEOs

PEOs May Save Your Practice Thousands

In the Preface, we discussed the administrative hassles of being a physician as a hindrance to your successful practice of medicine. We further urged you to work "On" your practice, not "In" your practice. By building a more efficient business, you will have more time to handle patients, make fewer malpractice-related mistakes, earn more money and reach your ultimate financial goals.

Unfortunately, residency programs don't teach you anything about running a medical practice. After you started practice, it was up to you to not only master your skills as a physician, but also to figure out how to be a business owner. Many classmates of ours from business school admitted that even after two years of school where the curriculum was designed around running a business, they still weren't adequately prepared for the challenges ahead. So, how can we expect doctors to handle the time commitment of being a physician with the full-time job of running a business — especially when doctors get absolutely no business training at any level?

Professional business people appreciate the economic and asset protection value of outsourcing their employees to professional employer organizations (PEOs). This trend has been widely accepted by business people nationally...and the trend is growing.

The purpose of this chapter is to introduce one option to you that may help you run your practice more efficiently, save you money on certain services and benefits, remove the employment liability from you as the employer, and potentially offer you access to some proprietary programs that may enhance your income in retirement. The topic we will discuss is the PEO.

Consider the following excerpts from the internationally recognized management expert, Peter F. Drucker:

"...the professional employee organization (PEO) was the fastest-growing business service in the United States during the 1990s. These businesses manage their clients'

employees as well as their clients' employee relations — including administration and human resources tasks associated with managing those employees. PEOs were virtually unknown only ten years ago but by 2000 had become the "co-employers" of 2.5 million to 3 million blue-collar and white-collar U.S. workers.

A more plausible explanation for the popularity of these trends is that both types of organizations legally make "nonemployees" out of people who work for a business. The driving force behind the steady growth of temps and the emergence of PEOs, I would argue, is the growing burden of rules and regulations for employers.

The cost alone of these rules and regulations threatens to strangle small businesses. According to the U.S. Small Business Administration, the annual cost of government regulations, government required paperwork, and tax compliance for U.S. businesses employing fewer than 500 employees was somewhere around $5,000 per employee in 1995 (the last year for which reliable figures are available). That amounts to about a 25% surcharge on top of the cost of employee wages, health care, insurance, and pensions...

Another way to reduce the bureaucratic costs is to outsource employee relations — in other words, to let a specialist do the paperwork. Aggregating enough small businesses to manage at least 500 employees as one workforce — which is, of course, what a PEO does — can cut employment-related costs by 40%, according to SBA figures."[1]

[1] Drucker, Peter F. "They're Not Employees, They're People," *Harvard Business Review*, February, 2002.

How Does a PEO Work?

Basically, PEOs use what is known as a "co-employment model." The PEO is hired to provide the employees to you. They manage the employees concerning all human resource issues. You, as the business owner, also employ and manage the employees, and manage all other aspects of the business. In this way, you will maintain a high level of control over your employees, but will not legally employ them.

As a business owner, what are the benefits of using a PEO? They can help you:

- Control costs

- Save time and paperwork hassles

- Provide professional compliance (e.g., payroll, IRCA, EEOC)

- Ensure compliance with government rules and regulations, which keeps you out of trouble and reduces the possibility of fines and penalties

- Reduce turnover and attract better employees

- Manage claims (e.g., workers' compensation, unemployment insurance)

- Provide better benefits packages, including options for you (the employer) that you didn't have in the past. These may significantly increase your retirement income.

- Provide professional human resource services (e.g., employee handbooks, forms, policies and procedures)

- Reduce accounting costs

Your employees will be much better off if you implement a PEO because it will offer them:

- Comprehensive benefits previously unavailable

- Better employer/employee communications

- Payroll that is on-time and accurate

- Professional assistance with employment-related problems

- Professional orientation and employee handbook

- Extension of statutory protection to more employees

- Up-to-date information on labor regulations and workers' rights, worksite safety

- Efficient & responsive claims processing

- Portable benefits (employees can move from one PEO client to another without loss of eligibility for benefits)

Many doctors ask us what would happen if they implemented a PEO. In other words, what the government (IRS, DOL, etc.) thinks about PEOs. They will be happy because the PEO offers the government:

- Consolidation of several small companies' employment tax filings into one

- More professional preparation and reporting

- Accelerated collection of taxes

- Extended medical benefits to more workers

- Expanded communication of government requirements and changes to small businesses

- Resolution of many problems before they reach court

- Allowance for government agencies to reach businesses through a single-employer entity

Conclusion

If you want to make your practice run more smoothly so you don't have to be involved or troubled with every minor concern, you need to implement systems and controls that will help you accomplish this goal. The Professional Employer Organization offers substantial benefits in the areas of efficiency, cost-cutting and liability reduction — these all lead to increased productivity and profit. If you are interested in learning how a PEO might be able to help your practice, contact your local Wealth Protection Alliance office at (800) 554-7233.

25

PROTECTING YOUR ACCOUNTS RECEIVABLE

As asset protection specialists, we know that a medical practice's accounts receivable (AR) is the doctor's most vulnerable asset when it comes to losing wealth in a malpractice action. This is because, when a partner gets sued for malpractice, both that partner and the medical practice as a whole will be named in the lawsuit. If the partner who was sued doesn't have enough insurance coverage to pay the judgment, the creditor will likely next go to the corporate assets to fulfill the judgment. What is the biggest (and possibly only) liquid asset that a practice has? The accounts receivable.

Are you the worst doctor in your group? This is a question we ask at every seminar we do. One oncologist in San Antonio responded by asking "Can we point?" All kidding aside (we think he was kidding), we ask because your partners and employees can cause you severe financial distress. Do you realize that one lawsuit against any of partners could cause YOU to lose all of your AR? Partners are great for sharing "call" and overhead but you must be aware of, and address, the financial risks associated with partners and employees. The accounts receivable has already been earned by your practice. You are only awaiting payment. Most physician practices "turn over" their AR every 60 to 90 days or so. This means the creditor only needs to wait two to three months, at most, to get access to the cash. It doesn't matter that the AR is used to pay salaries and expenses. Once there is a lien against the AR, it is the property of the creditor.

So, how do you protect your AR? You need to "encumber" or segregate your accounts receivable. By encumber, we mean you have to either sell (AR factoring) or take a lien against your AR (AR financing). In fact, by implementing one of these strategies, you may not only shield your AR, but you will turn a financially non-productive asset (the AR balance) into a productive one — by leveraging the AR into greater retirement income for you or death protection for your family. The asset protection value of this technique is maximized by use of a limited partnership or limited liability company. The leverage of the AR into a productive asset is similar to what we recommend you do with equity in your home in Chapter 18.

AR Financing means that the practice will receive a loan against its AR. The loan proceeds are NOT taxable income to the practice. The practice will then invest in a protected asset and transfer the asset to the physician, subject to certain restrictions. The key risk factors are the tax treatment of the transfer of the asset (or loan proceeds) to the physician and the deductibility of the interest on the loan. Most strategy "promoters" (most likely not licensed tax advisors like CPAs or tax attorneys) claim that the transfer to the physician is not taxable until retirement and the interest is fully deductible. *In our analysis, however, the exact opposite is likely to be the case when one of these deals is audited.* Issues like the lack of substantial risk of forfeiture, Section 83, interest deductibility under Section 264, and even the non-deductibility of the premium are all major risk factors to consider in any AR financing deal.

Typical Financing Arrangement
(not recommended)

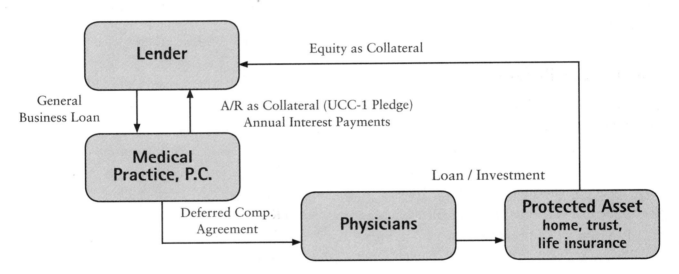

Economically, the client is told that the "cost" of doing this transaction is the interest on the loan from the lender to the practice. When you are told that your 5% to 7% loan (could be less) is going to be treated as a tax-deductible business expense to your corporation, the real after tax cost of the loan is supposedly only 2.5% to 3.7%. CAUTION: *Our analysis of the internal revenue code, private letter rulings and notices give us a very different conclusion which we will share with you briefly.* A longer discussion is given in our special report "How to Handle the Malpractice Crisis."

Since the loan does have to be repaid to the lender with after-tax dollars (ultimately), you need a mechanism for saving and paying back the loan (some may refer to this as a sinking fund). The mechanisms typically suggested are permanent life insurance policies with guaranteed minimum returns of 3% to 4% (and projected returns of 5%–7%). The strategy is to have very little downside because the guaranteed return in the insurance policy (which is tax deferred) should be equivalent or better than the purported after-tax cost of the interest on the loan to the corporation. Thus, there is little economic downside risk to the physician of implementing an AR Financing protection program — if all of the tax risks are ignored.

However, if you and your accountant follow the rules set forth by the IRS, the *interest will likely not be deductible.* Far worse than the lack of deductibility of the interest is the likely risk that the *transfer of the policy to the doctor will be fully taxable as income day 1* — as it is susceptible to attack under Section 83 and the rules and regulations surrounding constructive receipt of income and risk of forfeitability. As interest and penalties will more than wipe out any benefit from the transaction, this is a tax "bomb" waiting to explode. *We simply will not allow our clients to engage in this type of transaction. You should not either.*

Because of these potential pitfalls, we implement a financing program that involves a co-investment between the medical corporation and the physician, rather than a transfer of an asset. If you are interested in learning about the WPA's more conservative AR Financing strategy, contact the central WPA office at (800) 554-7233 and you will be directed to the financial planner and tax professional in your area so they can help you.

Further Tax Pitfalls

Many promoters of AR Financing strategies try to side-step these tax issues by arguing that the above does not apply if the physician has an S-corp or LLC (pass-through tax entities). They claim that because the S-corp or LLC receives the loan proceeds tax-free, it can then distribute those proceeds to the physician partners in a way that creates a loss to the corporation or LLC. This loss, they claim, offsets the taxable income to the doctor — because that S-corp. or LLC loss flows through to the doctors (through a K-1).

This claim is faulty on two levels. First, most physicians have little to no basis in their stock of the S-Corp (or LLC). This makes you different from business owners who may have capitalized their corporations with buildings, cash, furniture, etc. As a result of this roughly $0 basis you have in your medical practice entity, *the distribution of the loan proceeds to the doctor shareholders will NOT create a loss which passes through to the doctors.* In other words, *you will have to pay taxes on the loan proceeds out of your pocket.* If you are protecting $200,000 of AR, this tax cost could be almost $100,000 for doctors who have a combined marginal tax rate of nearly 50%. This, of course, blows up the economics of doing the transaction in the first place.

Even if you are one of the few physicians with adequate basis to cover the loss, by doing this, you will turn your practice's capital into a future tax hit, rather than a non-taxable return of capital. In this way, you will still pay a heavy tax hit, just when you retire, rather than right now.

Add this issue to those mentioned above (Section 83, constructive receipt of deferred compensation, creating substantial risks of forfeiture, the non-deductibility of interest on loans to fund life insurance, and the fact that you cannot implement a deferred compensation program after the work has already been done — no nontaxable payments can be made to doctor for "past performance") and one has a tax nightmare.

A Bird of a Different Feather — AR Factoring

Factoring means that your Group will "sell" the accounts receivable to a willing buyer (thus removing the asset from the practice) and distribute the proceeds to the doctors to hold in their own (hopefully) asset protected accounts. Of course, this will result in a tax liability to the doctor for receiving the payment from the group. Also, this transaction needs to be done periodically to make sure that very little AR is left on the books at any time. The big problem, or financial risk, is that most buyers will pay you less than you might otherwise be able to collect on your own. There is another problem — you can't sell Medicare receivables. There is, however, a solution to these problems.

Enhanced Factoring

The financial problems with factoring are two fold: 1) the doctor has an immediate tax liability; and 2) the factoring company generally pays you less than you would have received if you collected the AR yourselves. Sometimes, this reduction can be as high as 30%–50%. That's a big price to pay for protecting your AR.

At least one benefits company will purchase your accounts receivables on a recourse basis. They will only take a small percentage of what is actually collected. If you agree to collect the money for them (as part of their purchase of the AR), they will give you above market payout (80% to 90% of the anticipated collectibles) for your AR. The practice will collect the funds from the benefits company and use the proceeds to operate the practice (overhead, salaries, etc.). This portion of the strategy completely asset-protects the AR — as it removes ownership of the AR from the practice. Some benefits companies offer their clients ancillary benefits and very attractive loan programs that more than make up for the factoring discount.

A Third Option — Legally Separating Your AR from Your Practice

We were asked to design a strategy that separates the AR from the practice so doctors wouldn't risk their income over the next few months to acts of their partners or employees. Though we do recommend specific (not many) financing and factoring solutions for clients, we also have a strategy that removes the AR from the practice to each individual doctor. The keys to this strategy are:

1. Not generating a current tax liability

2. Not disrupting the normal collection and billing channels

3. Making sure the AR is ultimately owned in an asset protected entity or investment

The complex tax and legal components of this strategy are beyond the scope of this text. For information, call the WPA at (800) 554-7233 to schedule a meeting with the WPA member in your area.

26

PROTECTING YOUR
REAL ESTATE AND EQUIPMENT

There are four reasons to separate the ownership of the real estate and equipment (RE) from the operating practice. First, as with the AR, the RE are valuable assets that should be isolated from any liability created by the practice or the physicians. The reason why has been explained already in terms of the AR in the previous chapter. Second, the RE itself may cause liability — most likely, slip and fall claims from those coming and going on the premises or the equipment injuring someone. If the RE and the practice are operated by the same legal entity — all "eggs" are in the same "basket," exposing each to the other's potential liabilities.

By separating the RE from the practice, you have also asset-protected the practice better — by isolating it from any premises liability and equipment liability created by the RE. This way, each entity is a superior shield and the valuable "eggs" of the RE are not in the same "basket" as the medical practice. Other benefits or doing this type of planning are 3) potential income tax savings by "income tax bracket sharing" with lower income family members; and 4) estate tax planning. Chapters 34 and 67 explain these.

What This Involves

The actual tactic of separating ownership simply involves creating a new limited liability company (call it RE LLC) and transferring ownership of the RE to the LLC. Because the RE are no longer owned by the operating practice, patients or employees suing the practice have no claim against this RE LLC. Further, as you will learn in the next section, any claims against you or your partners directly cannot penetrate this LLC either if it established correctly — so the RE is shielded against lawsuits against you as well. So long as the transfer to the LLC is done properly, and the formalities of the new arrangement are respected (i.e., the practice pays rent to the LLC), this protection will hold.

NOTE: As long as the ownership of the P.C. and the LLC are the same, assets can be transferred rather easily and most likely without any taxes. If the ownership of both entities is not exactly the same, further planning related to valuation may be required. To be safe, check with a qualified attorney in this area first.

Your Financial Incentive

For simplicity sake, we will assume that you have a one physician medical practice — although these techniques work equally as well for group practices.

Own your business RE through an LLC that is initially owned by you and your spouse. Over time, you can gift ownership interests to children while maintaining 100% control of the LLC and the RE. Once the children are over the age of 14, their percentage of the LLC income will be taxed at their (likely) low income tax rates. If you can take full advantage of this, tens of thousands of dollars can be saved each year in income taxes. Stretched out over a career, the savings (and growth on saved dollars) can reach well into the six figures.

How to Structure Assets of the Practice for Maximum Lawsuit Protection

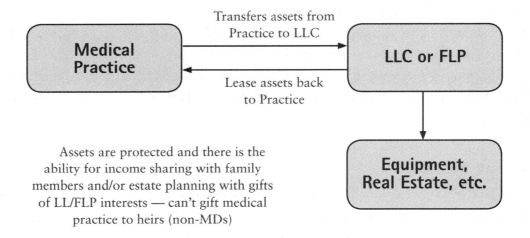

Obviously, this strategy helps you protect the assets of the practice from lawsuits against any of your partners or employees. An additional benefit of this strategy is that it can be utilized to reduce your income taxes through income tax sharing strategies (explained in Chapter 34). Lastly, this strategy can also help you more efficiently structure the buyout of retiring physicians. By letting retired physicians retain ownership of the LLC, they can still receive rental payments after they retire. Implementation of this fair and equitable way to compensate the forefathers of your group may actually help your partner meetings go more smoothly.

27

USING CAPTIVE INSURANCE COMPANIES (CICs)

Of all the Wealth Protection Planning tools we have encountered, the "captive" or closely-held insurance company (CIC) can be the most powerful for a successful business. It has the capability of shielding millions of dollars of a client's assets from significant risks and potentially lowering the need for third party commercial insurance. It asset-protects the funds accumulated in the CIC from both business and personal creditors. Finally, the CIC can produce powerful ancillary tax benefits as well.

The potential benefits of a CIC can only be achieved if the planning involved is justified by both economic and risk management need — and if the transactions involved are commercially reasonable. Further, it is crucial that one use an advisory team that specializes in this type of planning — as there are only a handful of experts in the country truly experienced in these matters.

What the CIC Is

The CIC we will discuss here is a legitimate insurance company. It is registered with the IRS for domestic tax treatment, but typically is based in an offshore jurisdiction such as Bermuda or the British Virgin Islands. Most CICs are established in these countries because of their favorable insurance laws and lower capitalization requirements, although the funds in the CICs can be maintained and managed in the U.S.

In fact, these offshore CICs have grown to number over 4,000 companies writing an estimated US$60 billion in premium per year. This represents more than a third of the total commercial insurance market in the United States. While Fortune 500 companies have long used CICs to protect assets and gain tax advantages, it is only in the last decade that individuals, small businesses, and professionals have begun to take advantage of them as well.

The CIC may insure any portion of the client's personal or business risks. These may include risks like wrongful termination, sexual harassment, professional liability, employer liability, business interruption, or even general liability (see following discussion of CIC as asset protector). In this way, a client who wants to participate in the risk of the business, but do so in a tax-favored way, should consider the CIC as an option. Alternatively, or in addition, the CIC might be used to insure relatively low liability risks like administrative audit or weather-related loss of electronic data. Thus, the CIC can be structured to have as much or as little economic risk as the client chooses.

CASE STUDY: *Tom and Dick Use CICs*

Tom and Dick each own surgery centers with similar revenues and each has about 100 employees. Tom feels like he is paying too much for his group's medical malpractice and commercial liability insurance policies. After consulting with attorneys and actuaries who specialize in advanced insurance strategies, he created a CIC to issue policies that cover the risk of the smallest, most common medical malpractice and commercial liability claims (under $100,000 per occurrence). This significantly reduces his existing insurance premiums because he now has much higher deductibles. Moreover, he gets a deduction for writing premiums to the CIC, which are available to pay claims as they arise.

Tom believed he could reduce his insurance premiums to commercial insurance companies, implement successful risk management programs, reduce the claims of the center, and reduce his overall payments and costs. Ultimately, he hoped that the CIC would help him increase the profits of the center. He was right! Tom deducted over $300,000 annually in tax-deductible insurance premiums to his CIC. While a significant portion of the $1.5 million in total payments was paid out to cover claims, there was still over $1 million in his CIC reserves after five years.

Dick had a different approach. He established a CIC to insure lesser risks that were not covered under commercial insurance. These policies included Medicare fraud defense, HIPAA litigation expense and malpractice defense policies (which is available only to pay for the company's legal fees, but not to pay claimants). As in Tom's case, the policy premiums are deductible to Dick's center. After five years, Dick's CIC did not pay any claims. At this point, the premiums are growing as reserves of the CIC to be used to pay future claims. If there are no claims, Dick may choose to close down the CIC. Any funds left in the CIC at that time may be treated as capital gains to Dick.

CIC as a Risk Management Tool

The CIC must always be established with a real insurance purpose — that is, as a facility for transferring risk and protecting assets. The transaction must make economic sense. Beyond this general rule, there is a great deal of flexibility in how the CIC can benefit a client.

First, clients can use the CIC to supplement their existing general insurance policies. Such "excess" protection gives the client the security of knowing that he/she will not be wiped out by a judgment in excess of traditional coverage limits. As wealthy individuals and businesses see more and more outrageous jury awards in areas as diverse as medical malpractice, sexual harassment, product liability, and breach of contract, this protection can be significant. Further, the CIC may even allow the client to reduce existing insurance as the CIC policy will step in to provide additional coverage, if needed.

Also, using one's own CIC gives the client flexibility in using customized policies which one would not get using large 3rd party insurers. For example, many clients would like a malpractice policy that would pay the client's legal fees (and allow full choice of attorney), but would not be available to pay creditors or claimants (what we call "Shallow Pockets" policies). This prevents the client from appearing as a "Deep Pocket" (a prime lawsuit target) — avoiding this appearance is a necessary asset protection strategy today. Many physicians considering "going bare" for medical malpractice should consider a CIC instead.

In addition, the CIC has the flexibility to add coverage for liabilities excluded by traditional general liability policies, such as wrongful termination, harassment, or even ADA violations. Given that the awards in these areas can be over $1 million per case, clients would be well-advised to use the CIC for this alone.

Further, entertainers and professional athletes can use these tools as well. See the following example:

CASE STUDY: *Mike the Professional Athlete Uses a CIC*

Mike is a professional basketball player, making over $8 million per year in salary and endorsements. As with any athlete, the risk of an injury interrupting or ending his career is significant. Mike would like to insure against this risk. While many of Mike's fellow players are advised to simply get an insurance policy from a specialty lines carrier (like Lloyd's of London), Mike gets better advice.

Mike is most concerned about a career-ending injury, not a relatively minor or even "average" injury. Mike decides to create a CIC that writes policies covering loss of income from all types of injuries (knees, ankles, wrists, hands, etc.) A reasonable premium for Mike is about $1 million per year, given his age and pre-existing conditions. Mike gets to deduct the full $1 million he pays to his CIC, which, in turn, re-insures the risk of the most serious injuries to Lloyd's for about $500,000 in premium. This way, Mike is covered for all injuries — he self insures for only minor claims against his own tax-favored dollars for minor injuries and gets the same coverage as his teammates for serious injuries. All of his dollars are treated in a tax-favored way and are asset-protected from his creditors.

The above case study demonstrates that clients can sometimes purchase policies like the ones from traditional 3rd party insurers through their CIC. The question for the client becomes:

If you are going to use insurance to protect your assets, why give away the potential profits, asset protection benefits, and tax savings to the insurance company when you could own the company yourself? Let's examine this more closely.

Compared with Self-Insuring: Annual Deductions & Superior Asset Protection

Because our society has become so litigious in recent years, many clients have been "self-insuring" against potential losses like the ones named earlier. These clients have simply saved funds that can be used to pay any lawsuit expenses that arise. This is exactly what physicians "going bare" do. While this planning may prove wise, the client would be better off using a CIC to insure against such risk. That is because — as discussed below — premiums paid to the CIC are fully tax deductible while amounts saved to "self-insure" are not. The CIC in other words, allows clients to get a tax deduction for putting money aside to protect the business against the same risks that were previously "self-insured" against without the benefit of a deduction.

Moreover, when the client "self-insures," the funds stay in his/her name or the name of the business. Thus, they are available to any lawsuit claimants, creditors, divorce proceeding party, bankruptcy trustee, or another creditor who may attack the client's assets. Simply put, there is no asset protection for the "self-insured" funds.

Conversely, using the CIC, the client has transferred such funds to an independent operating, fully-licensed insurance company. Further, this company is domiciled in an offshore jurisdiction — with all of the foreign hurdles to litigants described in other parts of this book. Finally, the reserves in the CIC are shielded by the insurance company laws, which are powerful barriers to outside threats (the funds are there, you must remember, to pay potential claims in the future). Thus, the funds in the CIC are ideally asset-protected against any litigation risks of the client.

CIC's Ancillary Tax Benefits

While the primary reason for using the CIC must always be economically justified and risk management-oriented, the CIC does carry with it powerful ancillary tax benefits. In fact, the CIC allows clients to build CIC reserves through tax-deductible contributions from their businesses. This is because premiums paid by the client or his/her business to the insurance company are deductible as ordinary expenses under the Internal Revenue Code section 162. These deductions for premiums can be over $1 million per year if justified by the size and risks of the business operation, far more than the set-up costs of the CIC.

Further, if the CIC is maintained as a tax-exempt or tax-favored company — which is quite often the case — there are numerous tax planning opportunities as well. While the applications are beyond the scope of this chapter, we can say that these entities can allow significant legitimate tax deferral and avoidance in extremely flexible ways.

No Loss of Control

When investigating the merits of a CIC, many clients are concerned with losing control of the funds paid to the CIC. While the clients' concerns are certainly justified, the proper CIC structure allows for complete control by the client. There is no need for the client to trust any other person or entity with the CIC assets. Further, while the CIC is typically established outside the U.S. — to keep administrative costs low — the CIC funds can remain in the U.S., in American stocks, mutual funds, money management accounts, or other approved investment.

Avoiding Land Mines

It is of the utmost importance that the CIC structure be properly created and maintained. If not, all risk management, asset protection and tax benefits may be lost.

For these reasons, using professionals who have expertise in establishing CICs for clients is critical — especially the accountants, attorneys, and insurance managers involved. The CIC should not simply be a straw corporation, lacking the necessary parties (such as actuaries and underwriters) involved to run an insurance operation. While using such experts and a real CIC structure may be more expensive than some of the cheaper alternatives being touted on the internet or at fly-by-night seminars, this is one area where "doing it right" is the only way to enjoy the CIC's benefits and stay out of trouble with the IRS.

Can You Afford a CIC?

Setting up a CIC requires particular expertise, as explained above. Thus, as might be expected, the professionals most experienced in these matters charge significant fees for both the creation and maintenance of CICs. Set-up costs are typically around $50,000 and annual maintenance costs another $25,000, although CICs can often be established for a group of partners for a lower cost per partner. It is even possible for two or more unaffiliated physicians to "share" a captive. While these fees are significant (and often fully tax-deductible), given the CIC's potential risk management, tax and asset protection benefits, they are viable options for many high-income businesses where such tax-favored asset protection is extremely valuable.

Conclusion: CICs Are Ideal Vehicles for Many Physicians

Because they have both significant and minor risks to insure against, because they generally have high income tax liabilities and can use significant tax deductions, and because they are interested in building tax-favored wealth over the long-term, many doctors can fully utilize the benefits that a CIC offers. In short, CICs should be considered as an integral part of any successful physician's Wealth Protection Plan.

28

ADVANCED ASSET PROTECTION
FOR YOUR PRACTICE

Turning Your Practice Into A Financial Fortress

Structure Your Practice for Maximum Wealth Protection

No matter what type of medical practice you own, you can transform it into a financial fortress. The challenge is to determine how to implement types of entities described earlier — professional corporations (PCs or PAs), debt shields to transform unsafe, nonproducing assets into asset-protected productive assets, and limited liability companies (LLCs) primarily — to your particular business. You then have the asset protection battle plan for your business. The specific blueprint depends on the structure and nature of your practice.

One Company with Multiple Business Units:
Use a Distinct Legal Entity for Each Business Unit

- A company that operates a restaurant and a catering service

- A lumber company that manufactures lumber products, sells its products at retail outlets, and performs construction consulting work

- A surgical practice with an in-hospital practice and an out-patient facility

What do these businesses have in common? They all have multiple business units that operate separately from each other. It would be a terrible mistake to operate these different business units under one legal entity. Instead, each should operate under its own corporation, LLC, etc. This way, a lawsuit or creditor of one unit is isolated from the assets of the remaining units. Consider this:

> **CASE STUDY:** *Westside Surgical Group: Before and After*
> The Westside Surgical Group rendered surgical services to a hospital and also operated a separate walk-in surgical center in a bordering neighborhood. Before consulting us on how best to structure their operations, the 6-surgeon group operated both

the in-hospital services and the walk-in clinic under their general partnership. In so doing, these well-intentioned physicians walked a liability tightrope. Any slip and fall accident at their walk-in clinic or severe collision by their clinic x-ray delivery car could threaten their thriving 10-employee, $4 million-per-year surgical practice. Similarly, an outrageous malpractice award or employment-related lawsuit in their medical practice could jeopardize their growing walk-in clinic. It was only a matter of time until one business threatened the other.

Fortunately, the doctors implemented asset protection planning before serious damage occurred. After learning about their business organization and company goals, we developed their "financial fortress blueprint," which had two phases. In phase 1, the doctors would reduce their personal liability arising from their surgical practice. While they could not use an LLC or limited partnership under their state law, professional corporations were used with each surgeon establishing his own professional corporation. The PCs then became the partners in the general partnership. That way, the personal liability of anyone physician was then limited to his own errors, not to the acts or omissions of the other partners. The doctors also had all of the control and tax characteristics as they had before.

In phase 2, we separated the surgical practice from the walk-in clinic. An "S" corporation was formed to operate the clinic, with each of the doctors a 1/6th shareholder in the new Westside Surgical Clinic, Inc. Each doctor's personal wealth was then protected from the liabilities of the clinic. Further, by incorporating the clinic, the surgeons effectively separated their business risks. Their clinic can no longer threaten their medical practice and vice versa. Moreover, because it is an S corporation, the doctors continue to enjoy pass-through tax status.

The doctors had not originally structured their businesses this way because: 1) they had not been advised to do so; and, 2) they incorrectly assumed the structure would be extremely expensive to set-up. In the end, the additional costs for the new fortress-like arrangement are less than $5,000 annually — less than .01 % of their annual revenues. This is very cheap insurance!

For One Business Unit with Multiple Locations or Outlets: Use a Distinct Legal Entity for Each Location or Outlet

- A dry-cleaning business with 16 locations throughout the state

- A chiropractic practice with four clinics around the city

- A taxicab company with 100 cabs

What do these companies have in common? They each operate one type business in multiple outlets. That's right — even the taxicab company has multiple locations because the business is conducted in different taxicabs. Do not put all your eggs in one basket. Create a separate protective basket for each business location. If one location fails, it is isolated to the one location…and the rest of your business continues unscathed.

CASE STUDY: *Metropolis Chiropractic Offices*

Metropolis Chiropractic Offices is partially owned by Clark, the chiropractor who set-up his first office over 15 years ago in a wealthy suburb. It was initially established as a professional corporation and continued to operate it as such. Throughout the first 10 years, Clark's practice grew, as did his good reputation with strong yet sensitive hands, and the opportunity arose to expand his practice to additional locations.

Over the next five years, Clark established three new offices, two in neighboring suburbs and another in the city's downtown business district. They operated under the original professional corporation. While the two suburban offices were relatively small, the downtown location was even larger than Clark's original office. Clark hoped the downtown office would be his real money-maker, but he was wrong. Within three years, the two new suburban locations were operating profitably, as was Clark's original location. However, the downtown location turned out to be a nightmare.

The downtown location could not attract patients. Perhaps it was because a renewal program for office's neighborhood never took hold or because most people left downtown after work and obtained care where they lived. Regardless of the reason, the downtown location operated deeply in the red, losing so much money that it threatened to financially cripple the entire corporation. Clark channeled cash from the other three offices to pay creditors of the downtown location. The cash crunch soon got so bad that Clark considered bankruptcy for the entire corporation.

Clark's problems could have been avoided had he established each chiropractic office under a separate corporation. While this may not have saved his downtown office from financial woes, it certainly would have isolated it. Its failure would be a bankruptcy of only that office, not Clark's entire operation. If the office had operated under its own legal entity, it is likely Clark could have negotiated favorable settlements with its chief creditors — the bank (on an operating cash loan), the landlord (on the lease), and medical suppliers (on equipment). By operating as one corporation, Clark precluded this possibility. After all, why should creditors settle when they can claim the assets of all four offices?

Learn from Clark's mistake and use multiple legal entities for multiple locations or outlets.

One Business Unit with a Single Location or Outlet:
Use At Least Two Legal Entities; One for Dangerous Assets and
One for the Safe Assets

- A men's clothing store

- A theater operator

- A single-physician medical practice

Each operation has one outlet and one line of business. But, like the businesses in the previous examples, these ventures can also benefit from multiple entities. These businesses can effectively segregate safe assets from dangerous assets by using multiple entities.

CASE STUDY: *Dave's Orthopedist Office*

Dave is an orthopedist who operates one successful medical office. Concerned after a friend suffered a devastating lawsuit judgment for a personal injury claim, he asked us how he could best protect his practice. We learned that in addition to owning expensive clinical equipment personally, Dave also owned the building housing the office personally.

First, we advised Dave to set-up a professional corporation in which to operate the business. This may help protect personal assets from future non-malpractice claims. Second, Dave formed an LLC to own his practice's accounts receivable. Third, we created a 2nd LLC to own the building. The LLC was owned by Dave, his wife, and his children and they leased the office to the PC. Should any patient sue, neither the AR nor the building would be vulnerable. Estate planning benefits and reduced income taxes were also achieved.

Even within a multiple-entity structure, each business unit or location should be as lawsuit-proof and creditor-proof as possible. This is the best structure: a multiple entity business where each unit segregates dangerous from safe assets. The added benefit of structuring your business in this manner is further illustrated by supposing that Dave's clinic became financially stressed and vulnerable to creditors. He could then sell the practice yet still realize income from his AR and from the lease of his building to the new owner. In effect, the income stream from these assets is protected even under circumstances where his business was a judgment debtor.

Assets Your Business Should Not Own

Your operating business or practice must never own its most valuable assets. Usually, this is the practice's AR balance. In other businesses, the most valuable assets may be real estate, copyrights, patents, or even high-tech equipment. Whatever the valuable asset, do not let the operating company own it!

Why don't you want your operating company owning this valuable asset? Because if the operating entity owns the asset, the creditors of the operating business can claim it. Your strategy: make your operating business as poor as possible. Then, creditors and lawsuit plaintiffs have little to gain by attacking the business. Establish other legal entities to own valuable assets and then lease or license these assets to the operating business entity. The following tactics illustrate this strategy:

1. If your business owns real estate: Create a separate entity to own the real estate and lease it back to the operating company asset. Make the tenancy month-to-month so it has the least valuable asset as an operating company. Remember: a lower value for the operating company means less attractiveness for creditors. Also, document the sale and lease-back and follow legal formalities (i.e., the business must pay rent to the other entity). See Chapter 26 for more here.

   For additional protection of the real estate equity, consider a "debt shield" as well. This may not only protect the real estate equity, but it might also help you build more tax-favored retirement wealth. Every physician can benefit from a debt shield against ALL real estate equity. You may be surprised to see how much additional income you can generate if you leverage your equity. See Chapters 17 and 18 for more on debt shields.

2. If your business has a valuable lease: Create a separate entity to own the lease and have your operating company sublet it on a month-to-month basis. This is especially crucial if your business depends on its location. Again, all formalities between the entities must be followed.

   If your business hits hard times, you can always close-up shop and your creditors cannot claim the lease. They can only claim the operating entity's sublet, until the end of the month. Next month, you can set-up the same business using a different legal entity in the exact same location! Your lease-controlling entity sublets the same location to your new business. You have effectively secured your valuable location while protecting it from creditor and lawsuit threats.

3. If your business owns other extremely valuable assets such as copyrights, trademarks, patents, high-tech equipment, etc., have another entity own these asset(s) and then license or lease them to the operating business. By now, you understand the tactic, but always follow legal formalities in the transactions. If not, you could lose your protection. See Chapter 26 again for more here.

4. Don't let an employee or partner lawsuit wipe out your next six months of income. For how to protect medical AR, see Chapter 25.

Conclusion

In this short chapter, we have truly just scratched the surface in terms of medical practice protection planning. As we noted at the outset of this section, planning for businesses is the most intricate and unique planning we do, as each business inevitably has very unique features. If you are interested in this type of planning, please contact us directly.

29

THE PERFECT CORPORATE STRUCTURE

Remove The Inefficiency Of Your Less Business-Savvy Partners

If the following scenario sounds too familiar, you should consider the perfect corporate structure.

The all too common scenario: (for offices with 2 to 200 physicians)

CASE STUDY: *Dr. Smith*

Dr. John Smith, age 40, is making $500,000 per year in income. He decides that he would like to implement a supplemental benefit plan. Dr. Smith is terribly excited about a plan that will allow him to put away $75,000 per year in a tax favorable manner for use at a later time.

Dr. Smith works in a 20-doctor practice. After researching the tax reduction plan, he tells his partners that he wants to implement the plan. To prevent objections, Dr. Smith tells the partners that they will neither have to pay for the plan nor participate in it, unless they so choose. However, the plan, like many non-qualified plans, requires "corporate participation" and Dr. Smith, therefore, needs to have the partners approve the use of the corporation to implement the plan.

Dr. Smith even tells the partners he is willing to indemnify the corporation should there ever be any adverse consequences of implementing the plan.

Out of the 20 physicians in the group, 5 are younger non-partners who are also interested in the plan. Unfortunately, 5 of the founding members (who also make up the Corporate Board for the group) are over the age of 55 and decide among themselves after little or no review of the plan that there is no upside to them and, therefore, tell Dr. Smith that they do not think it is a good idea. They vote to NOT allow him to implement the plan.

Dr. Smith is beside himself and joins the thousands of doctors around the country in a similar situation where they work in medical practices (or hospitals) either as owners or as employees where the main physicians or the CEO who runs the group regularly VETO any plan that does not have an upside for the managing physicians.

The above scenario is a sad situation that we have seen all too often. We would say that half the calls we receive on advanced topics are from doctors in groups in excess of five doctors (or who are employees of hospitals). Of those who want to implement advanced planning techniques, over half of them run into problems with their partners when asking for permission to implement a plan through the corporation. Of course, it is not always the older doctors who are difficult but most physicians tell us there are always a few in every group who make change very difficult.

For this reason, we have written extensively on what we call the "perfect corporate structure." In fact, this chapter is an expansion of an article that we have published in numerous medical magazines.

The Perfect Corporate Structure

The "perfect corporate structure" is fairly simple and several medical offices around the country already have implemented the structure.

Most multi-physician medical offices have a main company (usually a C or S corporation formed as a professional corporation — or "PC") that employs both physician and nonphysician employees. Let's call that the "mother" company. If a physician wants to implement any kind of plan, it must be done inside the "mother" company and, therefore, there must be an agreement of the partners to allow one or more physicians to implement such a plan. As we've stated above, it is virtually impossible to get five or more physicians to agree to anything (Insert ridiculous story about your practice here). Therefore, one physician has little chance of getting an agreement to implement any kind of advanced plan within the mother company.

With just the mother company in place, all the employees take their income from the mother company usually via W-2 income with a bonus at year end.

The "perfect corporate structure" exchanges a PC for the physician as the entity to receive income from the mother company. So instead of Dr. Smith receiving W-2 income from the mother company, the mother company would instead cut that paycheck to Dr. Smith, PC where the PC would, in turn, cut a paycheck to Dr. Smith.

Is it complicated to create a PC and have it paid instead of the physician? Absolutely not. If Dr. Smith has a contract with his medical office that says "Dr. Smith" will get paid whatever he is to be paid, Dr. Smith would simply re-do the contract to state that Dr. Smith's PC will be paid his normal W-2 income (plus the normal matching corporate payroll taxes the "mother" company would pay on his behalf) as a consulting fee.

In Dr. Smith's 20-physician group, Dr. Smith could be the only one getting paid to a PC or any or all of the other physicians (either owners or employee physicians) can do so as well.

Once Dr. Smith has money in his own PC, he can choose to do whatever he wants with that money without asking permission of the partners in the "mother" physician practice.

We've talked with practices lately where the physicians are not allowed to write off any portion of their automobile lease payment, their cell phones, or food. In the "perfect corporate structure" each individual physician can make that determination for him/herself.

The biggest benefit to the "perfect corporate structure" is the ability of each physician to implement his own income tax reduction plan without having to beg for approval from the partners in the "mother" corporation.

The Perfect Corporate Structure

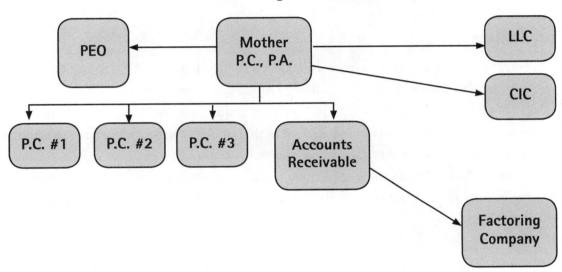

What Does This Accomplish?

- Each doctor has his/her own P.C. for independence and protection

- Practice lets PEO be employer of record of nonphysician employees — reduced costs, administrative headaches, and lawsuit risk.

- Leases equipment and real estate from LLC (protects from lawsuits)

- Deducts premium to CIC (see Chapters 27 & 39)

- Protects accounts receivable from lawsuits

Hurdles to Overcome

Like any endeavor that is truly rewarding, the process of moving your medical practice from any ordinary structure to the "perfect corporate structure" is not an easy one. In fact, there are two significant hurdles to overcome in implementing such a plan:

The political hurdle

As described above, most medical practices are extremely political. Often, some physicians have no interest in changing anything about the practice, certainly not its legal structure. Expect to face inertia from these physicians, as well as the practice staff (bookkeepers) and advisors (attorneys and accountants).

The regulatory hurdle:

Because changing to the "perfect corporate structure" involves a change in the legal entities involved in providing medical care, regulatory issues must be examined closely. Most problematic typically is Medicare. In many circumstances, the Medicare billing rules can present problems when changing from an individual physician to a PC. It is absolutely necessary that a qualified professional advise any practice that has a Medicare component.

Conclusion

Certainly, the perfect corporate structure makes sense for many medical group practices. If you can overcome the political and regulatory hurdles, it may be an ideal structure for your practice. If you are in a practice where you have no ability to do individual tax planning, you are costing yourself thousands in income taxes that could be saved or deferred via a non-qualified supplemental benefits plan. For a comprehensive analysis of your existing structure and potential changes you could implement to more efficiently and effectively reach your planning goods, please contact a member of the Weatlh Protection Alliance in your area (800-554-7233).

PART FIVE

TAX PLANNING

30

MAKE SURE YOU DON'T FOOLISHLY GIVE AWAY MORE THAN NECESSARY

You didn't have to complete the RFA to know that you would like to legally pay less in taxes. However, you did answer at least one question in the RFA that directed you to this section. You may be looking for ways to save for your retirement on a tax-deductible basis. You may wish to reduce the taxes on the capital gains from your investments. You may even like to explore the opportunities to provide benefits for you and your family on a pretax basis. Regardless of the reason, you are in the right section of the book. This section will help you understand how the tax planning portion of your Wealth Protection Plan can be utilized to improve your situation.

The famous judge Learned Hand once said: "No American is required to pay any more tax than the law would allow…there is not even a patriotic duty to do so." What you will find when reading the various chapters is that every legitimate tax-reduction strategy is allowed because the tax-deductible program is designed to offer some social benefit. When reading this section, you should look for a strategy that offers you and your family a benefit you need. The additional tax savings will be an extra incentive.

We are not recommending that you stop paying taxes. Rather, we recommend that readers work with conservative strategies that are based on Internal Revenue Code (IRC) sections and supported by revenue rulings, case law, or private letter rulings.

If you are not sure how taxes eat into your income and family net worth, you should read the next chapter entitled "Uncle Sam's Piece of Your Pie." The subsequent chapters will discuss many tools that may help you reduce, defer, or even eliminate some of these taxes while providing you, your family or your business an additional benefit.

These topics include: retirement plans, IRAs, insurance, annuities, closely-held insurance companies, private placement insurance, long term care planning and health insurance planning, among other topics. Read on and see how your taxes might be reduced this year.

31

UNCLE SAM'S PIECE
OF YOUR PIE

How Much Do *You* Really Get To Enjoy?

Before exploring the ways you can legitimately reduce your taxes, we must first understand how much money is on the table. If you thought you could only save a few hundred dollars per year, you might find the cost of this book and the time spent to read the book and create your individual Wealth Protection Plan to be worthwhile. If you thought you could save thousands, if not hundreds of thousands, of dollars from this book and its recommendations, you might take the exercises more seriously. Of course, if you thought you might save hundreds of thousands, if not millions, in taxes over your lifetime, you might even send us a thank you note or a holiday fruitcake. If you want to send us a percentage of the savings, we wouldn't want to insult you by refusing your generous gift (you can keep the fruitcake). With that said, let us begin by explaining the problems at hand and we will then move on to addressing them.

We all know that we pay income taxes on our salaries. Do you know exactly how income taxes are computed? Most people believe that they move from income tax bracket to income tax bracket — increasing the percentage they pay on each dollar earned as they move forward. The truth is that every individual (in the same filing category) pays the same tax rate on his/her first $14,000 or so of income. When someone makes money in a higher bracket, he pays the higher amount. Let's look at the 2003 tax table for a married couple filing jointly below:

Income Above	But Less Than	You Pay
$0	$14,000	10%
$14,000	$56,800	15%
$56,800	$114,650	25%
$114,650	$174,700	28%
$174,700	$311,950	33%
$311,950	upward	35%

Let's look at an example to see how this works:

Rob and Janelle are married and they file jointly. Rob makes $90,000 and Janelle runs an in-home business that generates $10,000 per year. For simplicity, let's assume they have no deductions and they live in a state with 0% state income tax. They have $100,000 of total adjusted gross income.

On the first $14,000 of income they pay 10% or	$1,400
On the next $42,800 (up to $56,800) they pay 15% or	$6,420
On the next $43,200 (up to $100,000) they pay 25% or	$10,800
Total tax	$18,620
Marginal Tax bracket	25%
Effective Tax Rate ($18,620/$100,000)	18.62%

Let's assume that Rob and Janelle spend $6,000/month on their living expenses and they save the rest.

Gross income	$100,000	
Income Tax	$18,620	
After Tax Income	$81,380	
Expenses	$72,000	
Savings	$9,380	for retirement

If Rob put away 10% of his salary into a tax deductible vehicle (like a retirement plan), it would look like this:

Gross income	$100,000
Deduction	$10,000
Taxable income	$90,000
Taxes	$16,120
Net income	$73,880
Expenses	$72,000
Savings	$1,880

Janelle and Rob have $10,000 in pretax retirement savings and $1,880 in after tax savings for a total of $11,880 in retirement savings instead of the $9,380 they had before!

Now that you pay your taxes on your salary, you're home free, right? Wrong!

You will either spend the money and pay sales tax or you will save the money. If you save the money, you have to put it somewhere. Children of the depression often put the money under their mattresses, in a safe, or buried it in their yards. Our generation is more comfortable with CDs, money markets, stocks, bonds, mutual funds, real estate and other investment vehicles. What happens to this money?

The investments are generally designed for income or for growth. In some cases, an investment may offer both. Income investments give you regular income. Your bank accounts, CDs and money markets give you an interest payment each year. If you own bonds, you receive a coupon every six months or year (we will not discuss zero coupon bonds here). If you own rental real estate, you collect rents. All of these interest payments, coupons and rent checks are ADDED to your income discussed above. If you are in a 25% marginal income tax bracket like Rob and Janelle, you will have to pay tax of 25% on those payments. If you are in a 35% marginal tax bracket, you will pay 35% in taxes on that investment income. Of course, if you are not in an income tax free state, you could pay up to 10% in state income taxes as well.

Growth investments are designed to "Grow" in value. These are typically stocks and some mutual funds. The money you invest with a company is used to grow the firm. The company may reinvest their earnings to potentially increase the net worth (value) of the company...and of course, the value of your shares. You do not receive a regular check from the company. This is at the discretion of the board of directors. If you need money, you have the right to sell your shares of the company. If you realize a profit on your investment, you are responsible for taxes on your "capital gains." There are two types of capital gains, short term and long term. Short term is defined as realized (sold) appreciation of an asset that you owned for less than one year. If you have a short term gain, it is treated exactly the same way (for tax purposes) as the interest, coupons and rents above. In Rob and Janelle's case, their short term capital gains would be taxed at 25% (plus any applicable state income taxes). Of course, if their combined incomes and investment income reach $114,650, then each additional dollar earned will be taxed at 28%.

If you hold an asset for more than one year, the government gives you a break. You can pay long-term capital gains tax rates. These rates are 10% of the growth (for individuals who are in the lowest tax bracket because you cannot pay a higher rate for capital gains than your marginal tax rate) and 15% for all other taxpayers (plus applicable state taxes). This benefit gives an incentive for investors to keep their funds in one place and not be constantly shifting them — which could significantly disrupt business. It also acts as a deterrent to short term, potentially unethical, trading.

Let's go back to the example, and assume Rob and Janelle invest $7,000 of their after tax savings into a 5% money market. This generates a $350 interest payment annually. They must add this $350 to their $100,000 of income. Because they are in a 25% marginal tax bracket, the additional federal income tax liability will be $87.50. The $350 growth will only really be $262.50 (3.75%, instead of 5% they thought they were getting).

So, you pay your income taxes, and sales taxes and taxes on investments. That should suffice. Right? Wrong again.

When you pass away, Uncle Sam has an estate tax for those of you who might be worth more than $1,500,000 when you pass away. That $1,500,000 may include the value of your home, retirement plans, real estate, brokerage accounts, and life insurance policies. At present, the federal estate tax rate is 48%. Some states have implemented state estate tax rates as high as 16%. Florida is the only state with a constitutional prohibition against a state estate or inheritance tax. More than half of what you leave your children could go to taxes. For a complete description of this tax, how it works, why the supposed repeal is a fairy tale, and how to avoid the unnecessary costs associated with it, please read the estate planning section later in the book.

Lastly, there is a combination of taxes that severely threatens those of you who hope to be worth over $1,500,000 and who might die with retirement plan or IRA money. There is something called IRD — income in respect of decedent. We will discuss this in great detail later. We just wanted you to know that it is very possible and highly likely that a $1,000,000 retirement plan or IRA could be worth as little as $170,000–$300,000 to one's heirs — after the IRS takes their (not-so) fair piece.

Conclusion

The average household income is less than $44,000 (Source: US Census). Most books, newspaper articles, websites and television reports and commercials are designed for the average American. As a physician, you are so far from average! You pay double the taxes of the Average American (as a %) and you likely pay ten times the absolute dollars (or more). Because of your tax rates, your planning will be very different than what the Joneses do. Pay very careful attention to this entire section of the book. It will be worth it.

32

IS YOUR TAX ADVISOR HELPING OR HURTING YOU?

David's law firm was recently retained to perform a self-audit by a long-term client. The client, an extremely successful businessman and real estate developer, was concerned when one of his business colleagues was found liable for back taxes and penalties because of some mistakes by his accounting firm. Nervous that he might become an IRS target soon, our client hired us to do an audit of his income taxes for the past 5 years, both personally and for his various businesses. What we found was shocking.

Even though this client had used four different accounting firms for his various returns (including a well-known 500+ person firm), the taxes he had paid were far from what he owed. Luckily for him, it was an overpayment. While, at this point, we do not know what the final numbers will be, we can write with confidence that this client will deserve a refund of AT LEAST $5 million.

That is correct. Because of the self-imposed audit which David and Celia's firm oversaw, the client will file for a seven-figure refund from the IRS and state tax agency. Lucky for him, he was concerned about poor tax advice and spent the money to hire us and to perform the audit (even though he thought he would owe more, not less tax).

Lessons to Be Learned

While the above case is extreme, it is not unusual. In fact, a recent study by the IRS found that the majority of audits resulted in a refund to the taxpayer. Thus, it is important for physicians to know all is far from lost simply because you are audited. Audits can be scary for taxpayers who are not tax professionals themselves. Nonetheless, it many cases, it is the client that wins in the end.

Even more importantly, the short anecdote above demonstrates the two ways millions of taxpayers (including tens of thousands of physicians) get into trouble with tax planning by relying on tax professionals who 1) incompetently cause unjustified underpayments of tax; or 2) are so conservative or close-minded that they actually "cost" the client through gross overpayments of tax.

As a physician, you likely pay income taxes at the rate of 40% to 45% once federal, state and even municipal taxes are considered. At these rates, the following question becomes very important: Does your tax advisor — CPA, attorney, or other professional — suffer from one of the drawbacks below? As attorneys and financial advisors who deal with physicians across the country (as well as with their advisors), we see the following problems every day:

Incompetence: Not admitting when an area is beyond their expertise

This is the most obvious issue for any advisor — do they actually know what they are doing? While it may be obvious to avoid the incompetent advisor, the signs of incompetence are not so apparent. If you do realize it, it is often too late (i.e., our client's "colleague" mentioned earlier).

More common is the situation where the client's advisor is skilled in one area of practice but not knowledgeable about another tax area. This is understandable. Tax planning is like medicine — each area has become so complex that one can only hope to become an expert in one discipline. In the medical arena, most patients and physicians realize this as different specialists are routinely involved. A gastroenterologist would no sooner make diagnoses of skin conditions than a dermatologist would if the situation were reversed. Yet this is what happens all the time in the tax arena.

We cannot overemphasize how many times we have seen the following scenario occur, to the detriment of the client. The client's tax advisor is quite competent with the run-of-the mill income tax strategies, perhaps even some sophisticated planning. Nonetheless, when it comes to the taxation of international entities or the estate tax planning for qualified plans, he/she knows relatively little. It simply is not what he/she does on a daily basis.

At this point, the advisor's choice is to 1) admit his/her lack of knowledge and refer the client to another expert, 2) try to quickly get up to speed on the issue (on the client's dime), or 3) simply reject any recommendations which he/she does not understand. Too often, we see tax advisors resort to the third option, rejecting a potentially beneficial strategy for their client because it is out of their area of expertise.

Over-conservativeness: "If everyone isn't doing it, then it isn't wise planning"

Although they may be competent in their field, many tax advisors are so conservative that they will not consider a strategy unless it has been around for decades or unless it is so common that every Tom, Dick and Harry employ it. In Chapter 31, we explained that families earning over $250,000 per year make up a very small minority of the population. Most of your advisor's clients are not like you! They don't have to be up to speed on advanced transactions to satisfy 90% of their clients. While we are certainly not advocating an approach on the other end of the spectrum (following every tax strategy that comes along), we are saying that either extreme position ends up hurting the client at the end of the day.

This pitfall, we believe, is the one which cost the client described at the beginning of the chapter about $5 million bill in unnecessary taxes. His previous advisors simply did not utilize planning techniques which could have legitimately reduced his overall tax bill by millions of dollars. The question that emerges, then, is how can you tell whether a tax strategy has any merit and whether an advisor should be considering it for their client? In our tax law there is a concept called "substantial authority." This means that, when the IRS examines all of the authority on a certain tax issue (statutes, cases, memoranda, etc.), a taxpayer who has more than 50% of that authority supporting their position is said to have "substantial authority" on his side. This is the litmus test for a tax strategy and one which your tax advisor should examine when evaluating a particular technique — not whether or not everyone else in the neighborhood is doing it.

Over-protectiveness: "Don't listen to anyone but me"

Closely related to an advisor's over-conservative disposition is the situation where a tax advisor is close-minded. Often, this is because he/she fears losing the client to another advisor if he/she admits that what the other advisor recommends actually makes sense. While the advisors will never actually tell the client not to listen to another professional, their behavior speaks for them when they reject another professional's suggestions with arcane arguments and references which he/she knows the client will not be able to evaluate on his own.

We saw this very recently regarding an offshore planning recommendation we made to two potential clients. They were accompanied by their present CPA, who obviously did not have an alternative plan for the clients nor completely understood the intricacies of our plan. He brought up objections that we could easily explain in our due diligence materials and remained extremely skeptical even after we sent him materials which answered his concerns. He failed to return our phone calls, refusing to take the time to actually evaluate the planning we recommended. When we later spoke to the clients, they related to us that their CPA had not suggested an alternative to paying the high tax bill and never explained, in understandable terms, why our plan was not acceptable.

How to Solve the Problem

Certainly, there is no easy answer to the dilemma of how to choose a tax advisor who is not overly-aggressive, not too conservative, and not close-minded. We are not suggesting here that you abandon your present CPA or tax attorney either. What we are suggesting is that you take an active role in your tax and estate planning, bringing new solutions to your advisor or — as happens with us quite often — bring in other professionals to assist your advisor in a coordinated team approach. This is especially important if you are working with a small law office or CPA firm (fewer than five people).

As you are the client who will ultimately pay for the planning (or lack of it) put into place by your advisors, it behooves you to make sure that your planning fits your needs and tax goals.

You may want to meet with a Wealth Protection Specialist and local attorneys and accountants who are sophisticated enough to review your situation and suggest alternative strategies. Part X of the book may give you advice on how to go about doing this.

33

RETIREMENT PLANS
An Essential Part Of Any Tax Plan

As you probably know, the IRS allows you to take deductions for contributing to your own retirement plan. The deduction is allowed because the government wants you to fund your own retirement and not rely solely on an under-funded Social Security program. As a tax-qualified retirement plan is often a cornerstone of a Wealth Protection retirement plan, we want to address it early in the tax planning section.

Though there are many types of tax-deductible retirement vehicles, they all fall into one of two categories: defined contribution plans or defined benefit plans. Defined contribution plans are plans that restrict the amount you can contribute to the plans on an annual basis. These are covered in great detail in Chapter 42. Conversely, defined benefit plans restrict how much can be in the plan at any time. These are explained in further detail in Chapter 43.

Because the retirement plan section covers all of these plans, keep in mind that the defined contribution plans usually allow you to deduct between $0 and $41,000 per year (depending on your income level and the type of plan you use). Although defined benefit plans only work best for folks near or over 50 years of age who also meet other criterion, they can be beneficial for people over 40 and can help achieve deductions as high as $60,000 to $200,000 or more.

Conclusion

The retirement plan is an integral part of any tax reduction strategy. As you learned in the asset protection section, qualified retirement plans are protected from lawsuits as well. A practical application of this is O.J. Simpson's outstanding $30+ million wrongful death judgment and his untouched, unattached pension from the NFL. Like all planning tools, retirement plans have their pitfalls as well. First of all, the plan assets cannot be accessed before you reach age 59½ unless you pay a 10% tax penalty. Second, and perhaps most dangerously, there is the hidden 70% tax that can occur if you die with funds left in these plans under certain circumstances. This is mentioned in Chapter 38 later in this section, explained in full detail in Chapter 68 and solutions are offered in Chapter 69. Practically speaking, most physicians who earn over $250,000 per year or who are worth over $3 million will be much better served utilizing nontraditional deferred compensation alternatives as they can access the funds sooner, with less tax cost and without having to pay for their employees.

34

HOW TO BORROW YOUR CHILDREN'S LOWER TAX RATES

Use FLPs And LLCs To Reduce Your Tax Bill

Two Centerpieces of Wealth Protection Planning

Of all the legal tools we use as part of a Wealth Protection Plan, by far the two we use most are family limited partnerships (FLPs) and family limited liability companies (LLCs). Of course, having family members play a role in these entities is common, which is why we use the word "family" in front of the LP or LLC. However, using family members in this way is NOT required. Whether family members are used or not, these entities can provide very good asset protection. As a convenience, we will use the abbreviations FLP and LLC throughout this chapter and the others in the asset protection and estate planning sections.

We have grouped these two tools because they are so similar. You can think of them as closely-related, like brothers or sisters, as they share many of their best characteristics. In fact, unless we make the point otherwise, we will use these tools interchangeably — if a case study refers to a FLP, you can assume that an LLC could have been used and *vice versa*. For more detail on the FLP and LLC, see Chapter 15 in the asset protection planning section.

Key Characteristics of FLPs and LLCs for Income Tax Planning

The following are the key characteristics of the FLP and LLC in terms of income tax planning:

They have two levels of ownership

Both the FLP and LLC allow for two levels of ownership. We'll call one ownership level the "active owners." These owners have 100% control of the entity and its assets. In the FLP, these are called "general partners" and with the LLC they are called "managing members." The second ownership level is the passive owner. They have little control of the entity and only have limited rights. These owners are called "limited partners" in the FLP and "members" in the LLC. This bi-level structure allows a host of planning possibilities because clients can then use FLPs and LLCs to share ownership with family members without having to give away any practical control.

They both have "pass through" tax treatment

In terms of income taxes, both entities can elect "pass through" taxation — meaning neither the FLP nor the LLC itself will pay any tax. The income will "pass through" to the owners. Thus, if the assets of an LLC make $100 in income this year, and you own 80% of the LLC interests, you will be responsible for paying taxes on $80 of income. Whoever owns the other 20% will be taxed on $20 of income.

How FLPs and LLCs Can Help You Reduce Income Taxes

FLPs and LLCs could save you tens of thousands of dollars, or more, each year in income taxes. This is accomplished by what is called "income sharing." This means spreading the income created by the FLP or LLC assets to the limited partners or members who are in lower tax brackets. Typically, these are children or grandchildren. In this way, the client gifts ownership of the LLC or FLP to children and grandchildren over time. As long as the children are over 14 (IRS rules), their share of the income will be taxed at their tax rate and not yours. Let's see how this works:

CASE STUDY: *Doug and Sheila's LLC Reduces Income Taxes*
Doug and Sheila had annual taxable income of $100,000 from their rental real estate, which was worth $1 million. In a 40% combined state and federal marginal tax bracket, their total income tax on this income came to $40,000. To reduce their taxes, they set up an LLC.

The LLC was funded with the real estate. Doug and Sheila declared themselves managing members, with 100% control. They gifted a 3% membership interest to each of their children (12% total). Because each child's interest would be valued at about $20,000 (3% x $1,000,000, less the minority valuation discount), no gift tax applied to the transfers to the children. Doug and Sheila made these 12% cumulative transfers to their children annually for 5 years.

Under the LLC agreement, the children were taxed on their share of the LLC's income; which, after five years, became 60%. Thus, in year five, 60% of the LLC's taxable income would be taxed at the children's lower tax rate. So, when the LLC assets earn $100,000 in income, 60% of that income will be taxed at the children's rate — 15%. Thus, their tax bill for operation of the LLC was $16,000 (40% tax on $40,000, the parents' share) plus $9,000 (15% tax on $60,000, the children's share). Doug's family tax savings would be as follows:

Total tax with the LLC, Year 5:	$25,000
Total tax without the LLC, Year 5:	$40,000
Year 5 family income tax savings with the FLP:	**$15,000**

It must be remembered that there were also savings in years one through four! What's more, under the LLC agreement, the managing members did not have to distribute any LLC income to the members. This was totally within the discretion of Doug and his wife as managing members. Thus, Doug and his wife could pay all LLC taxes with the income and re-invest the remaining proceeds.

Conclusion

FLPs and LLCs are some of the most powerful Wealth Protection tools we can use. Be sure to read Chapters 15 and 67 for more on FLPs and LLCs and how they can shield assets from lawsuits and save estate taxes, all while allowing you to maintain control of the underlying assets.

35

DEDUCTING LONG TERM CARE INSURANCE

How To Protect Your Family And Reduce Income Taxes

If you were directed to this chapter, or any chapter in the tax planning section, you have a desire to reduce income taxes. In this chapter, you'll learn how to reduce those taxes while providing an important Wealth Protection tool for your family — long term care insurance (LTCi).

Conventional financial planning wisdom tells us the reasons for buying long term care are threefold:

1. To make sure you have enough money to pay for potentially outrageous medical costs later in life (covered in the insurance section);

2. To protect your inheritance from high medical costs, so you can leave what you had planned to your children and grandchildren (covered in the estate planning section); and

3. To make sure those high medical costs don't destroy your retirement funds (covered in this brief chapter).

What's more, you can also deduct your long term care insurance premiums and reduce your taxable income. As an individual taxpayer, you can deduct up to the eligible amount of LTCi premium (IRC §§213(d)(1)(D), 213(d)(10)):

Eligible Tax Deductible LTCi Premium in 2004

Attained Age Limitations on Premiums	
Age 40 or less	$260
Age 41–50	$490
Age 51–60	$980
Age 61–70	$2,600
Age 71 and older	$3,250

If you have your own corporation, are a sole proprietor or own a limited liability company (LLC) or partnership, you can possibly take much larger deductions for LTCi. A C-corporation can deduct all LTCi premiums for owners and employees. If you do not have a C-corporation (you have an S-corporation, LLC or partnership), the key to deducting additional LTCi expenses is to cover select employees and their spouses. Theoretically, you could employ your spouse and achieve the maximal tax deduction you desire. The basic guidelines regarding LTCi paid through a business by the employer are:

- Employer provided LTCi treated as accident and health plan. IRC §7702B(a)(3)

- Deductible by employer (subject to reasonable compensation). IRC §162(a)

- Total premium excluded from employee's income (not limited to eligible premium). IRC §106(a)

The reason why deductions for long term care are allowed is because LTCi is considered to be a form of health insurance that pays for a variety of health costs which may or may not be covered by Social Security, Medicare, MediCal or your state plan. The details of long term care insurance and our recommendations on what to look for in an LTCi contract are covered in the insurance section. The purpose of this brief chapter is to explain why LTCi is an important part of any retirement plan and how purchasing LTCi in the proper way can save you taxes when purchasing an insurance product you need and would otherwise pay for with after tax dollars. The three chapters on LTCi should be read to get a full understanding of how LTCi will help you and your family.

Remember when you took the RFA? One of the questions you answered was "How much money might you need for retirement?" In making that calculation, you probably didn't factor in the possibility of $100–$300 per day for nursing home or in-home care, which you very likely will need when you get old. Even if you only need long term care for one year, it could cost $36,500 to $100,000, or more. This expense could take a very significant bite out of your retirement funds. If you need long-term care for 3–5 years, you could probably imagine it is possible that you could use all of your retirement funds just to pay for health coverage.

You may wonder "Doesn't my state or Medicare pay these expenses?" The answer is "Yes...and No." As an example, the State of California will not pay for a senior's medical bills until that individual has depleted all but a couple thousand dollars of his/her net worth. In lay terms, this means that if a retirement plan or any investments are titled to an individual or have been titled in the individual's name in the last 5 years, the state will require those assets to be sold to pay for medical costs. In addition, the state will then take all but a portion of the individual's income as reimbursement for the coverage.

It isn't hard to see how this so-called "Medicaid spend-down" could deplete someone's assets immediately. We don't know about you, but we could not live on $30 per day — let alone $30 per month — and we certainly wouldn't subject our parents to that poor of an allowance (though it might be a little fun to see them beg for a larger allowance). As a result, the two younger authors have purchased long term care insurance for their parents.

> **CAUTION:** The numbers above refer only to the state (Medi-Cal) or Medicare paying for some of your LTC. You should also keep in mind that Medicare only pays after you spend 3-days in a hospital, for nursing home care only (not in-home care), for needs that are "medically necessary" (custodial needs are the most common and are NOT covered) and for only 20 days. Thereafter, Medicare only pays a daily benefit of $105 and that benefit ceases if the patient is not improving.

36

⟡

USING CHARITABLE GIVING TO REDUCE INCOME TAXES
How Your Family And A Charity Can Both Benefit

Charitable Intent

The will to give is strong in many people. As a society, we cherish the right to give to the charitable institutions of our choosing. The will to give is what we refer to as "charitable intent." We want to give. The problem, many times, is that we do not know how to give or we assume that our family will suffer as a result of our giving. Our goal here, and in Chapter 72 of the estate planning section, is to show you some of the many ways you can make charitable gifts while benefiting your family as well. How is this possible? Because of the tremendous tax benefits the IRS grants for charitable gifts. Before we examine a few options for using charitable giving to reduce income taxes, let's take a look at the basic tax rules regarding charitable giving.

Tax Background

Direct Gifts

The federal tax code provides for current income tax deductions for gifts to charities that have qualified under 501(c)(3) as a charitable organization. The tax rules governing charitable giving are rather complex. Our explanation will be rather simplistic, but should give you a basic understanding. The IRS distinguishes between "public charities" (universities, hospitals, churches, etc.,) and "private charities" (private family foundations are most common). What's the difference? If the gift is to a public charity, you can deduct the amount of the gift against your adjusted gross income (AGI) up to a maximum of 50% of your AGI. If the gift exceeds this amount, you can apply the excess as deductions against future year's income for up to 5 years. If there is any unused "gift" after 5 years, it is wasted (from a tax deduction standpoint).

If the gift is to a private charity, then you can only deduct up to a maximum of 30% of AGI. This also can be applied forward 5 years. Let's see how this works in a real example:

183

> **CASE STUDY:** *Philanthropist Phil: Give to the foundation or the museum*
>
> Phil is a retired physician who created a small private family foundation a few years ago to give something back to the community. He involved his children in the foundation and realized some significant tax benefits. Now Phil has $50,000 worth of highly appreciated stock he doesn't need to support his retirement needs. As a result, he would like to make a gift to charity. His annual AGI is only $30,000 per year from the consulting work he does. Phil is considering giving the stock to his family foundation or to the local art museum, where he sits on the board.
>
> If he gifts the stock to the foundation, he will only be able to deduct $9,000 per year from his tax return (30% of AGI). If he gifts to the museum, he will be able to deduct $15,000 (50% of AGI). Because he can only carry the deduction forward 5 years, he'll only be able to apply $45,000 worth of deductions using the family foundation but he'll be able to use all $50,000 of deductions if he gifts to the museum.

Indirect Gifts (often called split interest or planned gifts)

The real beauty of charitable giving from the family perspective is that the IRS also allows tremendous tax benefits for "indirect gifts" — those left to charity through a trust or annuity. In fact, the IRS also allows deductions for indirect gifts through irrevocable charitable remainder or lead trusts and through charitable gift annuities which provide lifetime income to the donor that is guaranteed by the charity and monitored by the state. By using an indirect gift, charitable planning can truly be a win-win-win situation: you win, your family wins and your favorite charities win.

Common Charitable Giving Scenarios

The following are the most common scenarios where it makes financial sense for a family to consider charitable planning:

Sale of a highly-appreciated asset

If you invest long enough, you may eventually hold highly appreciated assets — usually real estate or stocks that have grown enormously in value over time. A problematic situation arises when there are few assets making up the bulk of someone's net worth. This is often the case where there is a closely-held family business or a family farm. Regardless of the asset, you may want to sell the asset but don't want to pay the capital gains tax, thus reducing the after tax value of the asset by up to 24%. Through the use of charitable planning strategies, you may be able to unlock some of the appreciation and significantly reduce the capital gains tax while benefiting a favorite charity as well.

Need to generate family income from investment assets

The past ten years have seen unprecedented growth of personal wealth in the form of port-folio appreciation. However, when clients seek to re-shuffle their asset allocation to produce more income and diversify their portfolios, they will be hit with a substantial tax on their gains. This gives you a chance to be creative in your approach to convert paper gains to cash flow, save taxes, and turn non-deductible items into tax deductible ones while addressing charitable objectives.

Estate Planning

The most powerful benefits of charitable planning can be enjoyed when used as part of a Wealth Protection estate plan. As you'll learn in the estate planning section, when you die, your family could pay as much as 48% in federal estate taxes, plus income tax on IRD assets such as pensions and IRAs. In Chapter 72, we'll address charitable planning as it pertains to estate planning.

The Most Common Charitable Tool: The Charitable Remainder Trust

Let's assume you have one highly appreciated asset you would like to sell but are reluctant to do so because of the significant capital gains taxes you would owe. At the same time, you are looking for ways to reduce your current year's taxable income while still generating a significant income stream through retirement. Finally, you would like to diversify your overall investment portfolio. Usually, this would mean selling that highly appreciated asset, paying the high taxes and reinvesting with a substantially reduced amount. In this situation, the Charitable Remainder Trust (CRT) may be an ideal option for you.

Used properly, a CRT can potentially:

- Reduce current income taxes with a sizable income tax deduction.

- Eliminate immediate capital gains taxes on the sale of appreciated assets, such as stocks, bonds, real estate and just about any other asset.

- Increase your disposable income throughout the remainder of your life.

- Create a significant charitable gift.

- Reduce estate taxes that your estate might have to pay upon your death, thus leaving more for your heirs after your lifetime.

- Avoid probate and maximize the assets your family will receive after your death.

- Protect your highly appreciated property from future creditors.

Think of a CRT as a tax-exempt trust that provides benefits to two different parties. The two different parties are the individuals receiving income and the chosen charity or charities. These individuals, known as "income beneficiaries" (usually you or your family members), typically receive income from the trust for either their lifetimes or a specified number of years (20 years or less). At the end of the trust term, the chosen charity will receive the remaining principal to utilize for their charitable purposes.

How a CRT works

A CRT is an irrevocable trust that makes annual or more frequent payments to you — typically until you die. What remains in the trust at the time of your death will then pass to a qualified charity of your choice.

A number of advantages may flow from the CRT. First, you will obtain a current income tax deduction for the value of the charity's interest in the trust. The deduction is permitted when the trust is created even though the charity may have to wait until your death to receive anything. Second, the CRT is a vehicle that can enhance your investment return. Because the CRT pays no income taxes, the CRT can generally sell an appreciated asset without recognizing any gain. This enables the trustee to reinvest the full amount of the proceeds from a sale and thus generate larger payments to you for your life.

The trust will be eligible for the estate tax deduction if it passes to one or more qualified charities at your death. If you wish to replace the value of the contributed property for heirs who might otherwise have received it, you could use some of your cash savings from the charitable income tax deduction to purchase a life insurance policy on your life. To maximize the after tax value of the insurance, the insurance should be owned by an irrevocable life insurance trust for the benefit of your heirs. This is called a "wealth replacement trust."

Often, through the leveraging effect of life insurance, it is possible to pass on assets of greater value than those contributed to the trust. In this way, your heirs are not deprived of property they had expected to inherit. In fact, your heirs may find it advantageous to receive cash, in the form of proceeds from a death benefit, as opposed to an asset that they did not wish or know how to manage. Let's see how this works:

1. You gift a highly appreciated asset to the Charitable Remainder Trust. You receive a current income tax deduction that you can use to reduce your income tax liability for up to 5 years.

2. The CRT sells the asset. Neither you, nor the CRT, pay any taxes on the sale. 100% of the value of the asset is preserved and invested in a tax-free environment.

3. You receive a larger annual distribution from the CRT than you would have received if you had paid taxes on the sale of the asset and invested the proceeds in a taxable environment.

4. Although the annual distribution is taxable, it is taxed in accordance with how it was earned in the trust. This form of taxation is beneficial given the lower dividend and long term capital gains tax rates. The income beneficiary will save a significant amount in taxes each year.

5. A "wealth replacement trust" can be funded with insurance to replace those assets given to charity and give the family even more than they would have received had no charitable planning been done.

6. After the death of all income beneficiaries, the remaining assets from the CRT go to your selected charity.

The CRT's "Cousin" — The Charitable Lead Trust (CLT)

When it comes to charitable trusts, CRTs seem to get all the attention. The cousin of the CRT, the charitable lead trust (CLT), also can provide significant charitable and tax benefits, particularly in an environment of lower interest rates.

With a CLT, sometimes called a "charitable income trust," you transfer cash or income-producing assets to the trust. The trust then pays out income earned by the assets to a designated charity or charities. The payout may be an annual fixed dollar amount set at the time of the transfer — called an "annuity trust" — or an amount based on a percentage of the assets in the trust at the time of each annual payout — called a "unitrust."

At the end of a specified number of years, the remaining assets in the trust are distributed to the non-charitable beneficiary, usually someone other than you or your spouse. It could be your children, grandchildren, other family members or a trust for the benefit and protection of any of these heirs. This timing is, in effect, the opposite of the CRT, in which the donor receives current income from the trust assets and the assets go to the charity at the end of the designated time.

Gift tax may be due at the time the assets are transferred to the trust, because non-charitable beneficiaries (your family) will ultimately receive the assets. However, this can often be planned so that no gift tax will be due. This is because 1) the gift is discounted — as the beneficiaries won't receive the gift for some time; and 2) you receive a gift-tax deduction because a charity is receiving the income from the assets (the deduction is based on the amount transferred into the trust and the amount of time the assets are to remain in the trust). Furthermore, the gift won't be taxed at all if its discounted value is less than your remaining applicable gift tax exclusion ($1.5 million in 2004; please refer to the estate planning chapters for future amounts).

Conclusion

If you have any charitable intent whatsoever and want to reduce current income taxes, capital gains taxes, or even estate taxes, then you should seriously consider charitable planning techniques. Often, you and your family will stand to benefit as much as the charity itself. A Wealth Protection Specialist or the gift planning department of your alma mater or favorite charity can likely assist you with this type of planning to make sure it is part of your overall Wealth Protection Plan.

37

⬥⬥⬥⬥⬥⬥

529 PLANS
The Tax-Advantaged Tool For College Savings

How much did it cost for you to go to college? A lot less than it does today, certainly. Did you know that the average cost of a 4-year education at a private college for a student graduating in 2000 was $85,356? With a 6% inflation estimate, the estimated cost of a 4-year private education for the graduating class of 2020 will be over $273,000. Of course, if your child goes to an Ivy League school, the total cost of the undergraduate degree could be over $500,000. If you consider that you may pay almost 44% in income taxes AND between 15% and 44% on your capital gains and dividends, it may seem almost impossible to save for a child or grandchild's education while also putting away funds for your own retirement.

If you have children or grandchildren who might go to college, graduate school, medical school or law school, recent tax laws make the 529 College Savings Plan the ideal vehicle. What are the benefits of the 529 Plan?

1. Contributions over $22,000 per year may be allowed — gift tax-free.

2. You, the owner of plan, control the withdrawals.

3. You receive the tax benefits.

4. You direct the type of investments.

5. You may change the beneficiaries.

6. The money grows tax-free.

7. Qualifying withdrawals from a 529 are tax-free.

Contributions Over $22,000 Per Year May Be Allowed — Gift Tax Free

You may already know that an individual can make annual tax-free "gifts" of $11,000 per year to any person and that a couple can make such gifts of up to $22,000 per year. With the 529 College Savings Plan, an individual can make 5 years worth of gifts in one year without paying gift tax. The 529 Plan allows you to allocate those gifts over the next five years. Thus, a couple can gift $110,000 tax-free in one year to a 529 Plan for <u>each</u> child or grandchild.

Total proceeds in a 529 Plan are capped. The amount differs from plan to plan but many caps are over $230,000. This means that a set of parents could gift $110,000 to a 529 Plan AND a set of grandparents could gift an additional $110,000 to the same child's 529 Plan and no gift taxes would be paid. Larger amounts could be gifted. but gift taxes might apply.

When you compare the 529 Plan to the Coverdell Plan (formerly known as the Educational IRA) whose annual contribution limit is $2,000, there is no comparison.

You, the Owner, Control the Withdrawals

Unlike a UGMA account or Coverdell Plan, you may change the beneficiaries of a 529 Plan. If one child doesn't go to college or receives a scholarship, you may change the Plan to benefit someone else. You can also make these changes as often as you like, as long as the beneficiaries are related. In fact, you can even name yourself the beneficiary if you plan to go back to school.

If you change your mind and want to withdraw the funds and use them yourself for something other than education expenses, you may do so. The only penalty is that you must pay a 10% penalty in addition to ordinary income tax rates on only the appreciation of the plan assets.

You Receive the Tax Benefits

Like a Coverdell Plan, the funds grow on a tax-free basis. Because annual capital gains and dividends are not taxed in the 529 Plan, the account balance has the potential to grow faster than if invested in comparable taxable investments. If you consider that dividends and short term capital gains are taxed at rates that may be as high as 45% in some states, the 529 plan could grow twice as quickly as a UGMA.

You may also be able to reduce estate taxes by using a 529 plan. The plan's high contribution limit provides a convenient way to effectively lower the taxable value of your estate. As you'll learn in the estate planning section, federal estate taxes start at 37% and quickly rise to 48%. In light of this fact, the ability to reduce your taxable estate while providing educational funding for family members should be very attractive.

> **SPECIAL NOTE:** Tax-deductible contributions can be enjoyed in some states. That's right! Some states actually allow an income tax deduction for contributions. That's a tax deduction to go along with the tax-deferral that accompanies the plan. If you're not sure if your state offers a deduction, feel free to visit a very informative website — www.savingforcollege.com.

You Direct the Type of Investments

Some 529 Plans allow you to invest in a variety of stock, bond, and money market funds. You may have a choice of a growth portfolio or a balanced portfolio. There's even a company that offers an "Age-Based Portfolio" that focuses on growth in the early years of the child and automatically re-balances every few years to focus more on capital preservation as college approaches. There is no extra fee for this added service.

For Those of You with UGMA Accounts

If you already have a Uniform Gift to Minors Account (UGMA), there's no need to fret. Congress has allowed for UGMA funds to be placed into 529 Plans and those funds will be treated with the same tax benefits as all other 529 Plans.

Shortfall of the 529 Plan

If you make your scheduled contributions, don't mind the risk of the stock market, and don't die, the 529 Plan is as good a plan as there is. However, we can't guarantee that you will live to see all of your children go to college or graduate school and we can't invest in a 529 plan without subjecting our funds to market risk. For these reasons, you may want to consider some type of life insurance as part of your college savings plan. There are two plans to consider. If you are going to invest in a 529 plan, you should also invest in a decreasing term life insurance policy. If you need $1,000,000 because your two young children will someday attend Ivy League schools, then you should buy a $1,000,000 decreasing term policy that reduces by your annual contribution amounts. See the following chart.

Year	Child's Age	Amount in 529 Plans	Amount of Term Insurance
1	2 & 4	$40,000	$1,000,000
2	3 & 5	$84,000	$950,000
3	4 & 6	$132,400	$900,000
5	6 & 8	$244,200	$800,000
10	11 & 13	$637,500	$500,000
15	16 & 19	$1,279,000	$0

If you are very concerned about the stock market's volatility and don't want it to have a significant impact on your children's educational funds, you should consider an equity-indexed universal life policy (see Chapter 57) for S&P returns with a 1% minimum annual return or a whole life policy with a AAA-rated insurance company. This is a very stable investment and will grow at a steady rate. Even in 2001, one of the worst years in recent stock market history, one AAA insurance company credited over 7.5% to the cash accounts of its whole life policies. From 2000 thru 2004, the equity-indexed policy returned an average return of nearly 8% per year. In addition to the tax-free cash accumulation inside such a policy, there is also a minimum death benefit to protect against an early death. When your children eventually attend college, you can then use tax-free loans to withdraw money from the policy and keep the death benefit intact.

Conclusion

If you have children, grandchildren, nieces or nephews you would like to assist in their educational funding or if you or your spouse might go back to school, you should seriously consider a 529 College Savings Plan for its tax benefits and flexibility. In many cases, a 529 Plan along with a life insurance component is an ideal strategy.

Comparison of 529 Savings Plan
to Other Educational Funding Alternatives

	529 Savings Plan	Coverdell Plan	UGMA / UTMA	529 Prepaid Plan
Income Litations	None	AGI limits apply	None	None
Maximum yearly contribution per beneficiary (all numbers double except IRA when gifts come from two parents or grandparents)	$50,000 in the first year of five-year period without exceeding the annual federal gift tax exclusion	$2,000	$10,000 without exceeding the annual federal gift tax exclusion	$50,000 in the first year of a five-year period without exceeding the annual federal gift tax exclusion
Account earnings	TAX-FREE, if used for qualified expenses	TAX-FREE, if used for qualified expenses	Taxable	TAX-FREE, if used for qualified expenses
Ability to change beneficiaries	Yes	Yes	No	Yes
Control of withdrawals	Owner of account	Transfers to child when child reaches legal age	Transfers to child when child reaches legal age	Owner of account
Investment options	Ready-made portfolios of mutual funds	Wide range of securities	Wide range of securities	Tuition units guaranteed to match tuition inflation
State tax deductible contributions	Varies by state	No	No	Varies by state
Qualified use of proceeds	Any accredited post-secondary school in the U.S.	Any accredited post-secondary school in the U.S.	Unlimited	Varies by state
Penalties for nonqualified withdrawals	10% penalty withheld on earnings	10% penalty withheld on earnings	No	10% penalty withheld on earnings
Taxation of qualified withdrawals	Tax-free	Tax-free	A portion may be exempt; income may be taxed at child's rate	Tax-free
Ownership of assets for financial aid purposes (may vary by institution)	Account owner	Student	Student	Student

38

INCOME IN RESPECT OF DECEDENT (IRD)

A 70% Tax Trap Awaits You

No tax discussion is complete without mentioning IRD or "income in respect of a decedent" (a deceased person). This is income which would have been taxable to the decedent had the decedent lived long enough to receive it. These items include unpaid salaries, bonuses and commissions (that the decedent would have been taxed on had he lived) as well as retirement plan and IRA balances and variable annuity appreciation. Statistically, the retirement plan and IRA balances are by far the most significant IRA assets.

Here is an example of how a retirement plan may be distributed at the time of death:

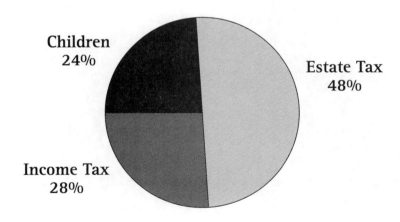

Distribution of IRD

Children 24%

Estate Tax 48%

Income Tax 28%

Because you don't know when you will die, you will may die with IRD unless you implement a plan to avoid this problem well in advance of your death. Please make sure you read Chapter 68 to better understand IRD and you read Chapter 69 to learn how to avoid this terrible problem.

39

TAX BENEFITS OF CAPTIVE INSURANCE COMPANIES

Before you dive into the potential tax benefits of Captive Insurance Companies (CICs), you must first understand the basics of the CIC. The paradox of that statement is that there is nothing basic about a CIC. The benefits that can be offered, including tax benefits, to owners of a CIC can be great if the owner understands and abides by all the rules governing captive insurance companies.

Chapter 27 is required reading for anyone interested in using a CIC. In Chapter 27, you will learn who qualifies for a CIC, what requirements exist for a CIC, what sections of tax code govern small insurance companies, and what kind of policies the CIC can offer. The purpose of this chapter is to give you just the tax benefits of small insurance companies.

The Internal Revenue Code (IRC) allows for certain benefits for small non-life insurance companies that qualify under either of two particular IRC sections: 501(c)(15) and 831(b). These benefits, in fact, were recently improved under 2004 legislation. The requirements for qualification, and benefits under each section, are discussed separately below:

Qualifications for CICs Created under IRC Section 501(c)(15)

- CICs total annual revenue (premium and investment income) does not exceed $600,000.

- Premium revenue is greater than investment revenue. In other words, the majority of all annual income (51% is fine) to the CIC results from annual premium revenue.

Income Tax Benefits for CICs Created under IRC Section 501(c)(15)

- No tax on premiums from insurance policies written.

- No tax on profit earned from insurance operations.

- No tax on investment income.

Qualifications for CICs Created under IRC Section 831(b)

- CICs receive annual premium less than $1,200,000.

- There is no cap on investment income.

Income Tax Benefits for CICs Created under IRC Section 831(b)

- No tax on premiums from insurance policies written.

- No tax on profit earned from insurance operations.

- Normal corporate tax rates apply to investment income.

Conclusion

There are significant tax benefits that can be realized when a company properly implements a captive insurance company. However, the pitfalls are great. You must first read Chapter 27 and then speak with an expert in this area. You may want to meet with a Wealth Protection Specialist in your area and with the local attorneys and accountants who have participated in a Wealth Protection Alliance training program on the CIC to see if this opportunity may benefit you and your practice or business.

40

━━━◆◇◆━━━

TAX STRATEGIES TO AVOID

We encourage our physician clients to take advantage of every legitimate and appropriate tax reduction strategy available to them under the law. The key words in that statement are <u>legitimate</u> and <u>appropriate</u>. We have seen so many doctors and non-doctors choose tax-deductible strategies while completely overlooking very important business factors. For example, real estate investors often look for property to buy as part of the 1031 exchange allowing them to further defer the capital gains tax on the sale of real estate. These real estate investors often look just at the price of the property to make sure they qualify for the tax deferral and disregard the profitability of the property. It's not hard to find ways to save taxes if you don't mind losing money in the process. Write-offs can be just a poor decision away.

Further, doctors are historically notorious for being terrible investors. Of course, not all of you are bad investors. We appreciate the fact that you are obviously of above-average intelligence. However, when it comes to tax planning, you are well outside your field of expertise. You need to consult someone other than the person who is trying to sell you the program, product or service that is designed to save the taxes. A good place to start for assistance in evaluating a potential strategy would be a tax attorney or CPA who is unaffiliated with the product being pitched.

The reason we added this chapter to this book is because a large part of Wealth Protection Planning is avoiding financial mistakes. We now hope to share with you some strategies that are either fraudulent, very poorly designed strategies, or misinterpreted applications of tax law and case rulings. It is true that many of the strategies we will mention do have a place in the Internal Revenue Code. However the bastardization of these strategies and misinterpretation of the language in the tax code have caused many taxpayers a great deal of stress as a result of having to deal with the IRS, their audits, and the tax penalties that can accompany them.

By no means is this an exhaustive list of the strategies for you to avoid. It is just a starting point. Remember that there is no substitute for having a qualified tax professional review every potential tax saving strategy you might consider for yourself.

419 Welfare Benefit Plans, VEBAs and Section 79 Plans

What vendors offer

The ability to deduct hundreds of thousands of dollars in the name of an employee benefit plan. The bulk of this money will go to a cash value life insurance policy for you or you and your partners and very little will be spent on policies for the employees. Some plans claim to allow you to take tax-free withdrawals from the policies as well.

The Truth is...

A very recent clarification from the IRS is that welfare benefit plans cannot purchase permanent insurance policies. Group term insurance, which has no cash value, appears to be the only safe deduction.

412(i) Plans

What vendors offer

The ability to create a defined benefit plan funded with guaranteed insurance and annuity products and that afford sizeable tax deductions. Then, the doctor can remove the insurance policy from the 412(i) plan (either by purchasing the asset or by closing down the plan and taking a distribution of the insurance policy) with the tax implication being very small because the cash surrender value of the policy may be 10% - 35% of the cash account value. The doctor can then gift the policy to the children or take out tax free loans and withdrawals from the policy.

The Truth is...

As of February 13, 2004, all insurance policies will be valued at the greater of the cash account value or premiums paid (roughly speaking). There is no foreseeable advantage to removing a policy from a qualified plan under this guidance. Furthermore, the IRS appears uncomfortable with the formula some are using to determine deductible contributions for 412(i) plans. Many 412(i) plans remain a safe, viable option. The key: creating and funding the plan properly.

Equity Disability and Equity Malpractice Trusts

What vendors offer

The ability to deduct hundreds of thousands of dollars in the name of supplemental disability or malpractice insurance coverage. These funds are invested and if you don't use the coverage, you get the money back as a dividend later.

The Truth is...

There are current cases and investigations against promoters of these strategies. Generally, the IRS does NOT recognize the deductibility of insurance if there is no real risk sharing. Moreover, the premiums have to be commensurate with the risk and in accordance with public policy. If your premiums were only $5,000 per year for DI and $25,000 for med mal, how did you justify "supplemental insurance" costs of $250,000 per year? You have to be realistic when you try to legally reduce your tax burden. One large promoter of such plans for physicians has had hundreds of millions of assets seized. You'd be wise to avoid such plans.

Global Leasing

What vendors offer

The ability to deduct hundreds of thousands of dollars by hiring a global leasing firm to be the employer of record for you and then have the firm lease you back to your corporation. You voluntarily reduce your compensation and the non-US taxpayer employer retains the earnings in a deferred compensation plan for you.

The Truth is...

We have had two doctors call us in the last six months telling us that not only was the IRS disallowing the deductions they took for payments to the "Irish leasing company," but they also were going to disregard the business deduction of the thousands of dollars in fees that they spent working with the attorney who drafted the operating agreements for the practice and the leasing company. Although we believe a Professional Employer Organization is an excellent opportunity for reducing costs in a practice, we do not recommend using international leasing of yourself to your own corporation especially when the company doing the "leasing" or "employing" does not pay taxes to a U.S. tax agency. Again, let's be reasonable.

PART SIX

RETIREMENT

41

———◆———

WE DON'T KNOW WHERE WE'RE GOING, BUT WE ALL WANT TO GET THERE

Most clients really aren't sure what they will do when they retire and many don't know where they will do it. However, the second most important reason most people give for working (after paying the bills) is to help them reach their lifelong goal — an enjoyable retirement.

We have analyzed thousands of physicians' financial situations in the course of our practices. From this, we can tell you that there is great variation in retirement ages and the amounts available in retirement for clients with the same professions or career incomes. You don't have to be lucky to retire early with plenty of money. You do have to plan intelligently, diversify your methods of saving, and avoid big mistakes along the way.

There are many different ways to save for retirement and even more pitfalls to avoid along the yellow brick road to retirement Oz.

The purpose of this section is to explain what tools can be used to help you maximize the amount available to you in retirement and to explain how to withdraw retirement funds to make sure you don't unnecessarily pay too much in taxes or expose yourself to unnecessary investment risk.

As you will see throughout the book, many of the tools and strategies have multiple uses and offer additional benefits. For that reason, it is imperative that you work with professionals who have multidisciplinary expertise and who can help you piece together your retirement, tax, asset protection, investment and insurance planning without unnecessary overlap, overkill, or overpayment! Keep this in mind as you read the retirement and other sections of your customized Wealth Protection Plan which resulted from your answers to the RFA.

42

DEFINED CONTRIBUTION PLANS
The Truth About Your 401(k), Pension, And IRAs

Of the two types of retirement plans, most of us are more familiar with the defined contribution ("DC") plans than we are with the defined benefit plans covered in the next chapter. DC plans allow us to put away certain amounts (on a tax-deductible basis), based on our annual salaries and by the type of plan created by our employer. These plans generally allow us some control over the direction of the investments within the plans.

Why Haven't I Heard the Term Defined Contribution?

We know the defined contribution plans by other names. 401(k) plans, 403(b) plans, IRAs, SEP-IRAs, Keoghs, profit sharing plans (PSPs) and money purchase plans (MPPs) are all types of defined contribution plans. They are all designed for different situations and offer different funding amounts. As you see below:

Employee Benefit Plan Limits (2004–2006 and beyond)*

Plan	2004	2005	2006	Increment
Defined Contribution Plan	$41,000	$42,000	$43,000	$1,000
401(k) and SAR-SEP Plans	$13,000	$14,000	$15,000	$1,000
Simple IRAs	$9,000	$10,000	$10,500	$500

Catch up provisions permit additional contributions for individuals over 50.

In addition to funding limits, there are also restrictions on who can create each type of plan and what investments can be purchased within each plan. If your employer creates the plan (and pays for it), your maximum contribution amount is rather low. If you are self-employed, the cost of a SEP-IRA is much less than if you created a PSP or MPP that would offer greater contribution amounts. If you are an employer, you have to provide something for your employees to get a larger benefit for yourself. This may mean creating a larger contribution plan, which is typically more costly to create and administer.

Other Benefits

Along with the tax deductions, there are other benefits that you get from certain plans. As you will learn in the asset protection section, retirement plans are generally excellent asset protection tools. This is especially true of ERISA-qualified plans (ERISA means Employee Retirement Income Security Act) covering non-owner employees (as well as owners) which are shielded under Federal Law. Even one-employee ERISA plans, non ERISA-qualified plans, and IRAs can be protected under state laws. For more on this, see the asset protection section.

By creating vesting periods, your employees do not technically "own" the contributions you make for them until they stay at your place of employment for a period of years. The amount you are vested may vary over a period of two to seven years. This usually helps employers retain employees a little longer because employees don't want to leave if they will lose thousands from the unvested portions of their retirement plans. If you have a retirement plan where you work, understand the vesting schedule before you even consider leaving. It could be more costly than you think.

Potential Pitfalls

While setting up a SEP-IRA for yourself or participating in your employer's 401(k) plan is fairly simple, properly administering a retirement plan for you and your employees is wrought with potential problems if you are an employer. When you combine the rules of the IRS, ERISA, and the Department of Labor, you can see how keeping the plan out of trouble can be harrowing. Regulations that prohibit discrimination and top-heavy plans as well as over-funding issues abound. If you are in this position, you must consult a professional who has a great deal of experience in retirement plan administration. It is truly one area where you don't want to skimp on fees for inferior knowledge and experience.

Beware The Tax Trap and Inflexibility

For young physicians or doctors with incomes under $250,000 who have a net worth below $3,000,000, retirement plans may be good Wealth Protection Planning tools. If you earn more than $250,000 per year or expect to ever have a net worth greater than $3 million, you and your family will be much better suited by exploring nontraditional deferred compensation plans and other nontraditional investments. These alternatives can offer tax reduction, asset protection or tax-efficient growth. Also, unlike traditional retirement strategies, these investments may offer income before age 59½, no 70% reduction in value at death, and possibly tax-free income when tax rates may be 35%–70% (depending on future law changes). Successful physicians owe it to themselves to explore these other options.

Choosing the Right Plan for You

Before you choose a plan for you or for your employees, make sure you contact a specialist with a great deal of experience in this area. You also should make sure you understand all the nuances of defined contribution plans, defined benefit plans (covered in the next chapter) and all other deferred compensation arrangements (some described later in this section). The benefits can be extraordinary, but the pitfalls are not to be taken lightly. Please contact a local Wealth Protection Alliance member to determine which retirement plan best fits your needs and to be introduced to a qualified plan administrator in your area who can best help you administer your plan properly.

43

DEFINED BENEFIT PLANS
Catch Up On Your Retirement Planning

Defined benefit plans are very different animals from defined contribution plans. Some actuaries might say they are actually "opposites." In a defined contribution plan, the amount you can contribute is restricted by both a percentage of income and by an aggregate cap ($41,000 in 2004). In a defined benefit (DB) plan, the "benefit" in retirement is the restricted total account value. An actuary calculates how much monthly retirement benefit you are entitled to based on your present salary and your desired retirement age. Then, the actuary calculates the anticipated rate of return on the investments to be purchased in the plan before making a final determination as to how much funding the plan will require to pay the benefit over your expected lifetime. This rate of return must be reasonable for standard DB plans even though the IRS has not provided us with a definition of "reasonable." For 412(i) plans, the rate of return used in the calculation is the guaranteed return of the annuities and insurance products that are used to fund the 412(i) plan (covered later in this chapter). With those assumptions, he will determine how much contribution you can make each year.

Rule of thumb: defined benefit plans are very attractive for individuals who:

- Are at least 37 years old (over 50 works best);
- Want to contribute more than the defined contribution limits allow;
- Have less in their retirement plan accounts than they should at this time; and
- Earn over $165,000 per year in adjusted gross income

Why would a physician have relatively low balances in his or her retirement plan? Our clients have shown many reasons, including, but not limited to, starting their careers later in life, not regularly contributing to a defined contribution plan throughout their careers, having lost a significant amount of retirement funds in a divorce, having a financial hardship that required them to liquidate their retirement funds for an emergency earlier in life, or having experienced very poor investment results inside their retirement plans.

> **CASE STUDY:** *Clayton Gets a Late Start*
>
> After working as a military physician for years, Clayton retired from the military (with a nice little pension) and went into private practice. After working for a hospital for 2–3 years, he started his own practice. At this point, he was 50 years old and had no retirement savings (the military pension doesn't count). We helped him create a DB plan for his professional corporation and our calculations showed that, based on his age of 50 and his salary of $175,000, he would be able to put away $123,000 per year (on a tax-deductible basis). This saved Clayton approximately $60,000 in income taxes and helped him begin recouping the time he lost in saving for his retirement. He also implemented other strategies that are described later in this section.

If you are a good candidate for a defined benefit plan, the reason for your present shortfall in retirement savings is not important. What is important is that the government allows you to "catch up" by contributing larger amounts per year on a tax-deductible basis with a defined benefit plan.

Are You a Good Candidate for a Defined Benefit Plan?

Unfortunately, there are many factors in determining the amount you can contribute to a DB plan and many of these change every year. For that reason, we must invite you to contact us to get an estimate. Most plan administrators will need to see a complete employee census that shows the names, dates of birth, sex, marital status, salary, years of service, and hours per week for every employee who has worked for the corporation over the past year in order to give you an accurate proposal. There are both sample and blank employee census forms available in the appendix of this book, on our website at **www.jarvisandmandell.com** and through your local Wealth Protection Alliance office.

412(i) Plans May Offer Even Larger Annual Contributions and Guarantee Income!

A 412(i) plan, or "fully-insured plan" is a type of defined benefit plan that is entirely funded by life insurance and annuity contracts. This plan works almost exactly the same way as the typical defined benefit plan. However, there is one major twist — the benefit in retirement is guaranteed! That's right. If you construct a 412(i) plan to give you a monthly benefit of $10,000 per month in retirement, it is guaranteed to be at least that high if you make the standard contribution. How is this done?

The 412(i) plan purchases annuities from insurance companies that may offer guarantees of 2% or 3%. With a 2% or 3% return guaranteed, the IRS allows you to use the 2% or 3% return in your calculation of the future value of the plan. Because the regular defined benefit plans may assume a non-guaranteed return of 6%–8% when determining the amount of tax-deductible contributions the owner can make and the 412(i) plans use a much lower 2%–3% return in the assumptions, the 412(i) plans can allow for significantly larger tax-deductible contributions annually. For example, it is possible for the same 50-year-old physician mentioned before to make tax-deductible contributions of over $150,000 into a 412(i) plan annually.

Why Would I Want Lower Returns?

You are not getting lower returns. You are just guaranteed a lower amount with the upside potential of greater returns. The annuities in the 412(i) plan may still give you 6%–8% or more per year. In fact, the 412(i) plan's investments will likely give you much more than the 2%–3%. However, we only have to use the guaranteed amount in our actuarial calculation. This is what allows some 60–65 year old physicians to make $300,000 in tax-deductible contributions per year into a 412(i) plan.

You are saving significant income taxes in your prime earning years, you are getting a guaranteed return on your investment, you still have the potential upside of the market and you do NOT have to have any employees to start a 412(i) plan. If you work for yourself, work in a small business with few or no employees, or implement one of the asset protection strategies mentioned earlier and create your own corporation, you can design a retirement plan that best fits your individual needs.

Pitfalls of Defined Benefit Plans

As with all retirement plans, the 412(i) can be a double-edged tax sword. You can save quite a bit of money if you qualify. However, if you die with a substantial estate and have money in any retirement plan, there may be a significant tax of up to 70% on those retirement plan assets when you pass away. This is covered in Chapters 68 and 69 later (If you presently have or intend to have significant retirement plan assets, please mark down that you should read those chapters as well).

Additionally, the 412(i) plan is not very flexible. Though the assumptions in the plan document can be altered if your situation changes, the 412(i) is commonly seen as a rather inflexible plan. Given that few physicians can accurately forecast income for one year, let alone every year until retirement, most doctors choose to forego the potentially higher deductions for more flexibility in the retirement plan.

> **BEWARE:** There have been some careless promoters of 412(i) plans who have clearly crossed the line with regard to the tax code. The 2004 Tax Facts warned: "The IRS is aware of and actively pursuing those taxpayers who use what they view as aggressive funding tactics. Characteristics of plans that the IRS views as abusive

include unusually high expense loads and unusually low cash values in early policy years, resulting in high death benefits based on these values. These arrangements conclude with a contract loan or distribution of the policy from the plan sometime after the first five policy years, followed by a sharp increase in the policy value." In a February 13, 2004 Notice the IRS made it clear that it does not agree that the value of an insurance policy (for tax purposes) is its cash surrender value. The IRS further clarified its position that taxpayers will not be allowed to "grandfather" more favorable valuations that were permitted under previous assumptions. The IRS got so tired of this strategy that it placed the 412(i) on its list of "listed transactions" under the category of "Welfare Benefit Plans." This means that you must let the IRS know that you implemented this strategy. This may be a reason for you and your tax advisor to choose the more conservative defined benefit plan over the 412(i) variation.

Tax Risk For Highly Successful Physicians

Just as we stated in the previous chapter, we do <u>NOT</u> advise successful physicians or physician families who are already (or expect to be) worth $3 million to <u>EVER</u> use qualified plans of any type. Though these plans offer deductions and asset protection, the funds are unavailable before 59½, all withdrawals are taxed at the highest rates, you have financial responsibilities to your employees, and funds may be taxed at 70% at death. Nontraditional investing will likely give you much more flexibility in your comprehensive Wealth Protection Plan.

Conclusion

If you have ever watched "This Old House," you undoubtedly heard Bob Villa tell you that it is very important that you "use the right tool for the job." This section includes many retirement alternatives. For those of you who have fallen behind in your savings for one reason or another, who want to achieve significant tax savings and who like the idea of "guaranteed" retirement benefits with further upside potential, and who are not anticipating being worth $3 million or more, the 412(i) plan can be invaluable in helping you achieve your goals.

44

VARIABLE ANNUITIES

Asset Protection, Tax-Deferral And
Capital Preservation For Your Retirement Funds

When it comes to retirement planning, many doctors ask us the following questions:

1. How can I reduce my taxes?

2. How can I protect my retirement funds from lawsuits?

The recent volatility in the stock market and the uncertainty of our political landscape has led to a third serious concern:

3. How do I protect my investments from depreciation?

We have devoted entire sections of this book to retirement planning, asset protection and investing and we mention variable annuities in all of those sections. For a complete understanding of all the benefits that are afforded variable annuities, you should read Chapters 14 and 53 as well. In this chapter, we will discuss how variable annuities can be an integral part of your retirement plan. Of course, you should read the remainder of this section so you understand some of your retirement planning alternatives. In addition, there is no substitute for meeting with a retirement specialist to determine the best mix of strategies and vehicles for meeting your retirement, asset protection, investment, tax and estate planning needs.

What Is a Variable Annuity?

A variable annuity is a personal retirement vehicle that brings together the features of investments and insurance. Money is invested in various investment options of your choosing, with potential growth treated on a tax-deferred basis. At retirement, the money in a variable annuity can be converted into income that is guaranteed to last for life (the payment of income for life depends on the claim-paying ability of the carrier issuing the annuity. For that reason, you should research the insurance company issuing the annuity).

Variable means that the return on your investment depends on the composition and performance of the investment portfolios you choose. These investment options, including stock and bond-based alternatives, give your assets the potential to grow more quickly than traditional fixed annuities and provide greater downside risk.

Will This Affect My Pension Contributions?

No. The typical variable annuity sets virtually no limit on the amount or frequency of your contributions (unless, of course, you are using a variable annuity to fund a qualified plan).

As you learned in the previous chapters of this section, you may be limited to $41,000 of tax-deductible contributions to a retirement plan. If you are earning much more than you need to live, you may be adding $10,000–$100,000 per year to your brokerage account. This brokerage account by itself offers no tax-deferral and no asset protection. The variable annuity may be the ideal tool for protecting your investments from lawsuits.

> **BEWARE:** Most doctors will <u>NOT</u> be in lower tax brackets when they retire. This means that variable annuities lock-up funds until age 59½, subject the doctor to maximum tax in retirement <u>AND</u> will be taxed at rates up to 70% at death. Nontraditional retirement plans are much better than variable annuities for doctors earning over $250,000.

Additional Benefits of Variable Annuities

Asset Protection. Variable annuities are "exempt" in some states. In these states, such annuities can be an ideal way to enjoy +4 / +5 protection. To find out if your state offers protection for variable annuities, speak with a member of the Wealth Protection Alliance.

Principal Protection. Generally, the insurance company issuing the annuity "insures" your heirs against lost capital at the time of your death. For example, if you put $500,000 into an annuity and the account is worth only $400,000 when you die, your heirs will receive the full $500,000 less any withdrawals taken.

Conclusion

Like every other planning tool discussed in this book, variable annuities have their proper place. In most cases, individuals who live in states where variable annuities are protected from lawsuits receive the most benefit from variable annuities. Most others find more benefit from using life insurance as a retirement tool. This will be discussed in the next chapter.

45

LIFE INSURANCE
AS A RETIREMENT TOOL

We consider life insurance to be the cornerstone of Wealth Protection Planning. This is because it can play so many roles in a plan, from death protection for a family to income tax reduction on investments, to asset protection, to pension tax reduction. These roles are covered in Chapters 14, 45, and 69. Here we will cover another important role of life insurance — its function as a retirement vehicle.

Would it surprise you to hear that life insurance is the only effective tax–deferred savings vehicle available to those who want to retire before they turn 59½?

Retirement plans and variable annuities both allow for tax-deferred growth. However, those benefits come at a price — you can't get to the funds before age 59½ without paying a 10% penalty in addition to the ordinary income taxes paid on the withdrawal. That could mean taxes of almost 60% in some states! In addition, when you die, the funds are completely income taxable before your spouse can get to them (with the same penalty applying before she turns 59½) and the funds may be taxed at rates of up to 70% before your children get access to any of the principal (covered in Chapter 38 on IRD).

The only retirement tool that allows for tax-deferred growth, tax-free withdrawals before age 59½, tax-free money for your heirs, and that protects your family from your premature death is life insurance. One thing you should realize after reading this book is that the key to inexpensive and effective Wealth Protection Planning is "flexibility." You want to implement tools and strategies that can help you in multiple situations. This way, you don't have to redo your plan every time one little part of your life changes. There are going to be many changes between now and the time when you pass away. A flexible plan that includes flexible tools and strategies, in particular life insurance, can change as your life changes and help you meet your new goals and objectives with minimal switching costs and aggravation.

Most people are very skeptical about life insurance because they may have had some unscrupulous life insurance agent sell them some terrible policy years ago. Life insurance is just like every other product or service. There are good and bad products and good and bad people who offer them. Just because some doctor harmed his patients, or even killed one in a hospital, doesn't mean that all doctors or hospitals are bad, does it?

What Are the Best Types of Insurance to Use for Retirement Planning?

Variable Universal Life, Whole Life or Equity-Indexed Universal Life policies may be used as a supplemental retirement plan, to compliment other retirement and investment programs, for investment diversification, or as protection against a premature death with the thought of using the cash values if they are needed in retirement.

Why use an insurance policy at all?

- The money invested inside the policy grows TAX- DEFERRED.

- The money inside is available to you, by way of loans, without penalty or taxes before age 59½ unlike most other tax-deferred plans.

- There is usually NO LIMIT to the amount you can have and therefore NO LIMIT on the amount you can invest. There are some limits but most people seldom reach them. You do have to qualify health-wise and financially in order to buy life insurance.

- All money in this type of policy goes to your heirs OUTSIDE of PROBATE COURT and totally INCOME TAX FREE!

- This is the ONLY investment other than a ROTH IRA that can possibly provide "TAX-FREE" (that's right FREE, not just deferred) growth on your money. It could become one of your primary investments for long-term retirement money.

- ASSET PROTECTION: In many states, all cash value life insurance products are "exempt" from creditors (+5 protection).

Why use a Variable Policy?

- All of the aforementioned benefits, plus...

- More investment choices. Some variable policies offer over 40 mutual funds while some 401(k)s offer limited choices.

- Not subject to the creditors of the insurance company (asset protected).

Why use an Equity-Indexed Universal Life Policy?

- Upside potential of the market.

- At least a 1% annual return every year (even if the market declines).

Why use a Whole Life Policy?

- All of the aforementioned benefits of insurance policies, plus...
- Whole Life Polices have guaranteed death benefits and guaranteed annual returns. This makes for a perfect compliment to the other investments you have that will vary based on the stock market. Remember, don't put all your eggs (or risk) in one basket.

CASE STUDY: *Jim and Janine Want to Retire Early*

Jim, 35, and Janine, 33, made the maximum contributions to their 401(k) plans every year and had put some money into variable annuities over the past few years. However, they knew that they would never be able to retire in their early to mid-50s with the projected amounts in their retirement plans — especially since the withdrawals from the 401(k) and variable annuities would be taxed and hit with an additional 10% penalty before age 59½. They were diligent at saving, putting an extra $1,000 per month away for their retirement (in addition to saving for vacations and home repairs on their Manhattan penthouse). They wondered where they should invest the $1,000 per month.

We explained that the average return of the stock market (S&P 500) was 11% per year over the past 70 years and that the average tax on mutual funds is 32% (not counting state taxes). They said: "So we should expect the average after tax returns to be closer to 7%." We told them that we had a better idea. Because they 1) have a $250,000 mortgage on their home, 2) will be having children very soon, and 3) have no life insurance yet, we told them we might be able to kill 3 or 4 birds with one stone.

We explained that a AAA-rated insurance company was presently crediting 7.5% on its whole life policies (all tax-deferred growth). In addition, if they put $500 per month away on each of their lives (into two separate policies), they would have $533,000 of coverage on Jim and $722,000 of coverage on Janine (who made more money). These amounts (which increase every year) would more than cover the mortgage on the home and a portion of the living expenses and college costs of their unborn children, should either of them die prematurely.

Perhaps more importantly, they were very excited that this investment would help them create a more diversified portfolio as all of their retirement plan assets were previously invested in mutual funds) and allow them tax-free withdrawals in their 50s — unlike their 401(k) funds which would require them to pay an additional tax penalty of 10% if funds were withdrawn before age 59½. When Janine turns 55 in 22 years, they will have over $500,000 in total cash value saved and available for tax-free withdrawals. This should help support their retirement until they turn 59½ when they can access their 401(k) and variable annuity funds. They will also have close to $1,700,000 in combined life insurance that they may wish to use to help meet their estate planning goals (if that becomes a concern by then). By purchasing life insurance now, when they both run marathons and compete in triathlons, they can secure excellent underwriting which will stay with these policies for the rest of their lives. If they wait to buy life insurance, there is a chance that their health might not be as good and insurance, if available at all, could be much more expensive. By doing this now, Jim and Janine have given themselves much more financial flexibility.

Conclusion

Any retirement plan that doesn't include some type of cash value insurance policy is probably subjecting the owner to unnecessary investment, tax and lawsuit risk and is probably costing the family great deal of planning flexibility that will have to be handled through increased estate planning costs. Please consult a member of the Wealth Protection Alliance to see how you can avoid unnecessary risk and provide the most flexibility in your planning by using life insurance.

46

DON'T RUN OUT OF MONEY (OR PAY TOO MUCH TAX) IN RETIREMENT

In the past few chapters, we have helped you look at ways to save for retirement. This and the following chapter focus on how to spend your retirement savings. No, we aren't going to try and sell you oceanfront property in Omaha or direct you to a website where you can buy discounted prune juice or MedicAlert bracelets so if you fall, you can get back up.

We are going to help you identify which assets must be spent down first and which assets should be left untouched for as long as possible. We will also show you a way to make sure that you don't run out of money in retirement. The reason this chapter is so important is because you don't know the exact day when you will die. Do you? Because you cannot predict that day, you will either die with money leftover for your heirs or you will run out of money in retirement. If you die with money leftover, we assume you would rather leave it to your heirs than to the federal government (this is where this chapter overlaps with the estate planning section). We also assume that you don't want to have to rely on your children, your children's spouses, or your grandchildren to support you (this is where this chapter will overlap with the insurance chapter).

How Can I Take the Stock Market and Interest Rate Risk Out of the Retirement Picture?

Retirement is a time for you to worry less, not more. You have already worked for 30 or more years, raised children, dealt with weddings (and maybe divorces), and handled thousands of day to day crises with your children, among many other troubles. The last thing you want to do in retirement is worry about how you're going to support yourself and still leave something for your children, grandchildren or your favorite charity. A strategy that we like to provide our clients eliminates the risk, "guarantees" the clients an adequate income in retirement and, if there is anything left, leaves as much as possible to the heirs and/or charities. In our best case scenario, we can do all of this while reducing, if not eliminating, the income and estate taxes in the process.

The life annuity (not to be confused with the variable annuity) is designed by actuaries to pay interest and principal back to you over your lifetime. The amount the insurance company pays you is "fixed" and will not decrease if the stock market crashes or if interest rates fall. Moreover, if you outlive your life expectancy, the insurance company continues to pay you or your spouse for as long as you are alive. This is a good way to remove the investment risk of your retirement plan assets and "lock-in" a fixed income in retirement.

How Much Income Can I Expect from a Life Annuity?

The following table shows some numbers for clients of ours (some individuals, some couples) at varying ages. Of course, these numbers are only examples and may differ based on a variety of economic and medical factors. However, once a life annuity is purchased, the monthly or annual income amount cannot change (unless they purchase a cost of living rider that increases the annual payout 1% to 3% annually).

Client	Cost of Life Annuity	Monthly Income for Life
Dr. B – age 82	$433,000	$6,243
Dr. F – age 65	$1,000,000	$7,900
Dr. and Mrs. G – ages 67 & 63	$1,500,00	$9,200*

Pays this amount as long as either Dr. or Mrs. G is alive.

How Do I Use a Life Annuity and Still Leave Something for My Children or Grandchildren?

A life annuity may pay you more than you need to cover your cost of living. We recommend you gift the "excess" to an irrevocable life insurance trust (see Chapter 66) and buy life insurance to replace the value of the pension assets. Because pension assets may only be worth 30% to your heirs after income and estate taxes (see Chapter 68), this solution almost always gives more to the heirs, reduces income taxes paid on withdrawals AND provides a fixed income stream in retirement. If you're not sure how this solution would work in your situation, please feel free to call us and we'll have a local Wealth Protection Alliance Member run an illustration for you.

Is There a Way to Get Tax-free Income with a Life Annuity?

Yes. If you purchase a life annuity with non-retirement plan assets, you will receive a significant tax benefit. Each life annuity of this type has what is called an "exclusion ratio."

This is the amount of the monthly or annual payment that is NOT income taxable. The older you are, the greater the tax-free percentage of the life annuity payment. For an 80-year old retired physician, 70% of the annuity payment may be tax-free. As an example, if you received annual annuity payments of $100,000 that were 70% tax-free, you would pay tax on only $30,000 of that payment per year. Assuming a tax rate of 25%, you would pay only $7,500 in taxes on $100,000 of income. For this reason, many retirees like to purchase life annuities rather than live off the interest of their savings and subject themselves to the risk of outliving their funds.

In the context of retirement plans, should you decide against utilizing the life annuity and take your chances with the stock market, it is possible that you could end up with a sizeable retirement plan balance at the time of your death. While you think this is desirable because it will benefit your children or grandchildren, you would be gravely mistaken. Many of your retirement plans will be subject to taxes of 70% when you die. Avoiding this hidden tax trap is a concern we will address in the next chapter.

A Smart Alternative — Annuities with a Charitable Element

Charities offer Charitable Gift Annuities (CGA). We cover these in Chapters 36 and 72. There are two major differences. First, you can create a CGA with appreciated assets where a commercial annuity must be purchased with cash. Second, you get a tax deduction when you create a CGA. You see similar returns and have some fringe benefits. Explore both when you go shopping for a guaranteed lifetime income for yourself, for you and your spouse, or for your parents or in-laws.

Conclusion

Retirement should be a time for you to worry less, not more. Unfortunately, there are many concerns our generation must consider that our parents and grandparents didn't. If any of these concerns in this or the next two chapters hit home for you, please take a step in the right direction and consult a WPA professional.

47

AVOIDING THE 50%–70% TAX ON RETIREMENT PLAN BALANCES

In Chapter 68, we will discuss the problem of Income in Respect of a Decedent (IRD). This is the dreaded 70% tax on your pensions that you were not made aware of before you started your retirement plan. You were simply told to "Save, save, save" and you will make it to a beautiful place called Oz otherwise known as retirement. This chapter is designed to help you avoid this problem. If you have any money left in your retirement plan and you don't want to leave only 30 cents on the dollar to your heirs when you pass away, this may be the single most important chapter in the book for you!

Because all of your contributions to retirement plans are income tax-deductible, all of your withdrawals from your plans will be fully taxable at ordinary income tax rates (as high as 44% in some states). Because of this tax, many clients are advised by their short-sighted advisors to "spend down other assets in retirement" and continue "deferring taxation on the pension assets" as a way of avoiding unnecessary taxes.

A *Wall Street Journal* article on April 15, 1999, explained why this strategy is a "tax trap" for many of us whose savings or investments mean we will not need a significant portion of our qualified plan to live on during retirement. Anyone worth more than $2 million should know that 70% of retirement plan assets can be eaten up by the combination of income and estate taxes due on IRD). Because losing 70% of your plan assets is the worst possible tax trap, we don't want to be penny-wise and pound-foolish and avoid 44% taxation just to leave a 70% tax bill for our heirs later.

Judge Learned Hand once said: "No person is obligated to pay as much tax as possible — there is not even a patriotic duty to do so." For this reason, we all look for ways to reduce our taxes. We must find a way to remove assets from your tax-disadvantaged retirement plan or subject ourselves to 44% or our heirs to 70% taxation. If you are concerned about this problem, make sure you spend some time reviewing Chapters 68 and 69.

48

DON'T LET MEDICAL CONDITIONS RUIN YOUR RETIREMENT

Purchasing Long Term Care Insurance Could Be Your Solution

Unfortunately, there are no tricks from Ponce de Leon in this chapter because we have not found the fountain of youth…yet. What we want to discuss briefly is the idea of using long term care insurance (LTCi) to protect our retirements, in addition to our inheritance and our children's inheritances, from the outrageous costs of medical care not covered by Social Security, Medicare or Medicaid.

Most baby boomers are saddled with the problem of having to take care of their children, themselves, and possibly their parents. The biggest financial disaster that may threaten your retirement is that you, your spouse, your parents, or your in-laws suffer significant health problems. In some states, the government will not pay for in-home or nursing home care until you have spent down all but $2,500 of your entire net worth. In addition, once they begin paying for your care, they may take the income to the person receiving the medical benefits. This would certainly destroy your retirement and any inheritances that might exist before the illness arose.

The cost of long-term care for one person can be hundreds of dollars per day. For this reason, many clients don't just purchase long-term care insurance on themselves and their spouses, but they also buy long-term care insurance on their parents and in-laws. This is a growing trend we are noticing with our younger physician clients. They are buying LTCi on their parents and in-laws as a way to take care of their parents and protect their own retirements. There are many different bells and whistles to consider and a variety of payment options ranging from single payment to 10-payment, 20-payment and life-pay programs. To determine which type of policy is right for your family, read Chapter 60 on long term care insurance.

PART SEVEN

INVESTING

49

YOUR MONEY DOESN'T
COME WITH INSTRUCTIONS

In the mid 1990s, many Americans decided that it was time to "jump into the pool" and try and invest on their own. They began investing their money in the stock market through mutual funds and then directly into stocks and bonds. We even had two clients who told us they were going to give up medicine for lucrative careers as day traders buying and selling options. For a few years, many of these new investors were likely very pleased. After all, it was pretty easy to make money in the stock market from 1993 to 1999 — almost everything continued to go up, and up, and up.

In the year 2000 came a rude awakening. The Dow went from 12,000 to below 10,000 by 2001, and the NASDAQ fell from a high of over 5,000 to below 2,000 over the same period. Billions and billions of dollars of wealth were lost and many of these "new" investors were left holding the bag. As a result, investors now realize that the stock market is hardly a "free lunch." Many of them are now afraid to get their feet wet again.

It may seem strange to have a section on investing in a book on Wealth Protection Planning. The section on tax planning showed you how to reduce taxes on your income. The asset protection section showed you how to protect your investments from lawsuits. The estate planning section will show you how to pass your wealth onto your heirs with as little tax and complication as possible. This section is going to help you avoid the most common investment mistakes by teaching you some basic investment fundamentals and by explaining some common, and some not-so-common, investment alternatives.

Specifically, this section will teach you the basic risk versus return theory of all investments, why taxes and inflation are important factors in your investment plan, why you need more than a Nobel Prize to invest wisely, as well as how and when to get back into the market. Finally, we'll introduce the ideas of using insurance, annuities, and other less common investment tools.

Like every other section of this book, you should be sure to read other chapters which are referred to here. This way, you can get a complete and fully-integrated Wealth Protection Plan tailored specifically to your situation.

50

UNDERSTANDING INVESTING

You Need More Than A Nobel Prize
To Help You Invest Wisely

Many investment advisors may boast that their strategy is based on a Nobel Prize-winning theory. Though this is impressive, it has two faults:

1. Nearly everyone's strategy is based on that same theory; and

2. The theory itself has a number of limitations that these Nobel Laureates acknowledge.

The purpose of this chapter is threefold. First, we will give you a very basic understanding of the aforementioned Nobel Prize-winning investment theory. Second, we will point out the limitations of the theory. Third, we will suggest how to make the theory work for your particular Wealth Protection Plan.

In 1990, the Nobel Prize in Economics was awarded to Harry Markowitz, Merton Miller and William Sharpe for their Modern Portfolio Theory ('MPT') and Capital Asset Pricing Model ('CAPM'). With apologies to Messrs. Markowitz, Miller and Sharpe, we would like to offer simplistic summaries of the Capital Asset Pricing Model and Modern Portfolio Theory. There are three concepts you must be able to grasp, before putting them together to form the CAPM and MPT. Those are:

1. Types of Risk

2. Risk vs. Reward

3. Diversification of Investments

Types of Risk

CAPM divides the risk of any investment into specific risk and market (or systematic) risk. Specific risk is unique to an individual investment while systematic risk affects all investments in the "market" and is also known as "market risk." Let's look at examples of each:

> Do you remember the Tylenol scare about 25 years ago? Someone tainted a number of bottles of Tylenol with cyanide. This obviously impacted the stock price of Johnson & Johnson, the maker of Tylenol. The risk of this type of occurrence is an example of specific risk because it didn't have an effect on all investments in the market, just on J&J's stock price.
>
> Do you recall the stock market crash of 1929? That incident affected all investments in the market. The risk of a crash is certainly the most extreme example of market risk.

When you make an investment, that investment is subject to both market and specific risk. In a portfolio of investments, you are subject to market risk, which affects the whole portfolio, and a combination of specific risks that affect each individual investment distinctly.

Risk vs. Reward

In a general sense, rewards are higher for those who take more risk. Individuals who start their own businesses and are ultimately successful will probably make considerably more money than those individuals who took the less risky route and went to work for someone else. The entrepreneur risked his time and money. If successful, he or she will be rewarded handsomely for the risks he took. Of course, the entrepreneur may make no money or lose money if the venture is unsuccessful.

Doctors bypass the opportunity to make money right out of college. Instead, they spend more money going to medical school and delay their income-producing careers by another 3–7 years. For this risk of time and money, you are generally rewarded with generous salaries when compared to other college graduates. Moreover, for those of you who pursued even more education and deferred income for another 2 to 5 years to become neurosurgeons, gynecologic oncologists or other specialists, you are obviously making more money than the average family practice doctor. This makes sense, doesn't it?

Diversification

Diversification is a business school term for "not putting all of your eggs in one basket." When applied to investments, it means investing in a combination of stocks, bonds, real estate, cash, and other investment classes. It also applies to investments made within each asset class — not investing in just a few stocks, not just a few bonds, not just one or two parcels of real estate, etc.

A few paragraphs back, we explained the idea that an investment portfolio is subject to 1) market risk, and 2) all of the specific risks for all of the assets in the portfolio. One interesting finding of the CAPM & MPT is that in a "well-diversified portfolio," all specific risks cancel each other out. In other words, specific risk can be diversified away. Investors can reduce the overall risk in their portfolios by spreading their risk across and within different asset classes. Although this may make perfect intuitive sense, the mathematical proof for this statement and the subsequent model for creating the "most efficient" set of portfolios was worthy of a Nobel Prize.

How Do the CAPM and MPT Work for You?

The CAPM and Modern Portfolio Theory provide a mathematical model for minimizing systematic risk in any investment portfolio. Once an investor determines the level of risk he is comfortable with (risk tolerance), he can follow the mathematical model to construct a portfolio that will optimize the risk-reward balance. In other words, by following this theory, the investor can maximize his expected return for any level of risk. All such "maximized" portfolios exist on what the financial people call the "efficient frontier."

Certainly, we are not going to contend that the findings of three Nobel Laureates are incorrect. Rather, we are going to point out the acknowledged limitations (by the authors themselves) in their theory and offer additional insights that might help you.

As acknowledged by the laureates, the CAPM and MPT are designed to work in a simplified world where:

- There are no taxes or transaction costs;

- All investors have identical investment horizons;

- All investors have identical perceptions regarding the expected returns, volatilities and correlations of available risky investments.

1st Problem — Taxation & Transaction Costs

Obviously, we consider taxation to be a significant concern of yours. If we didn't, we wouldn't have devoted an entire section of the book exclusively to this topic. If all of your stock investments are in a non-taxable account, like an IRA, you don't have to worry about taxes. You would maximize the returns on your portfolio for a given amount of risk and taxes would not become a factor until you withdrew the funds.

A common physician situation is to have a portion of a stock portfolio in a retirement account (or other tax-favored entity like those discussed in Chapters 53 or 54) and a portion in a taxable environment. If this is true for you, you will need to determine which investments will be made in the tax-favored accounts and which investments will be made in taxable accounts. If you are in prime earning years and are in the 35%+ federal income tax brackets, the following rules should suit you well:

1. Hold all interest-bearing assets within a tax-favored account. Otherwise, as much as 44% of the earnings will go to paying income taxes each year. You are better off deferring the tax and earning money on the government's dime.

2. Hold all long-term growth assets and dividend-paying investments in your taxable accounts. If you don't intend to sell these assets for at least one year, you will only pay 15%–24% capital gains taxes when you sell. If you hold these assets in a pension account, you would be taxed at 35% federal (plus state) when you make withdrawals. Why pay the government twice?

These are just basic strategies to supplement the CAPM and MPT when taxes are an issue. There is much more to be learned about taxes from Chapters 30–40.

2nd Problem — All Investors Do NOT Have Identical Investment Horizons

This is obviously a problem with the CAPM and MPT. Some investors need their money in 30 days and some don't need it for 30 years. The investor who needs his money in less than a month would be well served by a CD or money market. An investor who doesn't need the money for 30 years should have nearly 100% of his investments in equities (stocks) and other long term investments.

If you have assets that you do not need for five years, you can afford to take some risks with those assets and should seriously consider investing in the stock market. If you need the money in less than a year, cash equivalents are your best option. For the assets that need to be accessed in 1–5 years, some combination thereof may work well.

3rd Problem — All Investors Have Very Different Perceptions Regarding the Expected Returns, Volatilities, and Correlations of Available Risky Investments

In plain English, the environment where the CAPM and MPT work best is one where everyone has the same knowledge of all assets and the same access to purchasing assets. For stocks and bonds, where there is more research available than you could ever possibly read, perceptions of the risk of any given stock are broad. People can't even agree on the value or the risk of certain stocks.

As far as availability, there is a very wide gap. If you are only investing $100,000, you may be restricted to mutual funds that have very high transaction costs and taxes (see problem 1 above). If you have more than $500,000, you have access to unique products and your transaction costs are considerably lower relative to the smaller investor. If you have $5 million or more, you can access products that others can only dream of buying. These may include small businesses and initial public offerings, to name a few. Regretfully, we can only discuss private placements and other alternative investments with accredited investors (per federal securities law). If you are interested, please contact a local Wealth Protection Alliance member to see what investments you qualify for based on your income or net worth.

For those of you who have experimented with, or are experts in, real estate investing, you know the gap in knowledge between buyer and seller is a key competitive factor for the investor. Many professional real estate investors have admitted that a significant percentage of their profits are a direct result of a buyer not understanding the real estate market. The CAPM and MPT call for a percentage of your portfolio to be invested in real estate assets. However, for the real estate expert who understands this market better than most, we would deviate from the strategy and recommend he stick with what he knows best and profit from his advantage in this arena.

For the investor with little knowledge of real estate, we may recommend he/she avoid investing in real estate (other than your home) altogether for two reasons. First, the time necessary to manage the property or the costs to pay someone else to do so may decimate the earnings the property generates. Second, there is no reason to jump into a market where you have a distinct disadvantage. This adds risk to your portfolio instead of reducing it as you had hoped by utilizing the findings of the CAPM and MPT.

Conclusion

The Capital Asset Pricing Model and Modern Portfolio Theory have contributed greatly to the field of portfolio selection. In fact, these theories are the basis for a significant percentage of institutional investors and mutual fund managers. They have also played a large role in the field of financial risk management. However, as you saw from the chapter, there are problems with the practical application of these theories. You should consider working with one of the advisors in the WPA to help you with applying these theories to your individual situation. As you will learn from the remainder of the book, you may wish to invest in a vehicle that offers you other benefits such as asset protection, tax deferral, or protection against a premature death in addition to capital appreciation.

51

TAXES, INFLATION,
AND YOUR INVESTMENTS

You May Not Be Getting As Much As
You Think From Your Investments

"XYZ fund returned 18.6% last year." "My money manager has beat the S&P consistently for 5 years." "In this magazine, we'll profile the 'best returning' mutual funds." As financial professionals, we read and hear these types of statements on a daily basis. Why? Because everyone looks at the investment returns as the "currency" of investing. Most people use returns as a way of comparing money managers, mutual funds, CDs, bonds, etc. What most people fail to consider is the impact that taxes and inflation have on those investments. When you consider that ALL investments and financial professionals report their pre-inflation, pre-tax returns, it is easy to see why some people realize no additional purchasing power from their investments. They simply don't understand what they are really getting from their investments.

The last chapter discussed how taxes were not considered in Markowitz, Miller and Sharpe's Nobel Prize winning Capital Asset Pricing Model of investments. A new development in the mutual fund arena is that mutual funds may have to report AFTER-TAX gains, not pre-tax gains. How much will that change the numbers? A lot!

If you assume that half the gain comes from long term gains and dividends and half the gain comes from short term gains and interest, the taxes may account for 25–34% of the total gain. For example, if your mutual fund appreciated by 11% last year, it probably cost you close to 4% in taxes. Which number is more important to you, the 11% or the 7%?

Mutual funds are not the only tax problem. How many of you have CDs, money markets, or bonds? All of the income from these vehicles is taxed as ordinary income. This will likely be taxed at rates between 27% and 35%, not to mention up to 9% of state income tax. For this reason, 5% to 6% in dividend or interest income may only be worth 2.5%–4.0% after taxes. While this is depressing, it isn't the end of your problems.

You would always rather have a dollar today than a dollar tomorrow, right? There is an area of finance and economics that deals with this simple concept. They call it the "present value of money." When determining the present value of future dollars, many people want to know what a dollar in the future will buy them; i.e., what is it worth in today's dollars? What they are really talking about is inflation.

Obviously, things become more expensive as we get older. We have all heard our parents talk about a Coke (or pop) costing a nickel or a movie costing a quarter. The fact that a movie costs close to $10 today is because of inflation (though many might call it highway robbery given the quality, or lack thereof, of the films today). The average annual inflation rate over the past 70 years has been approximately 3.1%. This means that approximately every 22 years, things cost twice as much.

How Do You Calculate the Impact of Inflation?

The after-tax return that an investment achieves is called the "nominal return." This does not take inflation into account. When you divide the nominal return of an investment over time by the rate of inflation over that same period of time, you get the "real" rate of return, or inflation-adjusted rate of return.

Consider the mutual fund mentioned earlier — where an 11% pre-tax return meant a take-home 7% after taxes. That 7% return is actually more like a 3.8% REAL return (1.07 / 1.031 = 1.038), after inflation is factored into the result.

How Do You Invest to Plan for Inflation?

If they want to reduce taxes, savvy investors invest in the stock market through tax-managed investment accounts, variable annuities, variable universal life insurance, equity-indexed life insurance policies or through mutual funds or managed accounts if the funds are inside tax-deferred retirement plans.

However, if you want the most accurate hedge against inflation, then real estate would be the ideal investment because real estate almost always moves directly with inflation. Nowadays, most people own their home and the home represents a significant portion of their net worth. This is usually enough to fill up the real estate portion of their diversified portfolio. However, if you have significant wealth or just like real estate, you may want to purchase more real estate than simply a home. If you do, you MUST read Chapter 15 and 34 in the asset protection and tax sections, respectively, to make sure you don't unnecessarily expose yourself to lawsuit risk or pay too much in taxes.

Conclusion

When it comes to investing, there is no sure-fire method to avoiding inflation or taxes. However, there are a number of tools that are discussed in this section and in the tax section. The more you know about your options, the easier it will be for you to understand what you are really getting from your investments. Of course, there is no substitute for meeting with an investment specialist (or member of the Wealth Protection Alliance) who can help you meet all of your needs.

52

WHEN (AND HOW) DO I GET BACK INTO THE MARKET?

Dollar Cost Averaging May Be The Plan

In the opening of this section, we explained how many of the investors who poured their family savings into the stock market in the 1990's have pulled their money out (or at least not invested new funds in the market) since the start of the new decade. If you are one of these investors, you may be asking the question: "When should I get back into the market?" The truth is that we really cannot say for certain. Rather, your investing strategy should be determined by your answer to this question: "When do you need the money?"

When Do You Need the Money?

If you are saving your money to buy a house, pay for a child's education, or pay for a vacation in the next few years, then you have a short time horizon. With a short time horizon, you can't afford to lose money because you don't have time to wait for the market to turn. In these situations, you have to stick to CDs and money markets. If you are investing for more than 5 years (like retirement funds), you have a long time horizon. Obviously, the longer your time horizon, the more risk you can take because you can afford to "weather the storm" and ride out the tough times of the stock market.

What Are My Options?

If you want to remove some risk in your longer-term investments, you have the following options:

- Get a second opinion if you wish to ride out the storm
- "Lock-in" your retirement income
- Dollar cost averaging (with securities or with variable annuities)

Get a Second Opinion

If you are just going to wait out the down market, you may want a second opinion regarding your present investments. We have seen many physicians who believe they are in diversified portfolios (because they have 25 stocks or have 10 mutual funds). Unfortunately, all of their funds are heavily weighted toward the same sectors or stocks. One way to do a quick check is to look at the top 10 holdings of all of your funds. If there is overlap, you may not be sufficiently diversified and may be subjecting yourself to unnecessary risk with your investments.

"Lock-in" Your Retirement Income

If you are systematically selling a portion of your stock portfolio to pay your bills or are living on the dividend income of your stocks, the coupon payments of your bonds, or interest on your CDs or money markets, you may be subjecting yourself to too much risk. If the stocks do not perform or do not give you a large enough dividend, you will find yourself cutting into your principal. If the interest rates drop further, bonds and CDs (as well as money markets) may not pay enough. If interest rates go up, the value of your bonds will decrease. One popular alternative is the Single Premium Immediate Annuity (SPIA). The SPIA, unlike life insurance or variable annuities, can pay you (and/or your spouse) a fixed income for the rest of your life.* It does not change when the market does.

Both the income guarantees and the death benefit are dependent on the claims paying ability of the issuing company.

Dollar Cost Averaging (DCA)

DCA is not new. It is a strategy that has worked for years. The idea is to systematically spend the exact same amount per month to buy the same investment (stock, bond, mutual fund). By spending the same amount each month, and not by purchasing the same number of shares, you effectively reduce the average price paid for the investment. For example, if you spend $1,000 per month to buy shares of XYZ Company and the stock is trading at $20 one month, you will buy 50 shares that month. If the stock price goes up to $50 one month, you will only buy 20 shares at that higher price. If the price falls to $10 per share, you will buy 100 shares at that price. This is a good way to ease back into the market. Almost all mutual fund companies offer a DCA program and most insurance companies offer DCA on their variable annuities. See Chapters 44 and 55 for further benefits.

Of course, you need to realize that dollar cost averaging does not assure a profit and does not protect against loss in declining markets. DCA involves continuous investing in securities regardless of fluctuating prices. An investor should consider his/her ability to continue investing even in periods of low price levels.

DCA with Variable Annuities

A variable annuity is an insurance contract that offers a variety of investment options, including cash equivalents, stocks and bonds. The insurance contract protects the value of your initial investment at death. If you contribute $500,000 to a variable annuity and your investment drops 20% (to $400,000) at the time of your death, your family still gets $500,000, less any withdrawals you may have made. This is important for families who want to make sure their heirs have assets if the breadwinner passes away. Further, the variable annuity can offer a DCA program. If you put $500,000 into a variable annuity with a DCA strategy, the company will put your money into the investment you have selected systematically over a 6 or 12-month period. While the money is waiting to be invested, these companies will pay a fixed rate of return that adjusts periodically. If you want to ease back into the market, you may want to consider a DCA variable annuity strategy.

Variable annuities usually have mortality and expense charges, administrative fees and sales charges. These charges are in addition to the expenses normally incurred on the mutual funds that comprise variable annuity portfolio. Hence, variable annuities may be more expensive to hold than the typical stock or mutual fund portfolio. This additional cost must be weighed against the benefits that an annuity offers. It is our recommendation that you contact your local Wealth Protection advisor and ask him to run comparative illustrations between a mutual fund portfolio and a variable annuity comprised of the same fund portfolio over the same investment period. It should also be noted that investments in a variable annuity will fluctuate, so that your shares may be worth more or less than the original cost when redeemed.

53

———❦———

VARIABLE ANNUITIES
Asset Protection, Tax-Deferral,
And Capital Preservation

Variable annuities have their place in an investment portfolio. Typically, it is not because of their returns as you can invest in the same underlying investments of the variable annuity without the expenses of the variable annuity. It is because of the other benefits variable annuities offer. Remember, an important theme throughout the book is "flexibility." The more flexible the components of your total Wealth Protection Plan, the more flexible your overall plan. "The whole is greater than the sum of its parts!"

What is a Variable Annuity?

A variable annuity is a personal retirement vehicle that brings together the features of investments and insurance. Money is invested in various investment options of your choosing, with potential growth treated on a tax-deferred basis. At retirement, the money in a variable annuity can be converted into income that is guaranteed to last for life. The payment of income for life depends on the claims-paying ability of the issuer of the annuity. For this reason, you should research the insurance company issuing the annuity.

Variable means that the return on your investment depends on the composition and performance of the investment portfolio you design. These investment options, including stock and bond-based alternatives, give your assets the potential to grow more quickly than traditional fixed annuities with greater downside risk.

How Do You Like Those 1099s and K-1s?

You have undoubtedly received one of these forms from your non-pension investments this year. With mutual funds, money management accounts, and investment limited partnerships, a significant portion of your earnings may be subject to taxes even if you do not take any distributions. In fact, you may even realize capital gains during a year where your mutual fund investment *de*preciates.

If you hold a mutual fund that sells a stock for a gain, you have to pay capital gains taxes in that year even if you don't sell your mutual fund shares. With a variable annuity, all investment earnings grow tax-deferred until you access the money. This means you are free to move your money from one investment option to another without incurring a current tax liability.

You may already be in a high (around 35%–44%) marginal tax bracket. If so, the last thing you need is for additional taxes to be payable in April without having seen any cash flow on your part. The variable annuity can help mitigate this tax risk.

Are You "Stuck" Investing in One Company's Funds?

We hope you aren't. The variable annuities that we use and recommend for our clients offer 35–45 investment choices. These choices include "in-house" funds, but also many funds from "outside" mutual fund families. Part of what your investment advisor should do is to help you create a portfolio that meets your level of risk tolerance and your investment goals, without being tied to one company's products.

How Does a Variable Annuity Protect My Investment?

As we stated earlier, the variable annuity is a combination of investments and insurance. Generally, the insurance company issuing the annuity "insures" your heirs against lost capital at the time of your death. For example, if you put $500,000 into an annuity and the account is worth only $400,000 when you die, your heirs will receive the full $500,000 less any withdrawals taken. There are ways to increase the insured amount each year, all of which will be explained later.

What Additional Options or Features Are Typically Available with Variable Annuities?

Automatic Dollar Cost Averaging (DCA)

DCA is a popular investment strategy. It buys the same dollar amount of an investment each month. This means more units will be purchased when the price is lower and fewer units will be purchased when the price is higher.

Choice of Payment Method

In retirement, you can receive scheduled payments, income for life, or can choose to take out money as you need it. It's entirely up to you.

Automatic Portfolio Rebalancing

If you diversify your investments across a number of funds, you can expect the performance of each fund to vary. When funds grow at different rates, your allocation can get out of balance. This option automatically rebalances your investment for you.

Annual Ratchet Protection

If you purchase this death benefit option and your investment increases in a given year, this additional amount is then protected from that year forward. This reflects only positive performance and the insured amount never decreases. This is available for an extra charge.

Which Funds Are Best Suited for a Variable Annuity?

Before we tell you what funds to use, let us tell you what funds NOT to use. First, we wouldn't invest in a variable annuity within a retirement plan because you are already receiving tax-deferral in a retirement plan without the variable annuity. We do not recommend paying for the tax deferral twice. Unless your reason for purchasing an annuity is the principal protection or death benefit it offers you, avoid investing in a variable annuity through your retirement plan. Second, we would not invest money that you foresee needing before retirement (or age 59½), as there are penalties for early withdrawal.

The best funds to use are funds that are not in retirement plans which you would like to use for retirement. If you don't foresee needing more than 10% of these funds before retirement, then you should consider using a variable annuity. Additionally, we would consider rolling IRA funds into variable annuities in states where annuities are asset-protected and IRAs are not (see chapter 14). You maintain your tax-deferral that way AND get asset protection. Like every tool and strategy we present, the variable annuity has its rightful place in financial planning — the key is to use it when it makes sense.

Please keep in mind that every financial planning tool has its dangers. If you have over $1,000,000 of variable annuities and are worth more than $2 million, you may be subject to the 70% tax at your death. This problem is explained in Chapter 68 on IRD. If you have a large variable annuity portfolio and you want us to help you avoid that tax trap, you should probably contact a professional who is experienced in dealing with issues of IRD.

How Much Do Variable Annuities Cost?

Before you look at how much they cost, you must know exactly what you are paying for when you buy a variable annuity. First, if your investments decline below your initial investment at the time of your death, your premium payments are protected by the death benefit. Second, because of this insurance element, you get tax deferral on all short and long term capital gains, dividends and interest payments. If you are in a 35% tax bracket now and anticipate being in a 28% or 31% tax bracket in retirement, you may realize great tax savings from the variable annuity. Third, you may get excellent asset protection benefits from the variable annuity. When you consider that an asset protection plan may cost upwards of $10,000, this may be a significant benefit.

With these benefits in mind, now you can measure what they are worth to you. The costs of a variable annuity include the cost of the insurance element (and additional administrative charges) and the cost of the investment management. According to Morningstar, Inc., the average investment management fee was about 0.82% and the average administrative charge was 0.14% as of mid-1998. The insurance charge (or mortality and expense charge) averages around 1.1%. Additionally, there is a contract fee of $25–$40, which may be waived if your account size meets a certain threshold. Lastly, annuities have something called a surrender charge. This is similar to a back-load for a mutual fund and can be as high as 7%–10% in the first year before decreasing over time.

Generally, if your premiums remain in the annuity for more than 7 years, the surrender charge is eliminated. However, some variable annuities have rolling surrender charges that apply a new schedule of surrender charges to each additional payment. Lastly, some firms may have transfer fees, which may be applied if the client is making numerous investment changes.

Conclusion

In general, if you are looking at your annuity as a long-term investment, you keep the funds for over 7 years, and you don't make excessive fund transfers, you can avoid the surrender charges, the transfer fees and perhaps the contract fee. If it is worth paying a little bit more for the tax deferral, insurance, and potential asset protection, then you should at least consider utilizing variable annuities as part of your portfolio and retirement plan.

> CAUTION: For high earners who anticipate having significant taxable income in retirement and leaving and estate worth more than $2 million to heirs, there are more tax-efficient investments available. You can participate in market upside, have access before 59½, have access to funds tax-free, and leverage your estate. Please contact the WPA at (800) 554-7233 for the special report "The Unlikely Investment" — available free via email to *Wealth Protection MD* owners.

54

LIFE INSURANCE
AS AN INVESTMENT

In your study of investments or from talking with friends, you may have read or heard "Life insurance is a terrible investment" or "Mutual funds are better investments than life insurance." If you have, then you either read or heard something that was taken out of context or the source of that idea was not someone who espouses the ideas of "flexible planning" or "integrated planning" as we do.

Chapters 45 and 57 of the retirement and insurance planning sections will explain in great detail the benefits of life insurance. Also, it may benefit you to come back to this chapter after you have read the recommended sections on asset protection, retirement, insurance, and estate planning. Only then will you truly realize why you need flexible investment tools.

In a nutshell, life insurance is a very powerful investment because:

- Cash values and death benefits can grow tax-free.

- The cash value is available to you later without taxes.

- Rather than reducing in value by 50% when you die because of estate taxes (like every other asset you have), it appreciates when you die if you plan properly.

- It is the only asset that protects your family against your untimely death.

- Premium dollars are instantly leveraged upward into a higher death benefit and net worth.

- It is a +5 asset protection tool in many states.

Please read the other sections and keep in mind that a flexible, fully-integrated Wealth Protection Plan will include a sizeable investment in life insurance. If you would like a free special report "How Insurance out-performs other investments," please contact the authors or your local Wealth Protection Alliance member.

55

※

HAVE YOU OUTGROWN
MUTUAL FUNDS?

Individually-Managed Accounts May Be The Answer

If you are reading this chapter, it is probably because you have over $100,000 in cash or mutual funds. These funds may be inside or outside of your tax-deferred retirement plans. In previous chapters of this section, we have discussed alternatives to taxable mutual fund accounts for your non-retirement plan accounts. Some of these alternatives offer asset protection, tax-deferral, and death protection. In this chapter, we will discuss an alternative to mutual funds both inside and outside of retirement plans. Before we compare mutual funds and individually-managed accounts, we must first explain what they are.

Mutual Funds ("MF"s) and Individually Managed Accounts ("IMAs") represent two of the most popular investment programs used by individuals to create wealth. On the surface, at least, one could argue that they are not all that dissimilar. Both offer investors a professionally managed portfolio of securities, generally comprised of stocks, bonds or a combination of the two to provide ample diversification.

When looking beneath the surface, however, two distinctly different approaches emerge. Each offers particular advantages depending upon one's needs. Which is the more prudent choice? This is a question properly answered only by the individual investor. The information that follows is designed to help you make an informed decision, one with which you are comfortable and which, we hope, will prove over time to be the "right" choice.

What Are Mutual Funds?

A mutual fund is a company that invests in stocks, bonds and other securities on behalf of individual investors with similar financial goals. A "no-load" mutual fund is one that is sold directly to investors without an initial sales charge or "load."

Many financial advisors now provide access to no-load funds as part of a comprehensive range of services. However, the charge for the advisor's assistance tends to offset the lack of an initial sales charge, effectively minimizing any cost differences between load and no-load

251

funds. Of course, you get the assistance of an advisor that you would otherwise have to pay anyway. For purposes of this discussion, therefore, "no-load funds" will refer to funds purchased directly from the company without the help of an advisor.

Both load and no-load mutual funds are essentially "cooperatives" of investors who pool their money for a common purpose. Investors contribute to the pool by buying shares in the fund. Each share represents an equal percentage of ownership in the fund's assets.

The fund draws from the pool not only to make investments but also to pay for the services of a fund manager (who decides when and if to buy and sell securities for the fund based on its stated objective), marketing and distribution costs, custodian fees, and transaction costs. Mutual funds are not limited but generally hold several hundred different securities. No matter how many shares of the fund you as the investor hold, you cannot control the buying and selling of these securities inside the fund. You can only buy or sell the basket of securities the fund has by buying or selling your shares of the fund.

What Are Individually Managed Accounts?

Perhaps obviously, an IMA is an account that is individually managed by a professional investment manager who decides when to buy and sell securities based on YOUR stated investment strategy or goal.

Unlike mutual fund investors, managed account investors do not pool their money. Rather, they own the securities in their account directly. They may have many similar holdings with a number of their clients but each portfolio is separate. You, the investor, can direct the manager to buy only certain types of stocks or to avoid certain stocks (perhaps no tobacco stocks for moral reasons or no healthcare stocks because you work as a physician and enough of your income is tied to healthcare). This obviously gives you greater flexibility and control than you would have with a mutual fund.

Are Managed Accounts Worth the Money?

One of the most common problems we see with clients is that they are obsessed with the fee associated with any type of planning. If you took this approach to everything you bought, you'd only eat 99 cent Big Macs at every meal. There is truth to the saying "you get what you pay for." You should not be quick to dismiss the advantages of one investment strategy over another based purely on price. The recent popularity of no-load mutual funds is proof that many investors, particularly those who like a no-frills approach to investing, are doing just that.

You paid for this book, in hopes that it would help benefit you. That's $50 well spent, right? You are considering asset protection, insurance, estate planning, and retirement strategies that undoubtedly will cost you something. Why? Because the strategies will offer you something valuable in return. A prudent investor should consider differences in the following:

- The quality of service provided in return for the fee.

- How the accounts treat capital gains and losses relative to your situation.

- The effect that other investors may have on an investment manager's decisions.

- The methods used to report information.

- The way in which fees are handled.

These are very important factors to consider when comparing investment options.

Is Your Tax Situation a Consideration?

With IMAs, you pay taxes only on the capital gains you actually realize. Because you own the securities in your account directly, you can work with your tax advisor to implement planning strategies that mutual fund investors may not be able to duplicate. There are actually IMA firms who will call YOU to ask you how you want to end the year (more gains?, more losses?, balanced to $0 tax?).

With mutual funds, investors pay taxes on their pro rata share of capital gains experienced by the fund, whether or not they benefited from the sale of the security. The following hypothetical example serves to illustrate this point:

> Assume that a fund purchases stock at the beginning of the year for $25 per share. Over the next few months, the stock's price rises to $50 per share. Coincidentally, an investor buys shares in the fund just as the stock's price reaches this peak.
>
> Later in the year, the stock's price falls to $40 per share, and the fund sells its position. At the end of the year, the investor is allocated a pro rata share of the fund's gain on the stock (the difference between the purchase price of $25 and the sale price of $40), even though the investor did not fully benefit from the gain; in fact, the stock actually declined in value after the investor purchased shares in the fund at $50.

Over time, IMA investors and mutual fund investors who hold their investments for the same period and whose portfolio managers follow identical strategies will report little, if any, difference in capital gains taxes — at least on those particular investments. For the mutual fund investor, however, the point at which the gains are realized may be moved forward and that can affect the investor's tax planning strategy.

Comparing Individually Managed Accounts and Mutual Funds

	Individually Managed Account	Load Mutual Fund	No-Load Mutual Fund
Investment Portfolio	Tailored to meet investor's particular needs	Two-way communication, including in-person discussions with Financial Advisor. Can also call toll-free number.	One-way communication: Call toll-free phone number and talk to sales representative.
Establishing Investor's Goals	Investor benefits from Financial Advisor's help.	Investor benefits from Financial Advisor's help.	Investors determine on their own.
Investment Management Selection	Chosen by investor with Financial Advisor's help.	Chosen by mutual fund.	Chosen by mutual fund.
Investment Manager Evaluation	Screened and evaluated by investor and Financial Advisor.	Screened and evaluated by investor and Financial Advisor.	Investors must monitor on their own.
Performance Monitoring	Financial Advisor monitors on investor's behalf.	Financial Advisor monitors on investor's behalf.	Investors must monitor on their own.
Tax Planning	Investors have some control over the timing of capital gains.	Investors have little control over the timing of capital gains.	Investors have little control over the timing of capital gains.
Redemption Requests	Investors are not affected by the actions of others who use the same manager.	Manager may be forced to sell securities at undesirable prices to raise cash to meet redemption requests.	Manager may be forced to sell securities at undesirable prices to raise cash to meet redemption requests.
Reporting	Detailed monthly or quarterly statements; monthly letters; quarterly newsletters; periodic investment literature from manager.	General quarterly statements; semi-annual investment reports; possibly periodic newsletters.	General quarterly statements; semi-annual investment reports; possibly periodic newsletters.
Up-Front Costs	$0	Up to 6% of investment or an additional 1% per year added to the annual cost.	$0
Annual Costs	On average for a stock-based portfolio, between 2.5% and 3% of total investment.	On average for a stock-based portfolio, between 2% and 3% of total investment.	On average for a stock-based portfolio, between 1.5% and 2% of total investment.

So, What Do IMAs Really Cost?

Investors who open IMAs usually do so with a minimum investment of at least $100,000. At that time, the money in the account, less the initial quarter's fees which typically equal 0.75% or less of the opening balance, is invested by the portfolio manager.

Subsequent transaction costs are paid either by paying commissions on individual trades or by paying an asset-based fee on a quarterly basis. In addition to covering transactions, these fees encompass reporting, custody and the services of a financial advisor as well. For a stock-based portfolio, on average, total fees range annually from 1.3% to 3% of the assets under management. There are no additional charges.

Mutual funds have lower minimum investment requirements, often $1,000 or less. With a no-load mutual fund bought directly from the company, the entire investment is placed in the fund at the time of initial purchase. With a front-end load fund, on the other hand, the investor's money is placed in the fund only after deducting a sales charge. In the case of a 3.5% load fund, the fund would invest $965 of the investor's initial $1,000.

Beyond the initial sales charge or lack thereof, the difference in fee structure between load and no-load mutual funds virtually disappears. Management fees, transaction costs, custody fees, and distribution and marketing costs (known as 12b-1 fees) are deducted automatically from the fund's assets. These fees are usually not seen directly by investors but instead are specified in the fund's prospectus and statements of additional information. Mutual fund expenses for stock-based portfolios typically range from 1.5% to 2% per year for no-load funds and from 2% to 3% per year for load funds (with fees decreasing when you meet break points).

According to Morningstar, a third-party research publication that follows open-end mutual funds, the average diversified domestic equities fund incurs about 1.63% in annual costs, including a 1.32% expense ratio and 0.31% in transaction costs. Tack on an additional 0.94% annual sales charge on average for load funds or an estimated 1% annual charge for no-load funds purchased through a financial advisor, and that annual cost figure rises to approximately 2.6%.

Investors should note that transaction costs tend to vary depending on the type of securities in the fund. Trading foreign securities, for instance, can cost almost twice as much as trading domestic securities.

The Final Analysis

In the final analysis, only the individual investor can decide which investment program is the most appropriate for him or her. Those who work with a financial advisor will find only modest cost differences between no-load mutual funds, load mutual funds and managed accounts, with managed accounts providing the highest degree of service in relation to cost.

While one can save money by purchasing no-load funds directly from the company, such savings may not be enough to offset the loss of the value-added services which normally include investment planning, monitoring, communication and so on that only a financial advisor can provide.

Beyond cost differences, both load and no-load mutual funds require a lower initial investment than IMAs. However, mutual funds limit investors' tax planning choices and offer individual investors no control over securities in the fund. Additionally, fund performance can be affected by the redemption requests of other investors.

Individually managed accounts require a higher initial investment but, in return, provide more service, customization and flexibility. Furthermore, managed account investors are not affected by the actions of others who use the same manager.

Ultimately, both IMAs and mutual funds have their proper place among today's investment alternatives. What that place is in your investment plan is a decision best made only by you and your financial advisor.

PART EIGHT

INSURANCE PLANNING

56

AVOID THE BIGGEST PITFALL
Help Yourself And Your Family,
And Save Money in the Process

The insurance industry is a multi-trillion dollar industry. Next to taxes, insurance will be your biggest expense over your lifetime. You probably have auto insurance and health insurance. You more than likely have some form of homeowner's insurance and life insurance. Your bank accounts are insured by the FDIC.

We, the authors, have life and health insurance licenses in almost every state in the country. We have reviewed or sold insurance policies from dozens of insurance companies. Chris has worked in the actuarial departments of a number of property and casualty insurance companies who have very significant market shares in the auto, homeowners, business liability, workers compensation or malpractice sectors. While there, he determined insurance rates and rating mechanisms before he was hired by one of the world's largest auto manufacturer's to help them create two captive insurance companies.

We would like to turn our relatively unique experiences and insights into helpful advice for you. Insurance planning can help protect your family, provide necessary benefits, and reduce your tax burden. We will show you how to achieve these goals and show you some "tricks of the trade" that may help you reduce costs and avoid unnecessary fees or commissions.

In particular, we will cover, among other strategies:

- Ways to reduce your taxes with health insurance.

- What to look for in a disability policy.

- How to reduce your after-tax insurance costs.

- Why you need long-term care and what to look for in a LTCi policy.

- Secrets about malpractice insurance.

- When to consider and how to create your own captive insurance company.

57

⸺⬧⸺

LIFE INSURANCE

In Many Ways, The Backbone Of
Wealth Protection Planning

Would you be surprised to know that, in our opinion, Life Insurance is the most important tool in your Wealth Protection Plan? You shouldn't. No other financial, tax, insurance, or legal tool can play as many roles in a Wealth Protection Plan as life insurance.

Obviously, life insurance can provide death protection for a family. This is the role traditionally assigned to life insurance. Even beyond this, life insurance has a number of key characteristics you will see us refer to repeatedly throughout this book. Because of these characteristics (which you will see below), life insurance can play a number of other very important roles in your Wealth Protection Plan.

Because of these qualities, life insurance can be a tax-free wealth accumulator and retirement vehicle (see Chapters 45 and 54). It can also be an asset protected investment tool (see Chapter 14). It can provide liquidity to pay estate taxes (Chapter 66). And it can even be part of a solution to lower the 70%+ tax trap of pensions and IRAs (Chapter 69). Here, we will introduce the basic concepts surrounding the tool of life insurance. See the chapters enumerated above to learn about other important roles life insurance can play in your planning.

What Is Life Insurance?

Life insurance is a contract between you and an insurance company where the insurance company pays your named beneficiaries the "face amount" of the policy when you die. Some life insurance policies accumulate cash over time (permanent policies) and some do not (term policies).

Key Characteristics Making Life Insurance So Valuable

The following attributes apply to permanent (cash value) life insurance:

1. Amounts in life insurance policies grow tax-deferred

While investments outside of retirement plans and life insurance policies are taxed on income and realized capital gains, funds growing within a cash value life insurance policy grow completely tax-free. This is why life insurance is so attractive as a wealth accumulation and tax reduction vehicle. It can serve as another 'retirement plan' (for further explanation, see Chapter 54).

2. Account balances in life insurance policies can be accessed tax-free

When you take funds out of a retirement plan (pension or IRA), these withdrawals are always subject to income tax and may be subject to a penalty if withdrawn before age 59½. With a cash value life insurance policy, you can take tax-free loans against the cash value at any time. There is never a tax penalty and there is no tax on the loan so long as you keep the policy in force and the policy is not a modified endowment contract (MEC).

3. Life insurance is asset-protected

Most states give some measure of asset protection to cash value life insurance policies. Thus, this asset can play a role in your asset protection plan. Speak to a Wealth Protection Specialist (Part X of book) in your area to find out the level of protection life insurance receives in your state.

4. Life insurance has beneficial tax treatment

In dealing with the 70%+ tax trap facing pensions and IRAs, life insurance can play a very valuable role. The essence of this role is that life insurance enables the plan owner who would otherwise lose 70% of his plan holdings to estate and income taxes to instead leverage the dollars in the plan upward into a death benefit that will provide the plan owner's heirs far more inheritance from the plan net of tax. See Chapter 69 for more on this important benefit.

5. Life insurance pays heirs income tax-free

In most situations, we can structure the life policy to pay to beneficiaries 100% income tax-free.

Types of Life Insurance

Term Life Insurance

Given its affordability, term life insurance is the most common type of life insurance policy. However, because of it have a wealth accumulation component, term insurance can only play one role in your Wealth Protection Plan: death protection for a limited time for your family.

The premium on a term policy is low compared to other types of life insurance policies due to the fact that the term policy has no cash value. A term life insurance policy pays a specific lump sum to your designated beneficiary upon your death. The policy protects your family by providing money they can invest to replace your salary and to cover immediate expenses incurred as a result of your death. Term life insurance is best for young, growing families when the need for death protection of the breadwinner is high and excess cash flow is especially low.

Pros: Affordable coverage that pays only a death benefit, term life insurance initially tends to cost less than other insurance policies mainly due to the fact that, unlike other policies, it has no cash value.

Cons: Term life insurance premiums increase with age because the risk of death increases as people get older. Some term premiums may rise each year, or after 10, 20 or 30 years. Over the age of 65, the cost of a new term insurance policy becomes very expensive — often unaffordable.

Whole Life Insurance

Whole life insurance pays a death benefit to the beneficiary you name and offers you a cash value account with tax-deferred cash accumulation. The policy remains in force during your entire lifetime and provides permanent protection for your dependents while building a cash value account. The insurance company manages your policy's cash accounts.

Pros: Whole life insurance has a savings element (cash value) which is tax-deferred. You can borrow from this account free of income tax or cash in the policy during your lifetime. It has a fixed premium which can't increase during your lifetime (as long as you pay the planned amount) and your premium is invested for you long-term. Because it has the cash accumulation component, whole life insurance can offer tax reduction, wealth accumulation, asset protection, estate planning, and even reduction of the retirement plan tax trap.

Cons: Whole life insurance does not allow you to invest in separate accounts (i.e. money market, stock, and bond funds). It also does not allow you to split your money among different accounts or to move your money between accounts and does not allow premium flexibility or face amount flexibility.

Universal Life Insurance

Universal life insurance is a variation of whole life. The insurance part of the policy is separated from the investment portion of the policy. The investment portion is invested by the insurance company in bonds, mortgages and money market funds. This investment portion grows and is tax-deferred. The cost of the death benefit is paid for out of the investment fund. A guaranteed minimum interest rate applied to the policy that a certain minimum return on the cash portion of the policy will be paid no matter how badly the investments perform. If the insurance company does well with its investments, the interest return on the cash portion will increase.

Pros: The product is similar to whole life insurance, yet has more flexible premiums. It may be attractive to younger buyers who may have fluctuations in their ability to pay premiums. Because it is so flexible, universal life insurance can offer tax reduction, wealth accumulation, asset protection, estate planning, and even reduction of the retirement plan tax trap.

Cons: If the insurance company does poorly with its investments, the crediting rate on the cash portion of the policy will decrease. In this case, less money would be available to pay the cost of the death benefit portion of the policy and future premiums may be necessary in addition to the premiums originally illustrated.

Variable Life Insurance

Variable life insurance provides permanent protection to your beneficiary upon your death. The term "variable life" derives from the fact that you can allocate your dollars to various types of investment accounts (within your insurance company's portfolio), such as an equity fund, a money market fund, a bond fund, or some combination thereof. Hence, the value of the death benefit and the cash value may fluctuate up or down, depending on the performance of the investment portion of the policy.

Although most variable life insurance policies guarantee that the death benefit will not fall below a specified minimum, a minimum cash value is typically not guaranteed. Because of investment risks, it is also considered a securities contract and is regulated as a security under the Federal Securities Laws. It must be sold with a prospectus.

Pros: Variable life allows you to participate in various types of investment options without being taxed on your earnings (until you surrender the policy). You can apply interest earned on these investments toward the premiums, potentially lowering the amount you pay. Because of the ability to invest in more aggressive assets (mutual funds, etc.), variable life insurance is an ideal tool for accumulation and retirement planning, especially if you are looking for growth over a long time-horizon.

Cons: You assume the investment risks. When the investment funds perform poorly, less money is available to pay the premiums, meaning that you may have to pay more than you can afford to keep the policy in force. Poor fund performance also means that the cash and/or death benefit may decline, although never below a defined level if the policy so provides.

Variable Universal Life Insurancce

Variable universal life insurance pays your beneficiary a death benefit. The amount of the benefit is dependent on the success of your investments. If the investments fail, the policy may lapse and there may be no death benefit paid to your beneficiary upon your death. Variable universal gives you more control of the cash value account portion of your policy than any other insurance type. It has elements of both life insurance and a securities contract. Because the policy owner assumes the investment risk, variable universal products are regulated as securities under the Federal Securities Laws and must be sold with a prospectus.

Pros: Variable-universal life enables you to make withdrawals or borrow from the policy during your lifetime. It offers separate accounts in which to invest. Because it combines the flexibility of universal life with the ability to invest in mutual funds of the variable policy, universal variable can be the ideal tool for tax reduction and retirement wealth accumulation over a long time horizon. It also affords one another opportunity to invest in the equities markets on a tax-deferred basis.

Cons: It requires the policyholder to devote time in managing the policy's accounts. The policy's success is dependent on the investments you make. Premiums must be high enough to cover your insurance and your accounts.

A Hybrid: Equity-Indexed Universal Life Insurance

Equity-indexed universal life insurance (EIUL) pays your beneficiary a death benefit. The amount of the benefit is dependent on the success of the investments of the insurance company. If the investments fail, there is a guaranteed minimum death benefit paid to your beneficiary upon your death. EIUL gives you more upside than a traditional UL policy because the insurance company contractually agrees to credit the policy's cash value with the same return the S&P 500 Index realizes over the same period of time (subject to a cap). Because of the cap on the upside (two carriers we researched cap the investment returns at 17% per annum or at 30% per 24 month period), they offer a minimum annual return of 1% or 2% annually (which makes EIUL much less risky than variable insurance).

Pros: EIUL enables you to make withdrawals or borrow from the policy during your lifetime and it offers the investor the upside of the market (with a cap). It also, unlike variable life and variable universal life, offers the investor downside protection so the cash value will always see a positive crediting rate — even in a bad market. For a special report describing why EIUL may be a better investment than mutual funds for high wage earners, call your local WPA advisor (800) 554-7233.

Cons: EIUL policies vary from carrier to carrier. Some only allow for 50% or 75% participation of the rate of return from the S&P. This means that if the S&P 500 returns 10%, you may only get 5% or 7.5%. The policyholder must pay particular attention to the carrier's contractual obligations. Also, the minimum guaranteed returns are typically 1% to 2% which is much lower than most traditional insurance products that offer minimum crediting rates of 3% to 4%. EIUL is another case where you have to give up something to get something. Like all insurance policies, you need to understand what you are getting before you can make a smart decision.

Conclusion

This chapter is simply a thumbnail sketch about one of the most important tools in your overall Wealth Protection Plan. Be sure to read the other chapters referred to here to gain a more thorough knowledge of how Life Insurance can be the backbone of your Wealth Protection Plan.

58

PAY UP, SELF INSURE, QUIT MEDICINE, OR GO BARE

What Are The Opportunities During A Medical Malpractice Crisis?

You don't need us to tell you how terrible the malpractice crisis is. You already know that lawsuits are on the rise, jury awards are out of control, malpractice premiums are escalating to the point of being unaffordable and the practice of medicine as we know it is severely threatened.

What you do need are alternatives and solutions. To best judge the alternatives, you need to understand the pros and cons, as well as the costs and benefits, of each alternative. As authors of three books for physicians and contributing authors to over 200 medical journals, we get a lot of feedback from physicians who, like you, are fed up with what is going on today. The purpose of this chapter is to help you better understand what you can do so you can make an intelligent decision, take action, stop worrying and get back to the practice of medicine. So, what are your options?

Pay Up

The easiest alternative is to just pay the premiums offered by your malpractice carrier. We recently attended a conference in San Diego that was devoted solely to the "hard to place" medical malpractice market. As a result of the contacts we have made, we have helped quite a few doctors find malpractice coverage after they were cancelled or non-renewed. One of the organizations we met actually has the capability to help doctors in 30 states and they specialize in the high-risk marketplace. The key point is that, even if you think you aren't insurable, there might be a carrier out there willing to write a policy for you — thus preserving your privileges at the hospital and your relationships with your insurance payers. If you call us at (888) 317-9895, we can get you a medical malpractice insurance quote comparison and maybe you'll save a few thousand dollars or more!

Self Insure

Many large groups are considering self insurance. You can join an existing Risk Retention Group (RRG) or set up your own Captive Insurance Company (CIC). We have assisted hundreds of medical groups analyze the benefits of CICs over the years. Though most medical groups find alternative means of protecting themselves from medical malpractice, a growing number of medical practices are utilizing the risk management, asset protection, and tax-favored benefits of self insuring with CICs. Typically, medical groups use CICs to self insure for risks other than traditional medical malpractice. These risks might include: legal defense for malpractice, HIPAA violations, Medicare fraud, insurance fraud, loss of medical license, and other similar risks. Recent changes in the law on captives make it important for a physician to find someone with a great deal of experience in captive insurance and with the healthcare industry. We offer a more detailed description of CICs in Chapters 27 and 39.

Quit Medicine

Ahhhhh! A sigh of relief. Now, pinch yourself as the dream isn't over just yet. When the time is right, go see a Wealth Protection Advisor who can help you comfortably plan your well-deserved retirement. You might be surprised how close you actually are. Part VI of the book, Retirement, might help you better evaluate if you are there yet. If so, Hooray!!!

Go Bare

Though many doctors are considering this (especially in Florida and other high risk states), there are many pitfalls to going bare. The main benefit of going bare is that you will be a less attractive lawsuit target if you don't have insurance. This is true IF AND ONLY IF you have implemented a comprehensive asset protection plan prior to any action that could potentially result in a lawsuit. Placing assets in a spouse's name or into a living trust does NOT provide asset protection. Though some states offer tenancy by the entirety, some offer homestead protection, and some offer protection of insurance or annuities, it is imperative that you have an attorney research the recent case law in your state as the statutes often do NOT match the actual results in the courtroom. Furthermore, your brokerage accounts and rental real estate are NOT protected in any state! Lastly, your practice assets (like equipment, real estate and accounts receivable) may be at risk to lawsuits from the actions of you or any of your partners. Are you the worst doctor in your group? If not, then there is someone out there whose potential liability may cost you dearly.

A full scale discussion of asset protection is discussed in Part III of the book. We would seriously recommend that you read and implement all the possible asset protection techniques before going bare. If you aren't protected and you go bare, one small suit could wipe out all that you have worked so hard to accomplish.

59

DISABILITY INSURANCE

Inadequate Coverage Can Be More Costly
Than Death, Divorce, Or A Lawsuit

Wealth Protection Planning includes planning for the best possible future while protecting against the worst possible events. No doctor ever plans on becoming disabled although **half** of us will experience a long-term disability at least once in our lives. In fact, these odds proved true with the two lead authors as Chris missed months of work about 10 years ago when he injured his back playing basketball. It happened to one of us. It happens to half of the population. The odds are it will happen to you or your spouse. Though disability insurance may seem like a boring topic compared to some of the more "exotic" material in the book, this chapter may be the most important of them all because it deals with protecting your earning potential — typically your family's single greatest asset. This chapter explains not only why you need disability insurance, but it also explains what to look for in a disability policy.

If you are like most of our clients, the single greatest asset your family has is your earning power. Unless you are near retirement, if you were to stop working, your family would endure a significant financial strain. This reality motivates most people to buy life insurance as protection against a premature death. For most people, purchasing life insurance is "common sense."

While most people (with whom we speak) are underinsured, they do have at least some protection against a premature death. However, most professionals, entrepreneurs, business owners, and executives often overlook a more dangerous threat to their long-term financial stability — disability. What is the risk that the average individual will suffer a disability? According to one recent study,

> **"The probability of at least one long-term disability (90 days or longer) occurring before age 65 is: 50% for someone age 25; 45% for someone age 35; 38% for someone age 45; and 26% for someone age 55."**

In our opinion, disability can be more financially devastating to a family than premature death. In both cases, the breadwinner will be unable to provide any income for the family. In the case of death, the deceased earner is no longer an expense to one's family. However, if you are disabled, you still need to be fed, clothed, and cared for by medical professionals or family members. In many cases, the medical care alone can cost hundred of dollars per day. Thus, with a disability, income is reduced (or eliminated) *and* expenses increase. This can be a devastating turn of events — one which often leads to creditor problems and even bankruptcy if not planned for in advance.

If you are older (near retirement) and have saved a large enough sum of money to fund a comfortable retirement immediately, then you probably don't need disability income protection. Of course, you may have some long term care concerns but that is covered in Chapter 60. On the other hand, if you are under 50 years old, or if you are older than 50 and have several pre-college age children, you should consider proper disability insurance a necessity. The key question thus becomes: how do you determine what type of disability income policy is "right" for you?

Give Yourself a Check-Up

Here are some suggestions on what to look for when determining the adequacy of your present disability policies:

Employer Provided Coverage

If you are an employee of a corporation, your employer may provide long-term disability (LTD) coverage which must usually be paid for by the employer. The premiums are probably discounted from what you would pay for a private policy. We advise you take a good look at what the employer-offered policy covers and buy a private policy if you decide you need it. For many people, this makes a lot of sense because employer-provided group policies often limit either the term of the coverage or the amount of benefits paid. For instance, benefits may last only a few years, or benefit payments may represent only a small part of your annual compensation. Because this is most commonly an employer-paid benefit, the money received during your disability is taxable. For most, this would mean taking home less than half of your paycheck!

In your disability "check up," be sure to ask the following:

- How long does the disability coverage last?
- How much is the benefit? (Different plans may cap the benefits at $5,000 per month)
- What percentage of your income is covered? Generally, you cannot receive more than 60% of income and the benefit is capped at $7,500 or $10,000, depending on your age. Though most group LTD plans are good for the

purpose that they serve, they are only a partial cure. Because of the limitations or 'cap' in the plan, it has built–in discrimination against higher income employees like you!

- Who pays the premiums? If you pay the premiums yourself, and not as a deductible expense through your business or practice, your benefits will be tax-free. You may be seduced by the income tax deduction of the premiums, but the extra tax burden today is much easier to swallow than the tax burden will be if you suffer a disability and have a significantly-reduced income *and* increased expenses. When you and your family need the money most, you will have more available money if you bite the bullet and pay the tax now.

- Is the policy portable or convertible to an individual policy if you leave the group? If so, do you maintain your reduced group rate?

- If your practice distributes all earnings from the corporation at year-end in the way of bonuses to all owners/partners (typical of C-corps as a way to avoid double taxation), you should see whether these amounts are covered by the group policy? If not, and if bonuses or commissions make up a substantial part of your income, which we have seen to be the case with many people, you'll probably need supplemental coverage.

- What is the definition of disability in the group policy? Own-occupation, any occupation, or income-replacement? (Please see the discussion of these three terms below.)

- Are your overhead expenses covered if you are disabled? If you can't perform procedures, the insurance companies will not keep paying you. However, your expenses are still incurred, aren't they? For professionals, a business overhead expense policy also covers hiring an outside professional to replace the insured during disability for up to 2 years.

How Do I Get the Best Coverage for My Money?

Now that you have given yourself a check-up and realize that you need a new or supplemental policy, you need to know what to look for to give you the best coverage available at a reasonable rate. The following questions are important for you to ask when considering a disability policy. They are:

What is the Benefit Amount?

Most policies are capped at 60% of income. Some states and insurance companies have monthly maximums as well. You have to ask yourself how much money your family would need if you were to become disabled. Generally, you want to find companies that offer 60%

benefits with a maximum of $7,500 or $10,000 monthly. There are companies that can offer supplemental, or excess, DI insurance to much higher amounts.

What Is the Waiting Period?

The waiting period is the period of time that you must be disabled before the insurance company will pay you disability benefits. The longer the waiting period before benefits kick in, the less your premium will be. Essentially, the waiting period serves as a deductible defined by time rather than a pecuniary amount. You cover your expenses for the waiting period, then the insurance company steps in from that point forward. This is not unlike the deductible you have on your car, except that auto insurance deductibles are in the form of amounts paid ($100, $250, $500, etc.) and not relative to a period of time. If you have adequate sick leave, short-term disability, an emergency fund, and can support a longer waiting period, choose a policy with a longer waiting period. Although waiting periods can last as long as 730 days, a 90-day waiting period may give you the best coverage for your money.

How Long Will Coverage Last?

It's a good idea to get a benefit period that lasts until age 65, at which point Social Security payments will begin. Beware of policies that cover you for only two to five years as this is an inadequate period of time. Unless you are so young that you haven't yet had time to qualify for Social Security, a policy that provides lifetime benefits, at costly premiums, is generally not worth it. Often a long term care insurance policy (LTCi) is the most efficient way to protect yourself from health-related costs that may occur later in life.

What is the Definition of Disability in Your Policy?

The definition of disability in a policy used to be of utmost importance. The main categories are Own-occupation, Any-occupation, and Loss of Income. The Own-occupation policies are the most comprehensive, and of course, the most expensive. Two key elements to look for in an Own-occupation policy are:

1. Are you forced to go back to work in another occupation; and

2. Will you receive a partial benefit if you return to work slowly subsequent to full disability and still make less than you did before the disability?

These two benefits are of the utmost importance.

Does the Policy Offer Partial Benefits?

If you are able to work only part-time instead of your previous full-time hours, will you receive benefits? Unless your policy states that you are entitled to partial benefits, you won't receive anything unless you are totally unable to work. Also, are Extended Partial Benefits paid if you go back to work and suffer a reduction in income because you cannot keep up the same rigorous schedule you had before you were disabled? This is an important benefit for anesthesiologists, as you often work ridiculous hours in your younger years and most likely will work less after any disability.

> **NOTE:** Partial benefits may be added on as a rider in some policies and should be seriously considered as only 3% of all disabilities are total disabilities. Some policies even have a recovery benefit that provides benefits in the event that a business has lost clients and concomitant income during the disability period due to the insured's inability to service the clientele. The insured need not be disabled at all — there need only be a loss of income due to disability-related attrition.

Is Business Overhead Expense (BOE) Covered?

When you go out on your own, the last thing you think about is how you "won't" be able to pay your bills. Whether you have $10,000 or $20,000 of monthly disability benefit, you likely don't have enough to cover your lost income AND the costs of running the practice. Although most companies have limited how much an individual doctor can receive in monthly benefit (often 60% of after tax monthly income capped at $10,000 per month), many carriers still offer up to $25,000 or more per month to cover business overhead expense. Most physicians who contact us have failed to purchase this very important coverage.

Is it Non-Cancellable or Guaranteed Renewable?

The difference between these two terms is very important. If a policy is "non-cancellable," you will pay a fixed premium throughout the contract term. Your premium will not go up for the term of the contract. If it is "guaranteed renewable," it means you cannot be cancelled, but your premiums could go up. As long as non-cancellable is in the description of the policy, you are in good shape.

How Financially Stable Is the Insurance Company?

Before buying a policy, check the financial soundness of your insurer. If your insurer goes bankrupt, you may have to shop for a policy later in life when premiums are more expensive. Standard & Poor's top rating for financial stability is AAA. A.M. Best Co. uses A++ as its top rating for financial strength. Duff and Phelps rates companies on their ability to pay claims and uses AAA as its highest rating. Moody's uses Aa1 to rate excellent companies. There are no guarantees in life, but buying a policy from a highly rated company is the safest bet you can make and we would not recommend gambling on your disability insurance to save a few dollars.

Other issues include:

- Increased Coverage;

- Cost-of-Living Increases;

- Waiver-of-Premium;

- Return-of-Premium Waiver;

- Unisex Pricing;

- HIV Riders;

- Multi-Life Pricing Discounts; and

- Protection of Future Pension Contributions.

Conclusion

The likelihood of a disability is greater than the probabilities of premature death, a lawsuit, and bankruptcy combined. Disability insurance is the only way to protect your future income. We cannot stress enough the importance of having a comprehensive disability policy as part of any Wealth Protection Plan. When combined with other asset protection, tax, and estate planning, the proper disability coverage will help you sleep much more soundly.

Table 1. Disability Income Policy Options

Policy Option	Description of Option	For the Typical Individual
Benefit Period	Period of time the insurance company is obligated to pay the monthly disability benefits. Common periods are: five years, to age 65, and lifetime.	Lifetime is generally too expensive. To age 65 is ideal. Five years is too short.
Waiting Period	Period of time from the commencement of the disability to payment of monthly benefits. Common waiting periods run from 30 days to one year.	90 days
Extended Partial Benefit	Pays a partial benefit when the insured is not totally disabled. Partial benefits are a percentage based on the amount of income loss.	Highly recommended, but make sure you are not required to take a job in another occupation if you are qualified.
Portability / Transferability	If you leave your group, can you continue your existing policy with the reduced rate?	You want a group or multi-life policy that offers this benefit.
HIV waiver	Pays a monthly benefit (up to 2 years) to a healthcare professional who has tested positive for HIV, even if he/she is still working.	Worth considering. For high risk physicians, recommended.
Multi-Life Discounts	Different discounts can apply if you can get multiple people to apply at the same time for disability.	Cheaper is always better. See if anyone else in your group is interested.
Disability Trust (Pension) Option	Pays up to $3,333 and up to $3,000 over regular I&P limits to a trust, representing your lost pension contributions if you are disabled. If an employee with an employer match is disabled, this amount is considered for coverage also.	Not recommended for older physicians with large retirement plans. Good idea for younger doctors who can afford it.
Cost of living	Total disability and residual benefits each year are increased by a specific percentage or by the CPI; does not increase benefits prior to the commencement of a disability claim.	May not be cheap, but could be very valuable if you are disabled for a long period of time-inflation protection.
Future Insurability Options	The right to purchase additional amounts of monthly benefits at regular intervals without the insurance company inquiring about the individual's health.	Very useful for young doctors who expect future increases in income.

60

⟡

LONG TERM CARE INSURANCE
Protect Yourselves, Your Children,
And Your Parents

You are probably reading this chapter because either you or your parents are at least 50 years old. You may be reading this chapter because you don't find it acceptable for your in-laws or parents to move in with you for the rest of their lives, which could be a very short time if they got on your nerves "one more time!" Perhaps you are reading this chapter because you aren't sure if your children will be able (not to mention willing) to take care of you when you need it in your later years. If your children or family would like to take care of you, they would likely need to entirely change their lifestyle, possibly move, and probably have to quit their jobs.

As you now know, the key to Wealth Protection Planning is to integrate different components of your plan. For example, we don't want to save money, only to have it all go to taxes when we die or to an undeserving creditor as a result of a lawsuit. Similarly, we don't want to save for retirement or accumulate a nice inheritance for our children and grandchildren only to have rising medical bills wipe it out. This chapter covers one of the most underutilized, and very important, tools in a Wealth Protection Plan – long term care insurance.

What is Long Term Care Insurance?

Long Term Care Insurance (LTCi) covers health insurance costs for those people who cannot take care of themselves. These costs may include nursing home care, in-home care, and many other expenses.

Why Do I Need Long Term Care?

More than half of all Americans will need some form of long-term care during their lifetime. This means that next to life insurance, this is probably the single most likely insurance your family will need. Before you run off to buy insurance, you probably want to know how expensive Long Term Care insurance is.

277

We already know that half of us will need long-term care coverage at some point in time. This means that the odds are that one of your parents, one of your in-laws, and either you or your spouse will have a need for long-term care. In the U.S., the average stay in a nursing home is between two and three years. In some areas of the country, the cost of nursing home care or quality around-the-clock in-home care may be $200–$300 per day. This means that the average stay today costs between $150,000 and $320,000. Additionally, the U.S. Health Care Administration reports that costs are increasing 5.8% per year and are expected to more than triple in the next 20 years. At these projections, the costs may be $500,000–$1,000,000 by the time you or your spouse need long-term care. Are you sure that you, your parents and your in-laws all have hundreds of thousands of "extra" funds in your retirement and estate plans to cover this highly possible expense?

As you are probably very well aware, the advancements in medicine have helped to increase the average life expectancy. With this increased life expectancy, there is a greater chance that each person may suffer a debilitating illness that may require significant long-term care needs. With the trends of increasing life expectancies and increasing costs of medical expenses, the cost of long-term care can easily wipe out retirement savings and eliminate any inheritance you would have otherwise left your children or grandchildren.

Won't the Government Cover These Long Term Care Costs?

No. Not the way you would like them to. Did you know that in California an individual does not qualify for LTCi coverage until his/her net worth is LESS THAN $3,000. In addition, once that individual begins receiving LTCi benefits, the state takes all but $30/week of income from the patient. In a nutshell, you will have to spend every last dollar of your savings before you get any help. Though you may have more than enough saved to pay for these types of expenses, your potential health problem could wipe out your entire inheritance, which you hoped would go to your children or grandchildren. Incidentally, we see many of our physician clients buying LTCi on their parents because they know they will have to take care of their parents if the need arises. It can be a major financial and emotional problem to be getting ready to retire and have one of your parents or in-laws get sick and need $75,000–$150,000 per year of medical expenses. Unfortunately, this will most likely be paid with after tax dollars.

Why Don't Most People Have LTCi?

Most people do not want to bear the risk of self-insuring their long-term care costs. So why haven't more people purchased LTCi? In a word — Education(or the lack thereof). We see clients insure their lives, homes, cars and income but not events (like long term care and disability) that have the next highest probability of occurring in one's lifetime (behind only death). Why? Part of it is the "it's not going to happen to me" mentality and part of it is the thought of having to pay LTCi premiums for the next 20–40 years with only a chance that you will ever use the insurance.

What Should I Look for in a LTCi Policy?

Traditional LTCi policies feature benefits, options and riders that vary in availability and scope among carriers. They do not have cash value nor do they have a death benefit. Once eligible for benefits (inability to perform 2 of 6 Activities of Daily Living), this type of policy pays a daily reimbursement for approved expenses up to the maximum daily benefit chosen by the insured. Upper and lower limits vary among carriers but are in the $20–$300 per day range. Benefits can be received for life or for a period of time determined by a total insurance dollar value of the policy, often referred to as the pool of benefits. "Facility only" or "facility and in home care policies" are available. Elimination periods (deductibles) apply and can range from 0 days to 90 days. Other features, options and riders that vary among carriers are inflation protection, bed reservations, alternative plan of care, restoration of benefits, personal care advisor, respite care, joint policy discounts, premium waiver, rate classes, non-forfeiture benefits, indemnity benefits, caregiver indemnity benefits and 10 year paid-up, 20 year paid-up and non level payment options.

A major resistance to purchasing traditional LTCi is the possibility of paying premiums forever and never needing to use the policy. If this is the case, one should seek a carrier that offers paid up policies and/or non-forfeiture riders. Paid up policies will require yearly premiums for a specified number of years, usually 10 years or 20 years. After this time, premium payments stop and the insured owns the policy for life. Nonforfeiture riders allow the policy owner to name a beneficiary and, upon death, all premiums that have been paid are then paid to the named beneficiary even if benefits have been received. However, the policy must be in force at the time of death for the beneficiary to receive the paid premiums.

A different method of addressing long term care needs is to purchase a Universal Life Insurance policy with an attached rider that can accelerate all or a portion of the death benefit to be used for approved long term care costs should the need arise. Benefits are received in much the same way as a traditional long-term care policy. This requires a single premium payment and purchase of a paid up policy. In most cases, an existing cash value policy can be exchanged with no tax consequence (consult your tax professional regarding your particular situation). The larger the single premium paid, the larger the death benefit that can be converted to daily benefit maximums for approved long term care costs divided over a 2-year, 4-year or lifetime period at a decreasing daily maximum amount. The policy can be purchased to provide benefits for an individual or couple.

The most important feature of a good LTCi policy is a financially sound insurance carrier. Do not consider purchasing the cheapest LTCi policy that you can find. LTCi carriers must have the financial strength to sustain their ability to pay claims well into the future when the millions of baby boomers will begin needing LTCi benefits. In a nutshell, don't be pennywise and pound-foolish.

Would you consider paying for your LTCi if you could do so in a tax-deductible manner and do so in a finite period like five or ten years? Would you consider paying for LTCI if you knew that your heirs would receive every dollar of that premium at a later date? These possibilities are covered in Chapter 35 in the Tax Section. Your local Wealth Protection Alliance member can explain your LTCi options and help you integrate the purchase into your practice for maximum tax efficiency.

PART NINE

ESTATE PLANNING

61

MAKING SURE FAMILY
ASSETS AREN'T LOST TO
DISINHERITANCE, COURTS
OR THE IRS

As you now realize, something you answered in the RFA sent you to the estate planning area. Perhaps it was that you have neglected to implement wills, living trusts, or other basic estate planning documents. Perhaps it was that you hold property in joint ownership or that your life insurance policies are owned in your own name. Perhaps it was that your pension or IRA may suffer an 70% tax hit when you die. Regardless of the specific reason, you are here now and have the opportunity to understand how the estate planning portion of your Wealth Protection Plan can be designed to better meet your family's needs.

It is very likely that most of you reading these words haven't done much estate planning. This is so even though estate planning deals with life's two certainties: death and taxes. As an example, a major national magazine recently ran an article explaining that 95% of their readers did not have the basic estate planning tools in place. This same percentage could be true of you, the readers of this book. How many millions in unnecessary taxes will have to be paid by families like yours until it is realized that estate planning is crucial to an overall Wealth Protection Plan?

> **If you are one who thinks that estate taxes are no longer relevant because of the 2001 "repeal," or because you believe George W. Bush will eliminate the estate tax during his second term, then you should read the next chapter of this section. It will open your eyes to all of the hidden taxes lurking in the so-called "repeal."**

In any case, it's not just taxes one must avoid in estate planning. It's also the avoidance of disinheriting family members by mistake. Each year, millions of us title our property in joint ownership without realizing that this form of ownership supersedes our wills, leaving the property to our joint owner rather than to those we named in our wills. This "disinheritance risk" might be lurking in your estate plan right now.

The costs and delays of probate are also an important threat to avoid in estate planning. Remember the story of Chris's family back in the Introduction? When Chris's stepfather died, his estate was stuck in the probate process for over a year while Chris's family desperately needed the inheritance to pay bills. This threat caused Chris's mother to eventually file for bankruptcy.

In this section, you will read about all of the leading tools you can use to reduce and even eliminate estate taxes, avoid disinheritance risk, avoid probate, and even deal with "problem assets" such as pensions, IRAs, and family businesses.

62

THE TRUTH ABOUT
THE ESTATE TAX REPEAL

Before we get to the individual chapters of this section where specific solutions to particular problems are explained, we must first explain one thing: estate planning is more important now than ever before. Why is it so crucial that we mention this at the outset? Because many of you may incorrectly assume that the estate tax has been repealed and, therefore, estate planning is no longer important.

It is true that in a limited sense Congress "repealed" the estate tax as part of the 2001 Tax Relief Act. If you die in the year 2010 — and only in 2010 — the estate tax is indeed repealed. Beyond this simple statement, however, there is much uncertainty. Moreover, there is a strong likelihood that estates will be taxed heavily in the foreseeable future. Let's see how that will happen.

There Is No Estate Tax "Repeal:"
Only a Gradual Reduction of the Estate Tax Bite

As mentioned above, the full tax repeal, if it even occurs at all, will not take place until 2010. Before that time, the law reduces the estate tax on the estates of those who die during the intervening "transitional" period. It does this in two ways. First, in a provision that benefits all estates, it steadily increases the individual exemption amount (set at $675,000 for 2001) to $1.0 million in 2002 and 2003, $1.5 million in 2004 and 2005, $2.0 million in 2006, 2007, and 2008, and $3.5 million in 2009, the final year before repeal. Married couples, with proper planning, are able to take advantage of two exemptions in their estates. Thus, in 2005, a couple with a $3 million estate will be able to avoid the estate tax if they effectively utilize their exemptions and don't hold assets jointly.

The other tax-saving feature during the transitional period is a reduction in the top estate and gift tax rates, both 55% as of 2001. This change will help only wealthier taxpayers because these top rates affect only estates of more than $2.5 million. Effective January 1,

2002, the top rates of 53% and 55% were eliminated and replaced with a rate of 50% on taxable estates in excess of $2.5 million. The top rate will be further reduced by 1% a year until 2007, when it will be 45%, and it remains at that level until the tax is repealed at the end of 2009. In these ways, the 2001 Act has some effect on trimming the estate tax immediately, although this is clearly not a complete "repeal."

Will There Be Any So-Called "Repeal" at All?

In the fairy tale of Cinderella, if she did not return to her home by the time the clock struck midnight, her fine clothes would turn to rags and her carriage into a pumpkin. Similarly, the estate tax repeal becomes fully effective January 1, 2010. However, unless the entire estate tax repeal is re-approved by Congress prior to 2011 then the clock strikes for the repeal as well and the law that was in effect prior to the 2001 law change will be automatically reinstated. While the likelihood of there being a Republican-controlled Congress or White House can be cause for speculation, no one truly knows whether or not the repeal will be re-approved five years from now. One certainly should not predicate a family's estate plan on it.

It is important to understand that in the absence of a re-approval of the repeal, the estate tax is not simply reinstated at the lower tax rates and larger exemptions amounts enjoyed in 2009. Rather, the exemption amount is returned to the level allowed by the law we had in 2001 (a relatively minor $1 million per person exemption) and the marginal tax rates are again raised (to a top rate of 55%). In this regard, if the repeal is not re-approved in the next 5 years, most of the estate tax reduction gained over the 10-year period will be lost.

Even more likely, according to many experts, is that the "repeal" will itself be repealed before we even get to 2009. When Congress passed this legislation, the budget office was projecting multi-trillion dollar surpluses in the federal government. This was back in the spring of 2001, before the economy continued to falter, before the destruction of September 11, 2001, and before the prolonged military battle with terrorism at home and abroad. At the time of this writing, all of these surpluses had been eroded and an enormous deficit had already been amassed. The federal government can no longer afford to give away predicted future surpluses. In fact, it may have to take back some of the funds it has already given away.

Experts predict that the estate tax arena will be the first one targeted in this way, as the 2001 repeal only helped the richest 1% of taxpayers...a small enough minority that politicians won't be overly concerned about a public relations nightmare. Certainly, a rescission of the estate tax repeal would be easier to pass than a further reduction of social security benefits (which most people over age 65 utilize). Put simply, the dead no longer vote.

Even if the Estate Tax Repeal Makes it Through, the Gift Tax Remains

To the surprise of many experts, the 2001 Act did not repeal the gift tax. Even after the potential estate tax repeal, the gift tax will continue to be imposed on gifts in excess of the lifetime gift exemption. This exemption increased to $1.0 million in 2002 with no further increases slated.

The gift tax rates will be reduced to the same amounts applied to estate taxes and on the same schedule until 2010, when the maximum rate will become 35%. Incidentally, 35% was the top marginal income tax rate when the 2001 law was passed. There was good reason for this linking of the top gift tax and income tax rates. Congress decided to retain the gift tax to discourage taxpayers from making tax-free gifts of income-producing property to family members in lower income tax brackets. Such transfers would be an easy way to reduce the overall income tax burden on the family. Although it will still be possible to make such transfers after the potential estate tax repeal, the continuation of the gift tax will act as a "toll charge" for taxpayers engaging in this type of planning.

State Estate Taxes Will Appear

Prior to 2001, an estate was entitled to a dollar-for-dollar federal estate tax credit (subject to a cap) for any state death taxes paid by the estate. Under this scheme, individual states shared heavily in the tax revenue of the IRS. For the largest estates, the 55% tax was split — 39% to the IRS and 16% to the state. Thus, they had no need to impose their own estate tax other than a "sponge tax" equal to the federal credit. As of 2004, the 48% estate tax is split 44% to the IRS and 4% to the state.

This repeal has already had an effect in many states. States stand to lose billions of dollars annually by the repeal of the federal credit, and their tax revenues need to be replaced somehow. Already, a number of states have begun to levy a state estate tax — and many more will appear if Bush makes the repeal permanent. Expect 15% or more to be owed under state estate taxes — this number could be as large as 40%. So, in all states but Florida, the total estate and inheritance taxes have INCREASED and a complete federal repeal will not help you. We will explain later.

Any "Repeal" Means a Loss of Basis Step-up at Death

The *quid pro quo* for repeal of the estate tax was the loss of step-up in income tax basis at death. Currently, most property owned by a decedent for estate tax purposes receives a tax basis equal to its value at the date of death. Under the Act, property acquired from a decedent will generally retain the decedent's tax basis as of December 31, 2009. This is known as "carryover" basis. When the recipient of the property eventually sells it, he or she will be compelled to compute the gain using the decedent's cost basis. In most cases, the decedent's basis will be less than the date-of-death value, resulting in an increased capital gains tax.

The legislation contains two major exceptions to carryover basis. The first is for estates less than $1.3 million and the second is for property up to $3 million passing to surviving spouses. Nonetheless, for larger estates, the additional capital gains taxes will take a large bite out of any potential estate tax savings. Moreover, there will certainly be an increase in administrative difficulty and an increased cost in determining the cost basis of assets purchased 20, 30, 50 years ago or more by now-deceased relatives. Expect a 15% to 25% cost for capital gains taxes and administration.

The "Repeal" Leaves IRD Alone

In addition to the estate tax, income tax must be paid on certain assets left in a decedent's estate at death. This tax is levied on what is called "IRD" (income with respect to a decedent). Because combined federal and state income taxes — including those characterized as IRD taxes — can be as high as 45%, and estate taxes range from 45% to 60% during the transitional period, the combined tax rate can escalate to 75% or more on IRD. Which is the most common property subject to the high tax burden of IRD? Amounts left in pensions, profit-sharing plans and IRAs.

While there was much rhetoric in the 2000 campaign about reducing the "death tax" on a family's assets, the 2001 Act does nothing to eliminate taxes on IRD. Thus, it remains an area of extreme importance for Wealth Protection Planning. For that reason, we have dedicated an entire chapter to the problem of IRD and another chapter to strategies for avoiding this outrageous tax problem (see Chapters 68 and 69).

Conclusion

The supposed repeal has actually led to an increase in the total estate and inheritance taxes paid. A permanent repeal will still leave federal capital gains taxes and state inheritance taxes. We are currently participating in a war on terror that we can't afford. As a result, our deficit is escalating. State governments are in worse shape than the federal government. How can we possibly believe there will be lower tax rates? If we don't plan properly, we have only ourselves to blame.

63

⊰───◆───⊱

WILLS & LIVING TRUSTS
The Building Blocks of Every Estate Plan

You Can Either Have Your Own Will
or Use the Government's Will

Are you surprised to know that you already have a Will? Even if you have never written one or had an attorney draft one? It is true. That's because if you die without any Will, then you get the universal Will that your state government has written for all of its citizens. This is what is known as dying "intestate." While this may seem like a good thing, it probably is not…because there is no guarantee that the way the government will allocate your estate is the way you would want your property allocated.

While the precise rules vary among the 50 states, typically the laws are very rigid and formulaic. Usually, all of your nearest relatives get a piece of your property but no one else does…not friends, cousins, charities, etc. Furthermore, no one receives more than the state-allotted share, even if it's seemingly unfair. Often, this ends up hurting the surviving spouse. In this all-too-common scenario, the decedent's grown children may get some of the money meant for the surviving spouse, even if it means the surviving spouse then has too little to live on.

Moreover, the absence of a Will often leads to expensive and lengthy court battles by family members contesting the division of assets. Sometimes family members produce a questionable Will in court, trying to establish a rightful claim to a portion of the estate. Once again, this can be avoided by having a valid Will in place.

Finally, if you have minor children and both parents die without a Will, the courts will decide who becomes the legal guardian of your children. What parent would want to have an unknown judge make the decision of who will care for their children if they die? Avoid this tragedy and create a valid Will including an Appointment of Guardian sooner rather than later.

For a detailed description of one state's intestacy laws, see the Appendix.

289

Why Do You Need a Will AND Living Trust?
To Save Time and Money and to Keep Your Estate Private

While having a Will is certainly better than not having one, it is not enough. You also need a Living Trust. If all you have is a Will, then your entire estate will be stuck in the probate process, which is time-consuming, public, and, in many states, costly. If you combine a Living Trust with a short Will called a "pour-over Will," then the vast majority of the estate will avoid probate completely. Before we examine how a Living Trust works, we must first see why probate must be avoided.

The Pitfalls of Probate

Delays

Probate often takes between a year and two years to complete in many states. During that time, your beneficiaries must wait for their inheritance. Perhaps worse, the representatives of your estate may have to petition the court for permission to conduct any transactions involving your estate assets during this time. This process could make it difficult to sell estate property or invest estate assets during the probate process.

Costs

Probate can cost between 2% and 8% of your "probate estate" — the value of the entire amount of property passing under the Will. This pays the courts, lawyers, appraisers, and your executor (the person in charge of handling your affairs during this process), among others. In some states, these probate fees are paid on your gross estate — not taking into account any loans against your assets! In these states, if you die owning $1 million worth of assets that have mortgages of $800,000, your estate will pay probate fees based on the $1 million market value of your estate, or approximately $50,000. This is money which could have gone to your beneficiaries rather than to the courts and lawyers.

Privacy

Probate is a public process in all states. Anyone interested in your estate can find out who inherits under your Will, how much he or she inherits, the beneficiaries' addresses, and more. While you may not be famous or worry about the newspapers exploiting this information, think of your beneficiaries and surviving family members. They certainly will not appreciate the many financial advisors calling them with "hot tips" on investments. These salespeople find beneficiaries by examining probate records. They know who they are and how much "found money" they have to invest.

Another aspect of the privacy issue is that the intestacy rules require that each person who would be a beneficiary if you died without a Will have a chance to contest your Will as part of the probate process. These beneficiaries must each be given notice of the Will and have a chance to review it and make objections. If you die without close family surviving you, the beneficiaries who must be given notice of the Will may include people you haven't spoken to in decades, people you don't like or people you don't know how to find. Each of these people has to be tracked down, even if they live abroad, and provided with notice of your Will and the probate proceeding.

Control

In probate, the courts control the timing and final say-so on whether or not your Will — and the wishes expressed in your Will — are followed. Your family must follow the court orders and pay for the process as well. This can be extremely frustrating.

Double Probate

If you own real estate outside of your state of residence, your Will must be probated again (in an ancillary proceeding) in each state where the real property is located.

You are probably thinking, "How can anyone use a Will when probate is this unappealing?" It is hard to believe. We are continually astonished by how many families endure the time and expense of probate when it is completely avoidable. Remember reading our introduction? Chris' stepfather was an attorney and when he died, he only had a Will!

How a Living Trust Solves the Problem

A Living Trust, also called a "family trust" or "loving trust," is a legal document which creates a trust to which you transfer assets during your lifetime. A living trust is a revocable trust, meaning you can change it at any time. During your life, the assets transferred to the trust are managed and controlled by you, as the trustee, just as if you owned them in your own name. When you die, these trust assets automatically pass to whomever you designated in the trust outside of the probate process. Other benefits of the Living Trust include:

- Avoiding the unintentional disinheriting risked by joint tenancy (happens in most 2nd marriages).

- Preventing court control of assets or court appointment of a legal representative if you become incapacitated.

- Protecting dependents with special needs.

How to Transfer Assets to a Living Trust

When you transfer your assets to your Living Trust while you are alive, you maintain 100% control over these assets as though you still owned them in your own name. For your car, stocks, bonds, bank accounts, home, or any other asset, the process of transferring an asset to your Living Trust is the same. If the asset has a registration or deed, change the name on such a document. If the asset is jewelry or artwork that has no official ownership record, use an assignment document to officially transfer ownership to your Living Trust.

These ownership changes will transfer the name of the registration or deed to the "John Doe Revocable Living Trust" or "John Doe, Trustee of John Doe Revocable Living Trust," rather than "John Doe" as it now reads. As sole trustee of the Trust, you have the same power to buy, sell, mortgage, invest, etc., as you did before. Furthermore, because the Trust is revocable, you can always change beneficiaries, remove or add assets, or even cancel your Trust entirely.

It must be remembered that the transfer of assets to the Living Trust (called "funding the Trust") is a necessary activity. While it has no income tax ramifications at all (you are still treated as the owner for income tax purposes) it is crucial to gain the probate-saving benefits afforded to you at the time of your death.

You May Name Yourself or Someone Else as Trustee

You need not name yourself as the trustee of your Living Trust, although most people do. You could name an adult child, another relative or close friend, or even a corporate trustee, like a local bank or trust company. If you do not like the way the outside trustee is handling the Trust, you always have the power to remove him.

When You Die or Become Disabled, Your Successor Trustee Will Take Over

If you are the trustee while you are alive, you will name, in your Living Trust, someone (or a corporate trustee) as the successor trustee. That person or entity will take over trustee duties when you die or become disabled. If you have a co-trustee while you are alive, that person will complete trustee duties after you have died.

These duties involve collecting income or benefits due your estate, paying your remaining debts, making sure the proper tax returns are filed, and distributing your assets according to the Trust instructions. This person or entity acts like an executor for a Will. However, unlike a Will, actions under a Living Trust's directions are not generally subject to court interference.

You Decide When Your Beneficiaries Receive Their Inheritance

Another significant advantage of a Living Trust over a Will is that you, rather than the courts, decide when and how your beneficiaries get their inheritance. Because the court is not involved, the successor trustee can distribute assets right after he/she/it concludes your final affairs. This can take as little time as weeks or even days.

If you choose, assets need not be distributed right away. Instead, you may direct that they stay in your Trust and be managed by your individual or corporate trustee until your beneficiaries reach the age(s) at which you want them to inherit. One of the advantages to distributing assets in this manner is that while the assets remain in the trust prior to distribution, they are protected from creditors — a feature that may interest you if you have concerns about your heir's creditors or possible divorce.

The Successor Trustee Must Follow Your Trust Instructions

Your successor trustee (as well as your primary trustee if it is not you) is a fiduciary — a legal term meaning that he/she/it has a legal duty to follow the Living Trust instructions and to act in a reasonably prudent manner. The trustee must treat the Living Trust as a binding legal contract, and must use his or her "best efforts" to live up to the obligations of the contract. If your successor trustee mismanages the Trust by ignoring the instructions in your Living Trust, he/she/it could be legally liable to the Trust beneficiaries.

Conclusion

As you have seen, Wills and Living Trusts are a must for any Wealth Protection Plan. They are truly the estate planning "building blocks." If you do not have such documents in place yet, you should remedy this problem as soon as practicable.

64

❖

THE A-B LIVING TRUST

How To Save Almost $700,000 In Estate Taxes
For A Few Thousand Dollars

For the married couples of America, there is a tragic financial blunder hidden in their estate plans. It lurks because many such couples plan to provide for the surviving spouse by having the first spouse to die leave everything to the surviving spouse. Most Americans, in fact, don't know any other way to leave money to support the survivor. *This mistake may cause your family to pay hundreds of thousands of dollars in estate taxes — unnecessarily.* To understand why, you must first realize the two fundamental creatures of our estate tax system: the unified estate tax credit and the unlimited marital deduction.

The Unified Estate Tax Credit (UTC)

The UTC translates into a dollar amount which can be left by a decedent estate-tax free (commonly called the "estate tax exemption"). As explained in the opening chapter of this section, after the 2001 changes, this exemption grew to $1.5 million in 2004 and 2005, and will rise to $3.5 million in 2009. Today, an individual can leave $1.5 million of property at his death to anyone, without any estate taxes being imposed.

We often explain the UTC as a "get-out-of-estate-taxes-free" card. Every one of us gets one of these cards to use either during our lives (up to the gift tax exemption amount) or at the time of our death. However, the card is non-transferable and, if not used during your life or at death, it is lost forever.

The Unlimited Marital Deduction (UMD)

This rule means that a decedent can leave an unlimited amount to a surviving spouse without any estate tax — provided both spouses are US citizens. If you are interested in learning about the special estate tax rules applying to non-U.S. citizens, please talk to the Wealth Protection Alliance member in your city.

Unfortunately, when thinking about their estate plan, too many married couples look at the UMD as their solution. They simply leave everything to their spouse, using the UMD to avoid all estate taxes. While this effectively eliminates all estate taxes at the first death, it is a "penny-wise" and "pound-foolish" mistake. That's because the first spouse did not use his UTC or "get-out-of-estate-taxes-free" card. Because he didn't use it, it is gone forever.

While this seems innocuous when the first spouse dies, when the second spouse dies, the IRS gets you back. At that point, the surviving spouse's estate can only make use of one $1,500,000 exemption. That means everything over $1,500,000 will be subject to estate taxes at a current maximum rate of 48%.

Let's take a look at an example:

CASE STUDY: *Tina & Mike*

Tina and Mike own a home worth $500,000, have life insurance policies with combined death benefits of $1,200,000, have another $500,000 in a retirement plan, a business worth $300,000 and general investments totaling $500,000. They might not think of themselves as millionaires, but to the federal estate tax authorities they are.

If Mike dies and leaves everything to Tina there will be no federal estate tax, because of the UMD. Assume now that Tina has inherited the entire estate and lives off of the earnings for the rest of her life.

When Tina dies (let's assume in 2005), her Will leaves the entire estate to her children. In 2005, the children are not taxed on the first $1,500,000 worth of property they inherit from their mother because of the UTC. The children do, however, pay federal estate taxes on the amount in excess of $1,500,000, or in our example $1,500,000. The tax rate starts at 45% growing to 48% percent, meaning the children will be paying over $700,000 in federal estate taxes.

The terrible fact about this case is that the entire $700,000 of taxes could have easily been avoided. Moreover, Tina still would have been able to live on the earnings of what Mike left her during her last years. How is this achieved? By implementing an A-B Living Trust.

How an A-B Living Trust Uses Both "Get-out-of-estate-taxes-free" Cards

When using an A-B Living Trust, the property is divided into two "buckets," bucket "A" (or Trust A) and bucket "B" (or Trust B), at the death of the first spouse. Most people transfer assets that are the equivalent of the UTC amount into the bucket "B," which ultimately goes to the heirs. The balance of the property will be transferred to "Trust A" which will be the Trust for the surviving spouse. During her/his lifetime, the surviving spouse can be full legal owner of Trust A, as trustee, and can do virtually anything with the assets of the trust.

The concept of Trust B is different. The surviving spouse does not own Trust "B" technically but he/she will have an ability to draw income/interest from the trust. Moreover, the surviving spouse may be able to use the property (for example: live in the home), use the principal for support, maintenance, health and education, and typically use up to either 5% of the principal or $5,000 a year for any reason whatsoever.

After the death of the second (surviving) spouse, the Trust B assets directly go to the heirs without any estate taxes. This is true even if the value of the assets has grown to more than the UTC amount.

Trust A, which belonged to the surviving spouse, will also be distributed to the named beneficiaries. First, all the debts/liabilities will be paid off. Then the wealth that is equivalent to the UTC amount will be transferred estate tax-free to the beneficiaries. If the value of the Trust A assets exceeds the UTC amount, then that portion of the estate will be subject to estate taxes. After paying the federal and state estate taxes, the assets will be transferred to the heirs.

CASE STUDY: *Tina & Mike Revisited*

Let's now assume that during their lives Tina and Mike hire an attorney to create a joint A-B Living Trust and they fund it properly. When Mike dies, the trust creates the B trust and funds it with the UTC amount in 2004 ($1.5 million). During the rest of her life, Tina can access the principal for support, maintenance, health and lifestyle maintenance — nearly anything she needs. She can live in the home as well. The remainder of the property — $1,500,000 — funds the A trust, which Tina can access and spend for whatever reason she wants.

When Tina dies in 2005, the B trust pays out directly to the beneficiaries of that trust — their kids. Because the B trust qualified for Mike's UTC when it was funded, there is no estate tax on what is left in the trust, whether it has grown beyond $1.5 million or been spent down to less than $1.5 million.

Any property left in the A trust will qualify for Tina's UTC. Thus, if there is less than $1.5 million in this trust when she dies (and likely there is because she has been living on the interest and a portion of the principal of the $1,500,000), there will be no estate tax on this portion either. In this way, the A-B Living Trust would save Mike and Tina's family $700,000 in estate taxes.

Conclusion

Under our estate tax rules, any married couple whose total assets might put them above the estate tax exemption amount by the time they pass away (in 10, 20, or 40 years) should use A-B trusts. It is really that simple. Without such a trust, one spouse is throwing out his "get-out-of-estate-taxes-free" card for no good reason. If you see yourself or any family members in such a position, make sure that an A-B trust is used. Your family finances will be greatly enhanced.

65

AVOIDING JOINT OWNERSHIP & DISINHERITANCE RISK

Why Joint Ownership Is So Dangerous

Joint ownership is the most popular form of ownership in the United States for stocks, bonds, real estate and bank accounts. As we explained in Chapter 11 of the asset protection section, when one joint owner dies, property owned in joint ownership automatically passes to the surviving joint owner(s). In this way, jointly owned property passes outside of a will and avoids the expense of probate. Because it avoids probate, many financial and legal advisors recommend joint ownership as a form of ownership. What these advisors do not tell you, however, are the ways you can be burned by owning assets in joint ownership.

As you have seen and will see again here, using joint ownership as an ownership form is almost always a big mistake. In Chapter 11, you learned how joint ownership subjects you to lawsuit and creditor risks. Perhaps you should review that chapter again as a reminder of those dangers. In any case, now you will learn how joint ownership can frustrate your estate plan.

Joint Ownership Can Ruin Your Estate Plan

Joint ownership threatens to ruin your estate plan because any property you own jointly will pass automatically by right of survivorship to the surviving joint owner(s). In the eyes of the law, this automatic transfer takes effect the instant you die, before any will or living trust can dispose of your property. *In this way, your will or living trust will have no effect on jointly held property.* If you designated certain beneficiaries in a will or trust to receive your share of jointly held property, they will be "disinherited" and the surviving joint owner(s) will take it. This avoidable tragedy occurs everyday in this country because people do not realize the dangers of joint ownership and because their advisors are not giving them adequate information. Consider these stories:

William, a man in his late 60's, marries for the second time. Shortly after the wedding, he puts all of his significant property—his main home, his winter vacation condominium, and his stock portfolio—into joint ownership with his new wife. Within six months, William dies. The home, the condo, and the stocks all go to William's new wife. His three children and eight grandchildren inherit virtually nothing, even though William had made ample provisions for them in his will.

Susan's Will bequeathed her property equally to her son and daughter. Because her son lives near her and he pays her bills, Susan put her house, her safe deposit box, and her bank account in joint ownership with him. When she dies, Susan's son will get all of the money in the bank account and deposit box, as well as the house, regardless of the will provisions. Unless the son is extremely generous, the daughter will get close to nothing. Do you want to rely on your children's generosity to carry out your estate plan?

Assume in Susan's situation above that the son has serious creditor problems. Overdue on $15,000 in credit card debts and a defaulted loan, the son's creditors can come after the bank account, the safe deposit box contents, and likely the house the moment Susan dies. The only real beneficiaries of Susan's estate may be banks and finance companies.

Cecilia, a single mother in her thirties, is trying to build a college fund for her eight-year old daughter, Debbie. Cecilia has invested some of her excess income to buy old residential multi-family homes, which she and her partner fix-up and rent to owners. While her relationship with her partner has been strained at times, Cecilia nevertheless takes title to the investment properties in joint ownership with her partner without realizing that if she dies before they resell the properties, her partner will take them all and leave nothing for Debbie.

Why do well-intentioned people get stuck in these predicaments? Because they do not know any better and their advisors are not doing their jobs. Sometimes, owners may not even realize what type of ownership they have chosen. In other cases, people consciously decide to use joint ownership because they know it will avoid probate. Avoidance of probate is never a reason for affluent professionals to use joint ownership.

Never Use Joint Ownership to Avoid Probate — Use a Living Trust

Assets titled in joint ownership and assets titled in a living trust both avoid probate. As described in the previous chapter, your interest in these assets will pass outside the probate process at death by utilizing a living trust. Thus, if your goal is to avoid probate, use a living trust rather than joint ownership. You will benefit more without any of joint ownership's pitfalls.

> **NOTE:** The A-B Trust strategy discussed in the preceding chapter cannot be implemented if a couple owns property jointly. A-B Trusts can only be funded by separately owned property, (community property, or property owned as tenant in common).

66

DOUBLE THE VALUE
OF YOUR LIFE INSURANCE
Why Using An ILIT Is A Must

Many sophisticated Wealth Protection estate plans include life insurance. One reason is that clients can leverage today's wealth to create a very large estate (or cover the estate taxes on an estate) in the future. Just as important is the logic to using life insurance in estate planning. An estate plan takes effect when you die, and that's when life-insurance policies pay off. The IRS, unfortunately, doesn't always recognize simple logic and the unwary could face a huge tax TRAP. If you were sent here by the RFA, you may be one of these unwary taxpayers.

The problem isn't income tax because life insurance proceeds generally avoid income taxes. Instead, the proceeds from the life insurance may be subject to federal estate taxes where the rates are much higher than income-tax rates (up to 48% in 2005). Of all the money the IRS collects in estate tax, more comes from improperly owned life insurance than from stocks, bonds, closely held businesses and real estate!

> **EXAMPLE:** Let's assume you leave an estate of $1.5 million, plus a $500,000 life-insurance policy. That brings your total (taxable) estate to $2 million. If you die in 2004 or 2005, an estate tax will be owed on the amount over $1.5 million, as that is the estate tax exemption amount. The estate tax rate is 45% for estates worth between $1.5 million and $2 million. Therefore, your heirs owe an extra $225,000 in estate tax. In other words, you've paid for $500,000 worth of life-insurance but your family only ends up with only $275,000. You paid for that extra $225,000 needlessly!

If you could own your life insurance policies in a way that kept it out of your taxable estate, those policies would be worth close to twice as much. In the above example, the policy would go from being worth $275,000 to your family to $500,000...and the insurance would not cost you one cent more!

Removing the Insurance from Your Estate: Popular Mistakes

From the previous example, you can see how important it is to keep life insurance policies out of your taxable estate. The following are two popular "strategies" for doing so. Both have distinct drawbacks and pitfalls.

Having the spouse own the policy or be its beneficiary

One popular method of sheltering life-insurance proceeds from estate tax is to name your spouse as owner or beneficiary of the policy. This works temporarily but not in the long term. As you learned in the chapter on A-B trusts, the IRS is happy to have you pass everything to the surviving spouse so that you throw away one "get-out-of estate-taxes-free" card (unified tax credit) without using it. That's because when the surviving spouse dies, the IRS gets a piece of everything above only one exemption amount rather than only the amount above two combined exemptions.

A second pitfall of this approach is that you lose all control of the proceeds when you die. They will pass to your surviving spouse outright. If he or she spends them down foolishly, gets remarried and divorced, is sued, etc., then your planning just benefited someone other than your family members. **Note: The average time it takes to spend down an outright inheritance or lottery payment is 17 months!** As you'll see below, you can control the funds even after you're dead and keep them in the family for generations by using a special life insurance trust which dictates exactly how the funds can be used.

Having the children own the policy

A different approach is to have your children own your life insurance policy and provide that they will receive the proceeds at your death. They can apply for the policy, pay the premiums (with money you may gift to them) and receive the proceeds at your death. If the policy and the proceeds are outside your estate, no estate tax will be due.

However, there are some drawbacks with this strategy. These include the following:

- If the proceeds are paid to children, your surviving spouse may run short of funds to pay bills and support him/herself. This can be a very big problem in the situation of second or third marriages, as children may not agree to support a stepparent.

- If the policy is a cash-value policy (typical in estate-planning situations because it is permanent insurance) your kids may be tempted to borrow against the policy, thus reducing the death benefits payable.

- If there's a divorce, the policy may be considered a marital or community property asset of your children, and some of the cash value could end up going to an ex-son-in-law or ex-daughter-in-law.

- If a creditor has a claim against your grown child, the policy may be seized as part of their assets. For example, he may be a shareholder in a failed business with personal guarantees on the company's notes.

- If your children are still minors, the policy would have to be owned by a custodian or a guardian.

- If you have more than one child, co-ownership of a valuable insurance policy may prove awkward or a point of contention.

The Superior Strategy: Use an Irrevocable Life Insurance Trust (ILIT)

You can avoid all the above problems by creating an ILIT to be the owner and beneficiary of your life insurance policies. If the ILIT owns the policy, it's out of your taxable estate. Moreover, a properly structured ILIT can keep the proceeds from spendthrift children and their disgruntled spouses or creditors. The funds can then be used to cover estate taxes, provide an income stream, pay off debts and mortgages or notes and keep other valuable and needed assets intact for the family.

In many cases, the ILIT will use the insurance proceeds to buy illiquid assets, such as shares of a closely held business, real estate, or other assets from your estate, to keep them in the family. A purchase of this type is considered a tax-neutral exchange, so no tax will be due on the asset itself. Alternatively, the trust can lend money to your estate, with the loan secured by the estate's assets. This is sometimes done to use the money to pay the estate taxes that are due on the other assets. Because estate taxes are due within 9 months from the date of death, this ability to have liquid cash available is crucial to avoid selling assets in a quick sale where the family may not get the best price. This is what happened to Chris' mother when his stepfather passed away. The real estate market was depressed and interest rates were high — a terrible combination. Because we can't predict when we will die, we want to make sure we avoid all unnecessary problems.

In either case, the estate will receive cash that can be used in a variety of ways. Later, the trustee can distribute the assets to the trust beneficiaries, the surviving spouse and/or children. This can be done in a lump sum, or, if desirable, the assets can be maintained in trust for their later benefit and use. If kept in trust, these funds can be structured so that creditors of the surviving spouse, children, and even grandchildren will have no access to them — even in the case of potential lawsuits, bankruptcy and divorces. In this way, the ILIT can be an asset-protecting tool for many generations.

If the trust is structured for the long-term, it often makes sense to have its assets grow in a tax–efficient manner. This can easily be accomplished by having the trust purchase a variable annuity (see chapter on variable annuities in the retirement section). The bottom line: All the insurance proceeds are available to help pay estate taxes and provide cash for whatever need might arise. Your family keeps control over the assets and no distress sale is necessary to raise money to meet the estate tax obligations.

Requirements for Your ILIT

Your ILIT, for maximum protection, must follow these guidelines:

Make the Proper Transfers

You must fully fund the ILIT with the insurance policy in order to gain its protective value. Contact your insurance carrier and change the ownership of the policy to the trust. Make the trust the beneficiary of the policy as well. The trust beneficiaries (spouse, child, etc.) will eventually receive the proceeds as you instructed in the trust document.

If the policy is owned by you individually before transferring it to the ILIT, the policy will be "brought back" into your taxable estate if you die within 3 years of the transfer. This is called the IRS' "3 year look back" rule. It is therefore preferable for you to set up your trust to purchase an insurance policy from the beginning because the 3-year look back rule does not apply in that instance.

The Trust Must Pay the Premiums

One indication of ownership is who pays the policy premiums. If you continue to pay the policy premiums while the trust is the owner of the policy, the courts may disregard the ownership of the policy and consider you the owner. This allows creditors to "step into your shoes" and take the policy proceeds away from your family members. This would also mean that the policy proceeds would be in your estate for estate tax purposes. For these reasons, the trust must pay premiums out of trust funds. You will have to gift funds to the trust to pay the premiums. This can be done on a one-time or annual basis. You should be advised by a competent professional to minimize or eliminate any gift tax consequences of these gifts.

You Cannot be Trusted

If you are the insured, you cannot serve as the ILIT trustee. You may name your spouse, adult child, or another trusted individual as trustee but, if they are also beneficiaries, an independent trustee should be named instead. Corporate trustees are often preferred because of their familiarity with ILITs and their reliability in following trust instructions and paying premiums promptly.

How to Use an ILIT and Keep an Income Stream During Your Lifetime

Quite often a client will ask us if there is a way to use an ILIT to own life insurance and have access to the policy's cash values during retirement. The short answer is "yes." In order to accomplish this, though, we have to keep in mind the rules we explained above.

Essentially, the only persons who can access the cash values of policies owned by an ILIT are the ILIT beneficiaries. If the policy insures your life, then you cannot be the trustee or the beneficiary of the ILIT. Thus, you personally could not have access to the cash values. However, if the policy insures only your life, then your spouse could have access to the cash values if she were a trust beneficiary. Further, if the policy was on your joint lives (often called a "survivorship" or "2nd to die" policy), then the children or grandchildren could access the cash values to the extent they are beneficiaries or the trustee could utilize cash values to benefit them. This could include paying their college tuition.

An alternative for clients who wish to access cash values of their life insurance policies AND leave death benefits of the insurance policies to children in an asset-protected way is to use an ILIT-LLC model. A specially crafted LLC can own the insurance policies. The allocations can be crafted so that one member (the parents — YOU) has access to cash values and the other member (the ILIT drafted to protect your children from lawsuits and divorce) has access to the death benefits. This is an advanced technique the authors have designed. Given its flexibility, it has become quite popular with physicians wishing to asset protect millions of dollars, still have access to the funds, leave the funds to their children or grandchildren estate tax free and protect the funds from divorce at the same time. If this application intrigues you, contact the WPA at (800) 554-7233 to learn more.

Conclusion: Use an ILIT

We consider an ILIT to be one of the 3 building blocks of an estate plan along with a Will and a Living Trust (A-B or not). Do not ignore this tool. If you have a significant amount of life insurance, strongly consider an ILIT.

67

⟨━━━◆━━━⟩

FAMILY LIMITED PARTNERSHIPS AND LIMITED LIABILITY COMPANIES

The Triple-Play Tools For Estate Planning

By now, you may be familiar with family limited partnerships (FLPs) and limited liability companies (LLCs). Depending on your RFA analysis, you may or may not have already read about FLPs and LLCs in the asset protection section as these are two essential building blocks of any asset protection plan. You may have read about these tools in the income tax section as well, because both entities allow for powerful income tax leveraging between family members. If, because of your RFA analysis, you were not previously directed to either of the chapters on FLPs or LLCs, please do so now. Turn back and read chapters 15 and 34. This will give you important background on both types of entities — which you will need to make sense out of this important chapter. Also, it will explain how similar the two tools are, including why we can refer to them almost synonymously.

In this chapter, you will learn how FLPs and LLCs — in addition to being excellent asset protectors and income tax reducers — are superior estate planning tools. In fact, the FLP/LLC has three major benefits when it comes to estate planning. Let us examine each separately:

FLP/LLC Assets Avoid Probate and Continue to Operate

Assets owned by your FLP/LLC do not go through probate. Only your interest in the FLP/LLC will. However, if you structure your LLC so that your intended beneficiaries own most of the FLP/LLC shares when you die, these beneficiaries will control the FLP/LLC and its assets when you die. Your beneficiaries can effectively control the FLP/LLC assets or business while the probate process continues its deliberation over distribution of your remaining membership interests. Because probate can last several years, this continued control can be crucial for operating a business or real estate interests.

FLPs/LLCs allow you to get property out of your estate WITHOUT giving up control

Because your estate only pays taxes on property you own at death, a common tax-saving strategy is to gift your property away during your lifetime. The property goes to people you wish to inherit your assets at the time of your death and the government gets a smaller share. The main objection you might have to this type of planning is that you will have to give up control of the property while you are still alive. That's where the FLP/LLC comes in.

If the FLP/LLC owns the asset(s), and you are made the FLP general partner or LLC managing member, you get the best of both worlds. You can gift FLP/LLC interests to intended beneficiaries and remove the value of those interests from your estate yet you still control the FLP/LLC and all of its assets while you are alive. Let's see how this works.

CASE STUDY: *Robert's Mutual Funds*

Robert Whelan, a 63-year-old retired proctologist, owned almost $1.1 million in mutual funds. He set up an FLP to own the mutual funds, naming himself as the sole general partner. At the outset, he owned 2% of the FLP as general partner and 93% as limited partner, gifting 1% each to his five grandchildren. Since this 1% was worth approximately $11,000, the gifts to each grandchild were tax-free.

Robert can continue to gift each grandchild $11,000 in FLP interests each year, completely tax-free. If Robert lives to age 75, he will give $660,000 worth of FLP interests to his grandchildren ($132,000 each), tax-free. This equates to 60% of the FLP.

This $660,000 will no longer be in his estate, and not subject to estate tax. Moreover, any future growth of the gifted portion of the FLP will also be out of the estate.

Because Robert's other assets put him in the 48% estate tax bracket, his tax savings using the FLP will be $316,800 (48% x $660,000). Because he is the FLP's sole general partner, Robert retains control over the mutual fund investments while alive and can determine the amount of distributions (which should be pro-rated to all members/partners). In this way, Robert maintains significant control of his assets for his lifetime, pays less estate tax, and also provides more for his grandchildren.

Caution: The IRS is currently scrutinizing this technique closely in estate tax audits. The FLP agreement and operations, and the gift structuring, must be carefully crafted or Robert's retained control could be grounds for the gifted FLP interests being brought back into his estate for tax purposes. At this time the legal rules for estate inclusion of interests of improperly crafted LLCs and FLPs are not completely clear, but properly structured entities are still offering excellent benefits.

FLPs/LLCs Lower Estate Taxes on Assets They Hold

You may not want to gift your entire FLP/LLC interests during your lifetime or may start such a gifting program too late to "give away" much of your wealth. In either case, you will die owning FLP/LLC interests, which are then subject to the estate tax. The issue thus becomes what valuation will the IRS attach to your remaining FLP/LLC interests? It may not be:

your percentage ownership in the FLP / LLC	–multiplied– by	the fair market value of the FLP / LLC assets

This is because of powerful tax rules applying to FLPs and LLCs regarding valuation discounting.

Valuation Discounting Using FLPs/LLCs

An important estate tax benefit of the FLP/LLC is that FLP/LLC interests often enjoy discounted values by the IRS. The IRS recognizes that owning a percentage ownership of an FLP/LLC that owns an asset is generally worth less than owning the asset outright. If you own a $20 bill and hold it at death, then the IRS would assign an estate taxable value of that bill of $20. However, if you died owning a 20% interest in a LLC with four other family members, all with equal management rights, and the LLC owned $100, the IRS would allow a valuation of your 20% interest at a number well below $20! Here's why:

The IRS would first allow a *lack of marketability* discount to that interest, recognizing that your LLC interest is less marketable. Its value should be reduced for tax purposes. There is likely not much of a market for your 20% LLC interest when the other LLC members are all family members. Who would want to own part of an LLC worth $100 when the other owners are members of one family? What would an outsider pay for such an interest? This discount is available even if you retain all the management rights in the LLC.

Second, because you own less than 50% of the LLC, the IRS will also apply the *minority ownership* discount to your interest unless you have retained most or all of the management rights. Again, the IRS recognizes that there is very little market interest for shares of an LLC which others control.

Both of the aforementioned tax valuation discounts can be maximized by the proper drafting of the FLP/LLC agreement. Any provisions that restrict the transferability of any FLP/LLC interests may weigh toward a higher *lack of marketability* discount. Likewise, clauses that limit the control of minority interest-holders will substantiate greater *minority ownership* discounts. Further, the IRS allows different discounts based on the assets and the liquidity of the assets. Cash cannot be discounted very much, but real estate and life insurance can be discounted substantially. With proper drafting, FLPs and LLCs can often enjoy valuation discounts of *10% to 40% or more*. This can translate into an estate tax savings of millions of dollars in larger estates.

> **CASE STUDY:** *Robert Whelan's Mutual Funds Revisited*
>
> Assume that when Robert dies, he still owns 40% of his FLP interests after gifting 60% to his grandchildren during his lifetime. This 40% partnership interest, as part of his estate, is subject to estate taxes. Assume also that the mutual funds in his FLP have a value of $2 million when Robert dies. His 40% interest in the FLP is then economically worth $800,000 (40% x $2 million).
>
> For estate tax valuation, however, the IRS may agree that Robert's FLP interest is worth only around $500,000. The IRS will allow both the lack of marketability discount and the minority ownership discount. The lack of marketability discount exists because Robert's five grandchildren own the other FLP interests, so non-family members would not be interested in buying his interests. Also, under the FLP agreement, the FLP interests are not freely transferable. The minority ownership discount may be applied because Robert owns only 40% of the FLP when he dies, if he has gifted a majority of general as well as limited partnership interests. Even in this situation, he will retain de facto control if the other general partnership interests are split 12% to each grandchild because only one needs to side with him in a vote for him to control a majority!

These valuation discounts translate into an estate tax savings of about $100,000. More importantly, he retains significant control over his funds while he is alive.

If this same discounting technique is applied to the gifts made during Robert's lifetime, he can make tax-free gifts of 60% of his FLP more rapidly. Instead of the gifting program taking 12 years as in the case study, he may be able to complete it in 7 to 8 years!

Conclusion

The FLP and LLC are tremendous Wealth Protection tools. We have seen how they protect assets in Chapter 15, how they reduce income taxes in Chapter 34, and now how they reduce estate taxes. It is hard to imagine how anyone's total Wealth Protection Plan could be complete without at least one FLP or LLC.

68

<hr/>

WHY YOUR PENSION, 401(K) OR IRA MAY BE A 70% TAX TRAP

This could be the most dangerous threat to your Wealth Protection Plan

In speaking with most financial professionals, you'll find that the common advice is to contribute as much as you can to your retirement plans (pensions, profit-sharing plans, IRAs, 401(k) plans, etc.). The conventional wisdom is that because you get an income tax deduction and tax-deferred growth, these plans are a huge tax win for the client.

Unfortunately, for many clients — especially highly-compensated physicians — this "conventional wisdom" could have a catastrophic effect on your family's financial well-being. Retirement plans are a potentially dangerous tax trap for four reasons:

1. It is likely that the client will ultimately pay income taxes on distributions at the same or higher rates as the deduction saved them when using a retirement plan. This means there is no real tax arbitrage. It is merely a case of paying now or paying on the same percentage of a larger number later.

2. The client may not need most (or all) of the funds in retirement.

3. Perhaps most damaging, any funds left in these plans at death will be decimated by taxes. Quite literally, these plans act as "traps," capturing huge sums of money which are eaten up at tax rates of 70% to 80%.

4. If you need the money before age 59½, there is an additional 10% tax penalty on withdrawals.

If you can accumulate more in your pension, profit-sharing plan, IRA, or other retirement plan than you will use (because you have other assets, an inheritance, or die early), this chapter is a crucial one for your overall estate planning. If you have been directed to this chapter by the RFA, then this may be a real possibility for you. Let's see why this may be such a problem for your Wealth Protection estate plan.

You May Pay Tax At the Same — Or Higher — Tax Rates

A common misconception among working people today is that when they retire, they will be in a lower income tax bracket. Though this may be true for some, there are myriad reasons why this may not be true for you. One reason is that you may become accustomed to a certain quality of life that you don't wish to "scale back" when you retire. You didn't work hard in your career and as a parent so you could be put out to pasture and live on tomato soup and grilled cheese sandwiches. In fact, many retirees will increase their expenses and do the things they didn't have time to do when they were working 50, 60 or 70 hours per week. Most notably, the thing they do is travel. Nonetheless, even if you do scale back your quality of life, you still may have to pay MORE in living and entertainment expenses because of inflation.

Just 15 years ago we used to go to the movies for $3–$5 and we could go see the Red Sox play at Fenway Park for $34 (2 tickets at $17 per). Last week, we paid $12 per ticket to see a movie and the same World Series Champion Red Sox tickets in the Green Monster seats or on the right field roof are…$100 each!

Not only might your lifestyle, which you can control, increase your expenses (and taxes) in retirement but your plan itself might also contribute to increased taxes. The Internal Revenue Service has rules regulating what are called Minimum Required Distributions (MRD) from retirement plan assets. This means you MUST start taking money out of your retirement plans at age 70½, whether you need the money or not. Of course, if you take the money out of the plan, you must pay income taxes on those withdrawals.

You invest your funds inside the retirement plan and those assets grow on a tax-deferred basis. This means you get greater accumulation than in a taxable account. Consider this tax-deferral along with the stock market returns you may realize (despite current market conditions, the 70-year average is still 11.5% per year). The larger accumulation forces even higher MRDs. This can raise your tax bracket in retirement and result in taxation of your social security benefits as well.

Lastly, you may have other income producing assets like rental real estate, another business, limited partnerships, dividend-paying stocks, bonds and money markets. Each of these income-producing assets adds to your income and increases your income tax bracket.

Given the amount of invested assets inside and outside of retirement plans, and the continued long-term growth of the securities markets, many Americans will enjoy retirement incomes which put them in the same tax bracket as they are in now. For example, we have a client named Frank, a 50-year old dermatologist with $500,000 in his profit-sharing plan. By the time he is in his late sixties and begins his planned retirement, assuming 9%-10% annual growth, the plan funds will likely grow to $3 million. If Frank then withdraws only the interest from the plan from then on without using any principal or other sources of income (like social security), Frank and his wife will likely still be in the top tax bracket for the rest of their lives. Of course, his MRD requires principal withdrawal too so a $1.5–2.0

million pension is enough to put you in the highest tax bracket when you factor in MRD.

What this means is that for many highly compensated taxpayers, the value of the tax deduction and deferral are not as great as "conventional wisdom" would espouse. Clients like this have no tax arbitrage — they simply get the deduction at one tax rate and then pay the tax at the same rate. In fact, the plan may actually cause "reverse arbitrage" as distributions from the plan will be taxed as ordinary income (likely subject to a 35%+ federal tax rate for wealthier clients), while gains outside of a plan might have been subject to a federal capital gains rate capped at 15% or not been subject to any tax on appreciation if you chose to invest in cash value life insurance (for a free email special report on how cash value life insurance can be desgined to out-perform stock, bond and mutual fund investments, call the WPA at (800) 554-7233 or email goldfarb@wealthprotectionalliance.com). A Wall Street Journal columnist reviewed this comparison at few years ago, concluding that for many taxpayers qualified plans were a "fool's game" (April 15, 1999).

You May Not Need the Funds in Retirement

Because the amounts contributed to retirement plans are relatively small for highly compensated taxpayers, most will accumulate significant non-plan assets over their careers. If plan contributions are capped at $41,000 or less (in most cases), what happens to the rest of the after-tax earnings? Over a career, they end up in non-retirement plan brokerage accounts, ownership interests in closely-held businesses, rental real estate, precious metals, or any number of other investments.

Given the compounded interest on your investments in the securities and real estate markets over 10-30 years, these non-plan investments can throw off significant income in retirement — so much so that the retirement plan assets are hardly even needed. Though this is a problem we should all hope to have, it is a problem nevertheless and it needs to be addressed.

We see this problem with many of our clients, including, by way of example, our client Charlie, a 58 year-old software executive. He contributed $20,000 to his pension for each of the last 25 years. Meanwhile, he and wife Margie have also amassed $1.2 million in other investment accounts. By the time he retires, planning to do so at age 65, he should have enough in his brokerage accounts for a very comfortable retirement.

Charlie & Margie Won't Need Pension Funds to Retire

Clients	Charlie & Margie
Ages	Charlie 58; Margie 57
Average Pension Contribution	$20,000 for 25 years
Non-Pension Investing	$20,000 for 20 years
Present Pension Balance	$2.2 million
Outside Investments	$1.2 million
Planned Retirement Age	65
Forecasted Pension Balance, Age 65	$4.4 million (10% annual return)
Forecasted Outside Investments, Age 65	$2.3 million (8% post-tax return)
Post-Tax Earnings on Outside Investments, Age 65	$184,000/year ($15,000+/month)
Post-Tax Amount Needed for Retirement	$10,000 post-tax per month

As you can see from the chart, Charlie, who earned about $275,000 per year over the first 25 years of his practice, did not even maximize his pension contributions over that time ($30,000 per year was allowed). Instead, he chose to control some of his investments himself (about $20,000 per year) in a separate investment account. By the time he retires at age 65, Charlie will clearly have enough to fund his retirement (he and Margie need about $10,000 per month post-tax) just from his non-pension plan investments.

To be extremely conservative, let's advise Charlie and Margie to keep another $1.4 million of the pension funds secured for emergencies. That still leaves $3 million of the pension at age 65 which will continue to grow. Charlie and Margie think that this $3 million, plus most of this growth, will benefit their children and grandchildren as designated in their will and trust. As you'll see below, they are really benefiting the IRS and state tax agencies because over 70% of the funds will be eaten by taxes if they don't change their plan!

Any Funds Left Will Be Decimated By Taxes

So what happens to the assets left in the retirement plan if they are not used by the taxpayer and spouse during their lifetimes? Would you be surprised to know that the vast majority of these funds will end up with state and federal tax agencies? Did you think that after paying taxes for a lifetime of work, your "tax qualified" plan would be taxed at rates from between 70% and 80%? Most clients — when hearing these facts — are shocked, appalled, and want to learn how to do something about it. Let's take a look at how these taxes are levied and what you can do about it. The first thing you must learn is what "IRD" means.

The Basics of IRD

IRD means "income in respect of a decedent" (a deceased person). This is income which would have been taxable to the decedent had the decedent lived long enough to receive it. Whoever receives these items of IRD must report them as gross income and pay any resulting income taxes in the year in which the items are actually received — generally, the year of death (spouses are entitled to defer IRD until payments are actually withdrawn).

The IRD is taxable income which is assessed taxation in addition to any federal estate (death) taxes and state estate/inheritance taxes. To illustrate, it must be understood that federal and state income taxes (including those characterized as IRD) can reach up to 45% while estate tax is assessed between 45% and 48% (we'll assume 48% here), assuming no additional state estate tax (an increasingly unlikely assumption — see Chapter 62). When you combine both taxes, you can see how quickly taxation escalates. Although the rules provide for a partial income tax deduction for estate taxes paid, the total tax on assets characterized as IRD assets can be over 70% in some cases.

What types of assets qualify for the dreaded IRD treatment? Income earned by a decedent but not yet paid, like bonuses or commissions, qualify as IRD. Once they are paid to the estate or the beneficiaries, they'll be hit with income taxes and estate taxes under the IRD rules. What is the most important asset hit by IRD? Retirement plans, such as pensions, 401(k)s, and IRAs (to the extent contributions were originally tax deductible).

EXAMPLE: *How IRD Eats Up a Retirement Plan*

Let's take the simple example of Jim, a single professor whose other assets exceed the current estate tax exemption. His IRA is fully taxable as it was funded entirely with tax deductible contributions. The same illustration could be made for a married couple but the estate tax wouldn't be due until the second spouse dies if he/she were the plan beneficiary due to the unlimited marital deduction.

Assuming Jim's fully-taxable IRA has a value of $1,000,000 at his death, Jim's estate (or heirs) would first pay $465,000 in estate taxes upon Jim's death, and then pay another $251,212 in state and federal income taxes (i.e., 45% of the remaining amount after giving a deduction for federal estate taxes paid). Thus, only $283,788 is left out of the IRA for Jim's beneficiaries — less than 29%! Over 70% of the funds — built over a lifetime of working and paying income taxes — were taken by the IRD tax system. Let's see how that happened (assuming Jim lived in a state with only a "sponge" estate tax as described more fully in Chapter 62):

Jim's IRA: IRD Eats Up Over 70%!!

IRA Value – IRD Item		$1,000,000
Less		
Federal Estate Tax (95% of 46.5%)	($441,750)	
State Estate Tax (5% of 46.5%)	($23,250)	
Total Estate Taxes		($465,000)
Balance in Estate		$535,000
Income in Respect of a Decedent	$1,000,000	
IRD Deduction	($441,750)	
Taxable IRD	$558,250	
Income Tax (45%)		($251,212)
Amount for Beneficiaries		$283,788
Total Taxes		$716,212 (71.6%)

How to Avoid the Tax Trap

Because this topic is so important to your Wealth Protection Plan, it has been afforded its own chapter. Turn the page and let's see what your solution options are.

69

AVOIDING THE 70% RETIREMENT PLAN TAX TRAP

In the last chapter, you learned how pensions, 401(k)s, IRAs and other retirement plans can be 70% tax traps...among the most damaging threats to a successful Wealth Protection Plan. Undoubtedly, this is a huge threat for millions of Americans, many of whom have no idea what is facing them and their families when they die with funds left in such plans. Nevertheless, you now know the harsh reality. So what can you do about it? The answer to that question depends on where you are in your retirement plan funding.

If You Are Early in Your Career: Monitor Participation in Qualified Plans

For many Americans, it still makes sense to maximize participation in qualified retirement plans when they are working. In fact, this may be 100% true for your Wealth Protection Plan at this point. It really depends on an accurate financial analysis of what your plan balance is and what you project you will need to spend in retirement. If, after such a financial analysis, it looks like you now have more in your retirement plans than you will need in retirement, then you should consider ending participation as soon as possible. Ideally, you want to amass just enough in retirement plans to cover retirement expenses and a "safety buffer." Beyond this, you are simply accumulating 70 cents for the government for every 30 cents you will leave your family.

What if you have already built up a large balance in a pension or IRA and now realize that you won't need some or all of the funds in retirement (like our example of Charlie and Margie from the previous chapter)? Unless you want 70% or more of these funds to go to state and federal taxes, you must do something and the earlier the better.

Essentially, you have three potential strategies for attempting to reduce the heavy tax burden on qualified plans: "Stretch IRAs;" the "Liquidate and Leverage" strategy; and the "Pension Insurance Purchase" strategy. We will examine each separately.

Option #1: Stretch IRAs

Recently, stretch IRAs have been discussed as a viable tax-reduction option. Stretch IRAs lengthen the time over which distributions must be taken from retirement plans or rollover IRAs. They also allow you to leave the IRA to your heirs, who can then stretch out the distributions over their lifetimes and pay income taxes as they receive the funds. The common belief underlying this strategy is that "tax-deferred growth" is always a great idea. However, when you crunch the numbers you will realize that the stretch IRA is generally a bad idea for anyone who will have an estate tax liability and it may be only a minor benefit to everyone else.

There are at least two reasons why the stretch IRAs are not beneficial: 1) stretch IRAs completely ignore the estate tax problem, and 2) they may create additional unnecessary taxes for your heirs. Let's consider both problems briefly.

Stretch IRAs Ignore the Estate Tax Problem

If you think your estate will be worth more than $1 million when you die, you will probably have an estate tax problem. The stretch IRA gives your heirs the benefit of deferring their withdrawals and deferring their income tax liabilities. The IRS doesn't care that the children or grandchildren have not received the money. The value of the IRA is included in the estate and your heirs still owe the estate tax. Look at this case.

CASE STUDY: *Jeff leaves a business and a stretch IRA*

Jeff listened to his advisor, who told him to create a stretch IRA so he would avoid the 70% IRD problem at death. When Jeff passed away, his three children received his family restaurant and a stretch IRA worth $800,000. The total estate tax bill was $700,000. His children didn't want to sell the restaurant, so they took the $700,000 out of the stretch IRA to pay the estate tax bill. The kids should be happy because they now have the business and an additional $100,000, right?

Wrong. The kids now owe income taxes on the $700,000 withdrawal (income taxes are never waived or avoided with a stretch IRA). Their average state and federal income tax rates were 40%. Therefore, they owed $280,000 of income taxes because of their $700,000 withdrawal the year before. They used the last $100,000 from the IRA and took out a $180,000 loan against the business to pay the $280,000 tax bill. Then, they owed income taxes on the $100,000 withdrawal, another $40,000 to the IRS, and they owed another $15,000 of interest on the loan. This put them in the hole on another $55,000. Eventually the children had to sell the business to pay off their debts. Jeff's plan failed because he received bad advice.

Stretch IRAs Will Cost Your Heirs More Taxes

The stretch IRA may generate more taxes to your heirs for three reasons:

1. Your heirs may be in the same or higher tax bracket as you are by the time you die. If you die in your seventies, eighties, or nineties, your heirs will be in their prime earning years and will likely have other income to put them that higher tax bracket. You may be deferring 27% taxable income in lieu of 35% taxable income later.

2. All withdrawals will be taxed as ordinary income when withdrawn from the plan by you or by your heirs. The long-term capital gains rate of 15% doesn't apply to appreciated investments and the tax free accumulation and tax free loans and withdrawals from life insurance don't help you in a retirement plan because the plan will own the policy and you will still pay taxes on plan withdrawals after the plan takes a tax free policy loan. If you'd taken the funds from the plan and paid the taxes earlier, you would've had the opportunity to invest in long-term investments that may only be subject to federal tax rates of 15% or no taxes if you understand and take advantage of tax free withdrawals and tax free policy loans from life insurance.

3. You have no flexibility for intergenerational planning. You can only invest in securities inside a stretch IRA. You cannot buy life insurance. If you left the stretch IRA to your children and they didn't need it and wanted to leave it for their children, they would have to let the income taxable IRA appreciate. It would continue to be income and estate taxable until their children receive the money. If you had paid the taxes and left the children after-tax dollars, the children could have invested in tax-free life insurance or a tax-free 529 plan for your grandchildren. You wouldn't be handcuffing them with a stretch IRA.

In our opinion, the stretch IRA can be shortsighted, penny-wise and pound-foolish. Of course, if you or your spouse is completely uninsurable, if your IRA is your only asset, if your estate definitely will not be worth over $1 million when you pass away, then the stretch IRA may make sense for you. If you don't meet all those conditions, you should seriously consider another alternative.

Option #2: Liquidate & Leverage

The "liquidate and leverage" ("L&L") strategy is much superior to the stretch IRA. In fact, you can think of this strategy as allowing you to leverage your IRA, 401(k) or pension five to twenty-five times!

Assume that you and your spouse are 60 years old and have $1 million in your qualified plan. Because you have accumulated significant assets outside of your plan, you are sure that you won't need $600,000 of the funds, or the interest on those funds, in retirement. Let's assume that other assets will all but eliminate $400,000 of your estate tax exemption amount. In that case, more than 70 cents of every dollar in your plan will go to the government if you don't take action.

One L&L Method: One Time Gift

The L&L strategy will ensure that your heirs not only get the full $600,000, but also an additional $2.9 million as well. Best of all, they will receive the $3.5 million tax-free! The L&L steps are as follows:

1. Take $600,000 out of the plan and pay the $240,000 in income taxes (assuming a tax rate of 40%).

2. Use a portion of your estate tax exemption amount and gift the remaining $360,000 to a properly drafted irrevocable life insurance trust or to an ILIT-LLC combination structure if you still want access to the cash values — see Chapter 66 for further explanation.

3. The ILIT then purchases a second-to-die life insurance policy on you and your spouse. Depending on your age, health, net worth, and other factors, that policy might be worth $1.5 to $3.5 million.

4. When you die, the insurance company pays up to $3.5 million, income tax free, to the irrevocable life insurance trust. Then, all $3.5 million will be available to your heirs estate tax free as well. With an ILIT (Chapter 66), those funds can be protected from your children's creditors — including divorce.

If you consider that the $600,000 in your plan would have been worth less than $800,000 to your children and grandchildren (if you lived to age 80 and the funds grew at 8%), the L&L strategy left your heirs more than four times that amount — over $2.7 million more to your heirs after taxes!

8% growth for 20 years   =   4.66
4.66 x $600,000   = $2,786,00
After 72 percent tax, your heirs receive approximately $783,000

Wouldn't you rather leave your heirs $3.5 million than $783,000? The two reasons people don't do this are bad advice (which you can't claim now) and fear of needing the money. Chapter 66 discusses a way to give yourself a way to access the cash values if you need them.

Alternative L&L Method: Guaranteed Income/Annual Gifts

Many people don't like paying for insurance in one lump sum. Others already have life insurance policies that require annual premiums. Still others aren't sure how much of their retirement plans they need. They only know how much they need each month to pay their bills. For these people, the guaranteed income/annual gifts method of L&L is ideal. Consider this example.

CASE STUDY: *Marian's Guaranteed Income Allows Gifting*

Marian is 78 years old and has $800,000 in retirement plan assets. By purchasing a life annuity with the $800,000, she receives a guaranteed monthly income of $8,600. After taxes, she still has $5,400 per month. Because she has some income from her municipal bonds that are outside her retirement plan and additional income from Social Security, she only needs $2,000 of the retirement plan income to pay her bills and to fund the college savings plans she created for her grandchildren. This leaves Marian with $3,400 per month of excess income. She gives this $3,400 per month to an ILIT, which pays for a $1 million life insurance policy that is guaranteed to Marian's 115th birthday!

By using the steps, Marian took $800,000 of potentially 70% taxable money and turned it into guaranteed supplemental income for her and a $1 million guaranteed inheritance for her son and grandchildren. To "break even" with 6% municipal bonds, Marian would have to live another 24 years. The probability of Marian living to 102 is much lower than 50%. This is why she moved forward with this plan.

Option #3: Pension Insurance Purchase

The IRS and ERISA allow for certain types of retirement plans to purchase life insurance within the plan with pretax dollars. Typically, we use profit-sharing plans because the rules are most generous for these types of plans. Thus, for clients with roll-over IRAs, they will have to roll the IRA back into a properly-drafted profit-sharing plan (PSP) before being able to take advantage of this strategy. This provides better creditor protection for the large plan balances also.

From this point forward, let's consider that you have a retirement plan that you don't expect to completely empty before you die. What can you do? You can purchase life-insurance on yourself inside your retirement plan. When you die the insurance company will pay a death benefit to your retirement plan.

Savvy investors may say that this strategy is flawed because they feel that their investment choices can outperform the performance of a conservative insurance company. We do not argue that you may be able to outperform the insurance company. What we do argue (think back to Chapters 50 and 51 where we discussed that investment decisions should not be made in a vacuum and we shouldn't ignore taxes in our analyses) is that there is an opportunity to take advantage of tax benefits afforded life insurance. Let's look at an example.

> **CASE STUDY:** *Mutual Funds vs. Life Insurance — a Surprise Upset Winner*
> Let's assume that you could invest $500,000 into mutual funds inside your retirement plan. After 20 years, assuming a 7% return on your mutual funds, you would have approximately $2,000,000 in your retirement plan. If you died at that point, your spouse would have access to the funds but would have to pay income taxes on any withdrawals. If you assume a combined state and federal tax rate of 40%, the $2,000,000 pension is worth $1,200,000 to your spouse. If your children then wanted the funds, there might be gift or estate taxes to pay.
>
> If you invested the same $500,000 into a $1.8 million life insurance policy, you might think you would be at a disadvantage compared to investing in mutual funds. You would be wrong. At the end of 20 years, after paying for mortality costs and administrative expense of the life insurance policy, your policy only had $600,000 of cash value at the time of your passing. When the $1,800,000 death benefit paid to the pension, the Internal Revenue Code states that only $600,000 of the benefit will be income taxable to the spouse. $240,000 was due to the IRS and the remaining $1,560,000 went to the spouse tax free! That is 30% more money to the survivors. The same estate tax rates would apply, but 30% more money escaped the pension and the taxes associated with it. What's more, this strategy is not more aggressive than buying a home for the tax deductible mortgage interest. It is a benefit that is clearly spelled out in the Internal Revenue Code. It is simple, but very few people take advantage of it.

Conclusion

If you are accumulating wealth and fear that IRD may become a problem for your family, consider nontraditional retirement alternatives and tax efficient investing. If you have a sizeable pension balance, you don't need to worry terribly that your heirs will pay the 70% tax on IRD. What you do need to do is talk to professionals who are familiar with pension law, life insurance and estate taxes and ask them to help you with your planning. You may be surprised at how much you can accomplish when you work with a good team of advisors. The Wealth Protection Alliance has offices in 50 cities and the members train attorneys and accountants nationwide how to help avoid these problems and implement alternative programs for successful physicians, hospitals and medical practices.

70

"FREE INSURANCE"

You Can Use Other People's Money To Pay For Your Estate Planning

How do you think banks make money? They borrow money from people through deposits, certificates of deposit, checking and savings accounts, to name a few. They then lend money to people to buy homes or cars or to start businesses. Because they may only pay you 1%–2% for the money they borrowed from you and they lend money at rates of 6%–9%, they are making money…on someone else's money!!! This has worked around the world for centuries.

This chapter will show you how to benefit the same way that banks have benefited for years. All you need is a home, some real estate, a business, accounts receivable, a brokerage account, or a letter of credit from a bank and you can do your estate planning with someone else's money!

How Does This Work?

Ideally, you want to borrow money at a favorable, and possibly tax-deductible, rate. You would then use the loan proceeds to purchase a life insurance policy. Of course, the loan you take out has interest payments (that may or may not be tax-deductible). You also have to eventually pay back the loan principal. With insurance, you have dividends, cash accumulation, and a death benefit. If the cash accumulation (which may be tax-deferred or even tax-free) in the insurance policy is large enough to pay off the loan, you use tax-free loans from the policy to pay off the loan. The remaining death benefit in the insurance policy is yours!

An alternative method, after securing the loan and purchasing the insurance policy, is to use the dividends to pay the interest on the loan. If you borrowed $100,000 to buy a $500,000 life insurance policy and the dividends are large enough to pay the interest payments, you can agree to pay off the $100,000 loan with a portion of the death benefit from the insurance. In this case, your family still has $400,000 left. That's $400,000 that cost you $0 out of pocket.

Is This Really Possible?

In 2003, we had one client secure an interest only home equity loan as low as 2%. We had another client receive a loan on his brokerage account for as little as 1.3% (in a unique international loan program). We had many clients take out home equity loans at rates of 4%–6%. If you assume a 30% to 44% income tax bracket, these clients received tax deductions that reduced their after tax loan rates to 2.1% to 4.2%. At the same time, a AAA rated insurance company credited 5.5% (tax free) to its universal life policies and over 7% to its whole life policies. An equity indexed universal life policy credited even more than that! You can use the difference to pay down the loan principal, too. This will leave the entire death benefit to your family.

Another option that is becoming popular is the "Loan, Annuity & Life Insurance Triple-Play." The strategy is as follows:

1. You mortgage your real estate and borrow as much equity as possible (let's assume $500,000). This maneuver provides asset protection for the real estate (see Chapter 18). REMEMBER: the real estate appreciates at the same rate whether you have 1% or 100% equity. Any equity you have is not working for you. Why not leverage the equity?

2. You use the loan proceeds to buy a life annuity with an interest rate payout higher than your mortgage rate (see Chapter 46 on life annuities)

3. For the next ten years, the annuity payout will be partially tax-free (as return of basis) while you may be able to deduct the interest portion of your loan payment.

4. You will then use the annuity payment to fund a life insurance policy of say $1,000,000.

Under the right circumstances, there are cases where the annuity payment net of income taxes will be sufficient to make the premium payments on the life policy and the mortgage payment on the loan — you may even have a little left over! At death, the life policy pays the balance of the loan and there will still be over $500,000 in death benefit for your family which cost you...nothing. Of course, there are risks to every strategy. A variable interest rate on the loan could increase above the annuity payment. The life insurance policy could perform poorly (if you chose a variable policy and the market turned sour, for example). This is a complex strategy you should discuss with a Wealth Protection Specialist.

Is it Worth the Effort?

This is the growing trend with many multimillionaire families and businesses because they don't want to write checks for tens or hundreds of thousands of dollars to buy life insurance.

They like the idea of using someone else's money. They may have a lot of wealth, but not a lot of available money to pay premiums — especially if the money is tied up in a business or other investment. One WPA member, Vance Syphers, helped us design a debt shield program that helps physicians remove equity from unprotected real estate, fund insurance in an asset protected way, and generate cash values that can significantly enhance retirement income. This is covered in Chapter 18. Trust us, it's worth exploring.

Caution — Things to Look Out For

Interest is not deductible if the money borrowed is used to buy life insurance. Beware of any accounts receivable financing deals (described in greater detail in Chapter 25) that assume an automatic interest deduction. There are ways to make this work, but it can be very difficult.

Furthermore, borrowing money always increases your risk of loss of principal. If you borrow money and the investment you choose declines in value, you are still on the hook for the repayment. Always be conservative with the investments you choose when you are already leveraged. We typically recommend very strongly that investors not fall into the trap of investing in a variable insurance product with financed money as we believe the financial risk is too great.

71

⬥

LONG TERM CARE INSURANCE FOR ESTATE PLANNING

Protect Your Estate From Rising Medical Costs

You may have already read about the soaring costs of medical procedures and nursing home care. You may also be familiar with the folly of relying on the government to provide for your medical coverage and your comfortable retirement. What we will discuss in this chapter is how Long Term Care Insurance ("LTCi") plays a very important role in the estate planning segment of your Wealth Protection Plan.

Long term care is considered a type of health insurance because it pays for a variety of health costs that may or may not be covered by Social Security, Medicare, or your state plan. The details of long term care insurance and our recommendations on what to look for in an LTCi contract are covered in Chapter 60. The Tax Section of this book has a small chapter that discusses the retirement and income tax benefits of LTCi planning (Chapter 35). The purpose of this brief chapter is to explain why LTCi is an important part of any estate plan. The three chapters on LTCi should be read to get a full understanding of how LTCi will help you and your family.

If you met with your advisors recently to discuss your estate plan under the 2001 laws, you probably didn't count on having to pay $100–$300 per day for nursing home or in-home care. You also probably didn't factor in medical expense inflation rates of 5%–10% per year that could make a very mediocre $100/day nursing home in year 2005 dollars cost over $500 per day in 2025. If you need long term care for just one year, it could cost $182,500 of funds that you had hoped would go to your children or grandchildren.

Do you Need LTCi?

According to the Center for Long Term Care Financing, Americans face approximately a one-in-ten chance of spending at least five or more years in a nursing home after age 65. 48.6% of people age 65 and older may spend time in a nursing home. More startling is that

71.8% of people over age 65 may use some form of _home-health care_! Do you think the developments in medicine will help or hurt this situation?

The longer people live (as a result of these advancements) the greater the likelihood that they will eventually need some significant medical assistance on a long term basis. We may find treatments for cancer or osteoporosis, but that just increases the likelihood of eventually having Alzheimer's or some other debilitating disease that forces us to require significant, and very costly, care.

Here are some costs, by city, for nursing home care as compiled by the MetLife Assisted Living Market Telephone Survey 2002:

The Average Annual Cost of Nursing Home Care

Anchorage, AK	$120,815	Omaha, NE	$75,555
Los Angeles, CA	$63,875	Las Vegas, NV	$56,800
San Diego, CA	$68,620	New York, NY	$100,010
San Francisco, CA	$91,250	Cleveland, OH	$83,950
Stamford, CT	$126,655	Philadelphia, PA	$68,985
Miami, FL	$70,445	Providence, RI	$66,065
Honolulu, HI	$80,300	Nashville, TN	$46,355
Chicago, IL	$51,100	Dallas, TX	$52,195
Boston, MA	$88,695	Houston, TX	$52,195
Baltimore, MD	$58,035	Arlington, VA	$74,825
Detroit, MI	$45,990	Rutland, VT	$73,365
St. Paul, MN	$72,270	Seattle, WA	$74,460
St. Louis, MO	$54,020	Milwaukee, WI	$64,970

Nursing home care costs in most cities in this chart range between $5,000 and $8,000 per month. Some are as inexpensive as $4,000 per month and some can be as expensive as $10,000 per month or more. Is there any reason to believe that nursing home care will become less expensive? Are you willing to risk losing this much of your estate to nursing home costs or would you like to plan ahead?

The important point to take from this chapter is that you will eventually pay for long term care coverage. The question is: "will it be paid for in advance or will it be paid for from your intended inheritance or retirement funds?"

You may wonder "Doesn't the state or Medicare pay these expenses?" The answer is "Yes and No." As an example, the State of California will not pay for a senior's medical bills until that individual has depleted all but $3,000 of his/her net worth. If a retirement plan or a home or any investments are titled to an individual, or have been titled in the individual's name in the last five years, the state will require those assets to be sold to pay for medical costs. In addition, the state will then take all but $30 per month of the individual's income to pay them for their coverage.

It isn't hard to see how this could deplete someone's assets immediately. You are likely willing to buy insurance, create a living trust, and consider other estate planning strategies. Ignoring Long Term Care planning could be a potentially devastating mistake. Let's plan not to make it ourselves.

If you intend to leave an inheritance, then you may wish to purchase long term care insurance now, while you have the money. You can purchase an LTCi policy in one year, over 10 years, over 20 years, or make payments every year for the rest of your life. In Chapter 35, we explain how you can get a deduction for your long term care insurance premiums. You also have options to have all of your premiums go to your heirs at death...even if you collect on the policy during your life. In fact, there are policies on the market today which combine a universal life insurance guaranteed death benefit for your heirs with a guaranteed daily benefit for long term care costs. This can be an ideal tool to achieve two family Wealth Protection goals.

By purchasing long term care insurance, you are making sure that soaring medical costs don't take away the head start you wanted to leave your children or grandchildren or destroy the legacy you wanted to leave behind. It can be an important part of any Wealth Protection Plan.

72

CHARITABLE
ESTATE PLANNING

How To Get More To Your Family
And Benefit A Charity

"To give away money is an easy matter and in any man's power, but to decide to whom to give it, and how large and when, and for what purpose and how, is neither in every man's power nor an easy matter"

— Aristotle

In Chapter 36, we introduced the topic of charitable giving. There, you learned the basic tax rules that make charitable giving so attractive for family Wealth Protection purposes. In that chapter, we also explained the basics of the two leading tools used to make charitable gifts: charitable remainder trusts (CRTs) and charitable lead trusts (CLTs). Because charitable planning is such a vast topic, we can only hope to give you a tiny hint of the types of planning we implement for our clients.

Rather than ramble on about a series of planning options, we think it best to be succinct and show the power of charitable planning through the following case study:

> **CASE STUDY:** *Steve and Martha use a CRT*
>
> Steve (56) is an orthopedic surgeon and his wife Martha (48) is an OB/GYN. They have two boys, both finishing graduate school. As a result of prudent investing, good luck and some great investments in some start-up businesses, Steve is considering early retirement so he can travel and enjoy his hobbies of flying and sailing.
>
> In addition to his significant retirement plan account, Steve has $3 million in essentially zero basis stock in his friend's company (that he helped finance in return for stock) that was recently acquired by a public company. He is in line with qualified stock options to acquire an additional $5 million over the next three years. Faced with planning for the disposition of an estate of $10 million (almost all of it in an undiversified portfolio), Steve and Martha decided that they'd like part of

their Wealth Protection Plan to be paying $0 in estate taxes, if that were possible. In short, they're willing to give to charity those assets that would otherwise default to the IRS in the form of estate and capital gains taxes.

As a part of this strategy, they will also use FLP's to make aggressive gifts of stock to their two sons and other family heirs over the next few years, (FLPs explained in Chapter 67). By freezing estate growth and squeezing the value of the assets, we hope to be able to eliminate all unnecessary estate taxes. Additionally, our plan will provide an excellent retirement income stream through the use of a charitable remainder trust (CRT).

Examine the following chart carefully, as we will refer to it below:

Steve and Martha Use a CRT to Benefit Charity & Their Family

	Sale	CRT
Net fair market value (FMV)	$3,000,000	$3,000,000
Taxable gain on sale	$3,000,000	
Capital gains tax (20% federal + state)	$600,000	
Net amount invested after sale	$2,400,000	$3,000,000
Annual return of reinvested portfolio	10%	10%
Reinvested for 10% annual income produces annual retirement income of	$240,000	
Trust payout of 5% (averaged with 10% returns over trust term of 40 yr.)		$452,999
Annual average after-tax income (at 39% tax and 20% capital gains rate for CRT payout)	$146,400	$321,622
Years – projected joint life expectancy	40	40
Taxes saved with $616,290 deduction at 39%		$240,358
Tax savings and cash flow over 40 years	$5,856,000	$13,105,233
Total value of asset in estate in 40 years	$2,400,000	$0
Estate taxes on this asset at 48%	$1,152,000	
Net value to family	$1,080,000	
Total insurance expense – wealth replacement	$0	($530,000)
Insurance benefit in wealth replacement trust	$0	$3,000,000
CRT remainder value to family charity	$0	$20,415,96

What is happening here? The stock that Steve owns is publicly-traded, so its value is readily ascertained and is easily transferable to the Charitable Trust. This CRT will take the highly appreciated stock and sell it without being taxed on its sale. It will then reposition the proceeds into a more balanced portfolio of equities designed for both growth and security.

The CRT, with Steve as co-trustee, will buy and hold stocks and mutual fund shares so that most of the portfolio will continue to appreciate while Steve and Martha, as income beneficiaries, receive quarterly payments of 5% of the trust's value every year. They've made the decision that leaving each daughter with a $5 million inheritance is part of their family's financial goals and have placed some stock and life insurance in an irrevocable life insurance trust (see Chapter 67), so the two girls will be well protected in the future.

Everything else in their estate will be either spent during retirement or left to their favorite charity when they pass away. After examining the numbers, Steve and Martha felt that it made great sense to re-exert control over their social capital and follow through with their plan. Because Steve felt a need to sell in order to diversify his unbalanced portfolio, the only comparison to be made was between 1) selling, paying tax, and reinvesting the net proceeds and 2) contributing the stock and reinvesting inside the CRT. We have made such a comparison in the "sale" and "CRT" columns.

You can see that the benefit to their family of the CRT is significant. Steve and Martha will enjoy $175,622 in additional annual retirement income in the CRT scenario ($321,622 post-tax versus $146,000 post-tax). Over their joint life expectancy, this difference will amount to over $5 million!

Furthermore, because of the use of life insurance in a "wealth replacement trust," their kids will get more out of that asset than in the "sale" scenario ($3 million of estate tax-free insurance proceeds income vs. $2.4 million asset netting $1.08 million to the family after estate taxes).

By combining a charitable remainder trust with a wealth replacement trust for their heirs, Steve and Martha were able to enjoy a greater retirement income than they had anticipated, leave a substantial legacy to their children and pay nothing in estate taxes. As if that were not enough, they were able to leave over $20 million to charity. This is quite an accomplishment.

Conclusion

Although you may not have the wealth of our clients Steve and Martha, this doesn't mean that charitable planning is not for you. From everyday families to the wealthiest benefactors in the nation, charitable planning can play an important role in Wealth Protection. Make sure to consider it as part of your plan.

73

KEEPING THE ESTATE ALL IN THE FAMILY

It is common knowledge that more than 50% of marriages end in divorce. Do you love everyone that your children and grandchildren have ever dated? Maybe a better question is "Have you like ANY of the people your heirs have dated or married?" Regardless of how much you like the spouses of your children or grandchildren, you undoubtedly don't want to leave your inheritance to them if they are no longer part of your family.

In the thousands of cases where we have been brought in, we have NEVER seen an estate plan adequately protecting the heirs from divorce. What many families don't know is that you can protect heirs who are already married from losing an inheritance *without* requiring a prenuptial or postnuptial agreement. We recommend that you read Chapters 19 and 66 to learn how irrevocable trusts can be used to protect your heirs from divorce.

The cost of implementing this type of planning may be a one time cost of a few thousand dollars. Given that so many marriages end in divorce, this type of planning seems like very inexpensive insurance for your family.

PART TEN

IMPLEMENTING YOUR WEALTH PROTECTION PLAN

74

WHAT IS THE WEALTH PROTECTION ALLIANCE?

The Wealth Protection Alliance ("WPA") is a national network of independent financial planners, attorneys and accountants who work collaboratively as a multidisciplinary team to bring comprehensive integrated asset protection, tax reduction, insurance and investment planning, business and practice planning, and estate planning to physicians, business owners and high net worth families.

The Wealth Protection Alliance is a high-end boutique planning network that does not advertise or actively recruit advisors. The clientele and network of advisors is developed exclusively through word-of-mouth referrals and *educational* programs. The WPA has expanded into 50 markets nationwide. Although the WPA is not in every metropolitan market, we do have professionals licensed in all 50 states. Although it may be more convenient to work with someone whose office is only 2 miles from your home, many WPA clients are willing to sacrifice a little convenience for the level of attention, experience, and expertise members of the WPA provide.

The WPA was created by Chris Jarvis and David Mandell of Jarvis and Mandell and Dale Edwards of Agilis Benefit Services. Their combined experiences and careers in the fields of actuarial science, law, investment banking, financial planning, investment advisory services and insurance helped them develop their vision of integrated wealth protection planning.

Physicians, as a group, appreciate the value of having specialists in addition to generalists working on a case. Doctors often prefer having a local advisor who is supported by a national team of experts. This is similar to how medicine is practiced around the world and it ensures excellent local service and high-end, cutting-edge technology. At the WPA, this is what we offer you:

What Do You Get through the Wealth Protection Alliance?

First, you get a local team of advisors:

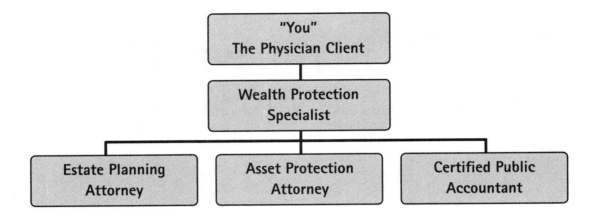

Second, you get a national support team that designs advanced strategies, oversees the local advisors, and is available to you, the client, as needed:

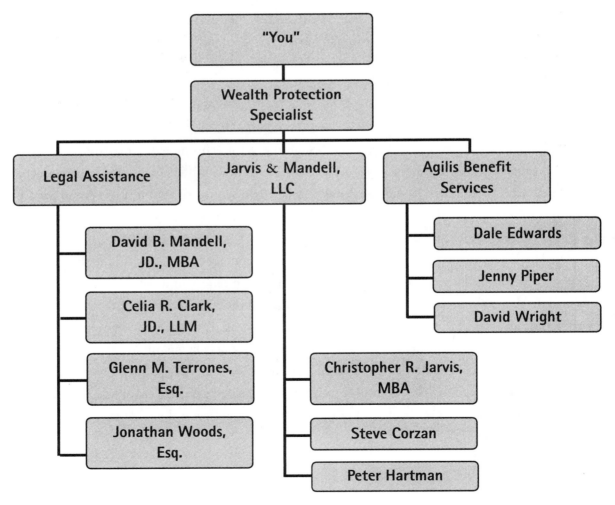

What Services Are Offered through the Wealth Protection Alliance?

Accounts Receivable Factoring

Accounts Receivable Protection

Benefits Analysis & Products

Business Overhead Expense

Buy-Sell Agreements

Buy-Sell Funding

Captive Insurance Companies

Charitable Planning

Comprehensive Estate Planning

Comprehensive Financial Planning

Deferred Compensation Planning

Disability Insurance

Domestic Debt Shield Structures

Dynasty Trusts

Equipment Protection

Family Limited Partnerships

Fee-Based Financial Planning

Individually Managed Accounts

International Debt Shield Structures

International Financial Products

International Insurance Products

International LLCs

International Trusts

Investment Advisory Services

Irrevocable Trusts

Life Insurance Products

Life Insurance Review

Life Settlements

Limited Liability Companies

Living Trusts

Long Term Care Insurance

Medical Malpractice Insurance

Mutual Funds

Non-profit Deferred Compensation

Practice Formation

Practice Restructuring

Premium Financed Insurance

Private Placement Life Insurance

Professional Employer Services

Property & Casualty Insurance

QPRTs and Other Home Protection

Real Estate Protection

Retirement Plan Analysis

Retirement Plan Implementation

Variable Annuities

Wills

529 College Saving Plans

75

<hr/>

WORKING WITH THE WEALTH PROTECTION ALLIANCE

Wealth Protection Planning requires multi-disciplinary expertise that one person or firm is likely unable to provide. It requires a collaborative effort from a number of specialists with the oversight of a local generalist who can quarterback the process and regularly meet with you. The local Wealth Protection Specialist can help you understand what is being done and, most importantly, make sure all of the work being done is integrated for your maximum benefit.

As we described in Chapter 1, in putting together this book, we worked with a series of advisors from the Wealth Protection Alliance — a national network of top financial advisors to physicians. These advisors not only have their own successful practices in 50 cities throughout the U.S., but they have also been have been trained by us in the areas of asset protection, tax planning, and advanced business issues that specifically effect medical practices. By working with the Wealth Protection Alliance, you will have access to the expertise and experience of a number of experts in various fields through your local Wealth Protection Specialist. If you already have an attorney or accountant, he/she can be integrated into the process for maximum flexibility and convenience.

If you would like to take the first step to implementing your Wealth Protection Plan, please complete the Confidential Data Form and Asset Questionnaire in the Appendix and fax it to (888) 317-9896. A Wealth Protection Specialist will review your information and contact you to discuss your situation and how working with the Wealth Protection Alliance might benefit you. Expect to spend only ten minutes of your time completing and faxing the form, there is no expense in taking the first step to comprehensive Wealth Protection and financial freedom.

We hope you found this book helpful and we look forward to assisting you.

Wealth Protection Alliance

To request a meeting with a member of the WPA, arrange to have a WPA member or principal speak at your association or hospital meeting, or to receive the schedule of upcoming web-based educational programs for physicians,

Contact us toll free at (800) 554-7233

APPENDICES

Appendix A

⸺◆◆◆⸺

THE TEN COMMANDMENTS OF OFFSHORE

Despite the pitfalls and mistakes involved in offshore planning explained in Chapter 17, one can still achieve many legitimate goals offshore. They key is to follow our "10 commandments of offshore." For update information on offshore planning, including common scams, speak to an attorney who works closely with the Wealth Protection Alliance.

1. Consider Offshore as an Option

Any client with over $500,000 in liquid wealth should consider offshore planning. You simply cannot achieve the same level of protection — or claim discouragement — by using domestic structures. When one considers the stability of the offshore financial centers, and the security of the large fiduciaries typically utilized, most clients' skepticism about offshore planning melts away.

2. Do Not Intend on Saving Taxes through Offshore Planning

As noted above, 95% of offshore planning is not designed to, nor will it achieve, tax savings for U.S. taxpayers. If you intend to save taxes offshore, you'll need a particular plan designed to legitimately reduce, or defer, taxes. General asset protection plans will aim to be tax-neutral. If you intend to save taxes by not declaring income, realize that this is tax evasion, punishable as a felony.

3. Do Not "Hide" Assets or Income Offshore

Whether your goal is asset protection, tax reduction, privacy, or investments, you must intend to disclose everything you are doing offshore to the relevant U.S. government agencies. If not, you run the serious risk that you will need to perjure yourself to keep the existence of offshore assets (and their income) a secret. As above, this is a felony punishable by a long vacation in the steel chateau.

4. Use Structures Respected under U.S. Law (Trusts, LLCs, Real CICs)

If your asset protection plan is ever challenged in the U.S., you want judges to understand and respect what you have done. This is a much easier task if the structure you utilize is part of estate or business planning in the U.S. The best structures: LLCs, certain types of trusts (generally, where there are 3rd party beneficiaries, such as children and grandchildren), and captive insurance companies.

5. Use Transactions that Have an Economic Substance

Again, U.S. judges are becoming increasingly skeptical of offshore transactions which do not make economic sense (i.e., funding a foreign trust with most of your net worth while claiming you no longer have control of the trust). This warrants the use of entities that allow a real exchange of economic value. The leading personal entity which experts use to gain this benefit: the foreign LLC. Strategies using captive insurance companies are also excellent if they are only used when there is economic justification to do so.

6. If It's Too Good to Be True, It Is

This is an old adage — but nowhere is it more true than in offshore planning. You simply cannot expect to achieve mind-boggling returns without risk offshore, nor can you hope to create complex offshore arrangements on the cheap. You will simply get what you pay for — and you will not like what you get if you choose a cheap, poorly constructed plan.

7. Use PFICQEF Mutual Funds

Making sure your offshore entity is tax compliant is only the first part of the tax battle. You must also make certain that the investments you choose are U.S. tax compliant as well. The best bet in this regard is 1) to use a large established mutual fund which makes the effort to comply with the complex PFIC QEF rules (they aren't many that do) or 2) to invest in a legitimately U.S. tax-deferred life insurance policy or annuity. We can recommend a number of such products if you contact us.

8. Rely on Established Fiduciary Firms

You want to make sure that the fiduciary firms you rely on are established, have adequate references, have insurance and are bonded, if applicable. In most offshore centers, it will not be difficult to find some of the largest accounting, investment and banking firms in the world. Don't skimp on these services...the security of your funds depends on it.

9. Walk before You Run

It is always a wise to move wealth offshore gradually, as you become increasingly comfortable with the process. We typically recommend that one begins with less than 25% of the amount one eventually intends to move offshore.

10. Find an Experienced U.S.–Based Attorney

Of all the commandments, this one is paramount. That is because an attorney who is an offshore expert will make sure that commandments 1 thru 9 are followed. Further, this advisor will have the contacts and experience to make the planning process seamless and understandable for the client. Finally, an attorney is the only advisor with an absolute client privilege respected by the courts. CPAs and "financial advisors" have no such privilege and can be forced to divulge any and all information you have given them. In the sensitive area of offshore planning, it is always wise to use an attorney just for this reason alone.

Appendix B

FRAUDULENT TRANSFER LAWS

Why You Must Avoid Running Afoul of These Laws

Fraudulent transfer laws give creditors the right to undo certain transfers that debtors have made so that the transferred property can be seized by creditors (including judgment creditors). In other words, under certain circumstances, the courts invalidate sales or gifts you make to hinder those suing you. Whatever you sold or gave away is transferred back to you, allowing the creditor to seize the property. These laws have been enacted so that debtors cannot transfer property to defraud their creditors.

Fraudulent transfer laws are important because they may partially, or totally, destroy your asset protection plan. Asset protection is achieved by titling your wealth beyond the reach of creditors. Fraudulent transfers laws are obstacles to that goal because they allow a creditor to get at your assets even when you no longer own them in your name. This is extremely important — fraudulent transfer laws separate valid legal asset protection from illegally disposing of assets. A fraudulent transfer challenge often becomes the true test of your asset protection plan.

When a transfer is "fraudulent"

Courts find two types of fraudulent transfers, each explained separately:

1. Fraud in fact — or "actual fraud"
2. Fraud in law — or "constructive fraud"

Actual Fraud

For actual fraud, your creditors must prove that you actually intended to hinder, delay, or defraud your creditors. This may be very difficult to prove directly as they must prove your state of mind or get you to confess fraudulent intent. To assist creditors, the courts recognize signs of fraud or "badges of fraud" which, if proved, can allow the court to infer fraudulent intent. These include:

- The transfer was made to a close family member or friend.
- The transfer was made secretly.
- The transfer was for less than fair value.
- The debtor continued to use or possess the property after the transfer.
- The debtor disappeared.
- The debtor had been sued or threatened with a suit before the transfer.
- The debtor concealed assets.
- The transfer was around the same time the debtor incurred a large debt.
- The transfer left the debtor with no property.
- The transfer left the debtor insolvent (unable to pay debts as they came due).

Even if a creditor proves these "badges," it does not always mean that the judge will automatically find the transfer to be fraudulent and allow the creditor to recover the property. These badges only "infer" fraudulent intent; that is, they are evidence that can allow the judge to conclude that you had fraudulent intent when not admitted..

Constructive Fraud

Because actual fraud is so difficult to prove, even when certain "badges of fraud" exist, creditors more often rely on constructive fraud to undo transfers by debtors. Constructive fraud occurs when there is *a gift or sale of the debtor's property*:

- **For less than fair value** (also called *fair consideration*)
- **In the face of a known liability**
- **Which leaves the debtor insolvent**

Factor A: "For Less than Fair Value"

Creditors must first show if they want to prove *constructive fraud* that the transfer was for less than fair value. While this is not a problem when the debtor makes a gift, proving an actual sale was for less than fair value is more difficult for the creditor, because of the way a court defines fair consideration.

Fair consideration is a price that a reasonably prudent seller would obtain using commercially reasonable means. This may not mean the fair market value; it depends on what type of item or property is involved. For stocks or bonds of publicly-traded corporations or commodities, fair value does mean fair market value. Exact value of the stock/bond/commodity can easily be determined by looking to the quotes of the day of the transfer. If the debtor transferred the stock/etc. for less than its price that day, then the sale would be for less than fair value and might be a fraudulent transfer.

For items that are more difficult to value precisely, like real estate, stock in a privately held business, antiques, vehicles, and others, fair consideration may be much less than fair market value because reasonable minds differ about the exact value of a piece of real estate, or a painting, or a business. Also, as the debtor, you may not have the luxury to wait through a series of negotiations or for the right buyer willing to pay full fair market value price. You may want to settle for less than optimum price in return for fast cash. For these reasons, courts typically conclude that real estate which is over 70% of fair market value satisfies fair consideration. For other items, like jewelry or closely-held businesses, courts will look at all the facts — especially certified appraisals — for whether the payment was in the ballpark.

Factor B: "In the Face of a Known Liability"

Even if a creditor attacking a transfer shows that it was a sale for less than fair value or a gift, he must still show that you made the transfer "in the face of a known liability." What does this phrase mean? Courts define it to mean that you cannot transfer assets to protect against future *probable liabilities,* but you can make a transfer to protect yourself against future *possible liabilities.* Again, it is difficult to precisely define the difference between *probable liabilities* and *possible liabilities.* The courts look at the facts of each case, focus on the timing of when the act creating the liability occurred and when you realized that you may be liable for that act.

Factor C: "Which Leaves the Debtor Insolvent"

Even if a creditor attacking your transfer can show it was for less than fair value, and even if they can show you made the transfer when a probable liability existed, the court will not undo the transfer, unless it left you *insolvent. Insolvent* means the market value of all of your assets is less the amount needed to pay your existing debts as they come due. In other words, you are left in the position where you cannot pay your debts.

> **To summarize: You cannot safely transfer your property for less than fair value, when a probable liability exists, and when your remaining wealth cannot cover your debts as they are due.**

How to Avoid Fraudulent Transfer Claims

These are more common ways to structure asset transfers to insure that they will not be judged to be fraudulent:

Transfer before the liability arises.

Simply put, there cannot be a fraudulent transfer if you make the transfer *before* a probable liability arises, underscoring why it is so important to set up your asset protection plan sooner rather than later.

Show that the transfer was for purposes other than asset protection.

Support your transfer with adequate correspondence and documentation that the transfer was part of an estate or investment plan. Often we put language in the legal documents — or *preliminary recitals* — which confirm that the transfer was for purposes other than creditor protection alone.

Document what you receive in the transaction — higher is better.

This is especially important if the transfer was made for past services. Be prepared to prove that the value you received satisfies the fair value requirement. If you received property, obtain favorable appraisals.

Document the value of the property you transferred — lower is better.

For the same reasons, shop around to document the lowest appraisal of transferred property. Emphasize defects or damage to the appraiser to help insure a low value.

Utilize overlapping asset protection techniques.

Good attorneys use *overlap* techniques to protect certain assets. For example, in addition to transferring rental property to a family limited partnership, the attorney might also recommend a mortgage on the property to an uncle for the $15,000 owed an uncle. Now, a creditor must attack the transfer to the partnership, and also the mortgage.

Continue your regular gifts and donations.

Even if you gifted property when a liability existed, it may not be fraudulent if it was part of an established pattern of gifting. For example, if you always paid your children's college tuition, you can probably continue without incurring sanctions.

Why an Asset Protection Expert is So Important

Laws against fraudulent transfers are complex. They create a tremendous gray area — as most challenged transfers are neither clearly fraudulent nor clearly legitimate. An asset protection specialist will understand the complexity and the nuances of fraudulent transfer laws. The specialist understands how transfers can be justified. Further, a specialist knows how to structure a transfer so that the very documents which create the transfer, any claim of a possible fraudulent intent is eliminated.

An asset protection plan's ultimate test is often a fraudulent transfer claim by a frustrated creditor. An experienced asset protection specialist can ensure that your plan will survive such a fraudulent transfer attack. If you don't know of an asset protection attorney in your area, contact the local WPA member to be introduced to one.

Appendix C

INTESTACY

What Happens If You Die
Without A Will Or Living Trust

If you die without a valid document disposing of your property — either a Will or a pour-over Will and Living Trust — your state will decide exactly how your estate should be divided. Each state has a statute which controls the distribution of a decedent's property in these circumstances. Such a statute is called an "intestacy" law because "intestacy" is the legal term for dying without a valid Will (or pour-over Will and Living Trust).

As we stated earlier in the book, dying without a Will is the worst estate planning mistake you can make. Not only do you lose estate tax benefits and lose the probate fee savings of a Living Trust, but *you also lose all control of how your property will be given away when you die*. Instead, you allow the politicians to decide how your property is divided. And they usually make a mess of things — as you might have guessed.

READ THIS DISCLAIMER:

The following is a general description of how property is divided under California's intestacy laws. Use this description to give you a general understanding of what intestacy laws are. Check with an attorney familiar with the laws in your state for particular legal advice. Or, better yet, set up a Living Trust and a pour-over Will and rest easy knowing this law will not apply to you.

Sample Intestacy Law

If you die intestate, your property Will be divided as follows:

1. If you have a surviving spouse, but no surviving issue (descendants), parent, brother, sister, or issue of a deceased brother or sister, the surviving spouse gets everything.

2. If you have a surviving spouse, and any of the following are true, the surviving spouse gets one half of the estate:

- You also are survived by one child (that child gets the remaining half); or

- You also are survived by the issue of one pre-deceased child (that issue takes or splits the remaining half); or

- You leave no issue but are survived by one parent (he/she gets the remaining half); or

- You leave no issue but are survived by the issue of one parent (they either take or split the remaining half); or

- You leave no issue but are survived by more than 1 parent (they split the remaining half).

3. If you have a surviving spouse, and any of the following are true, the surviving spouse gets one third of the estate:

- You leave more than 1 living child; or

- You leave one child living and the issue of a predeceased child; or

- You leave issue of two or more predeceased children.

There are also issues here about how much the issue (descendants) of predeceased children should take — and state laws do differ on this point.

4. If you do not leave a surviving spouse, then your entire estate Will pass to your heirs in the following priority:

- To your issue (descendants);

- If you have no surviving issue, then to your parents;

- If you have no surviving issue or parents, then to the issue of your parents;

- If you have no surviving issue or parents or issue of your parents, then to your grandparents, or their issue;

- If you have none of the above, then to the surviving issue of your predeceased spouse, if any;

- If you still have none of the above, then to your "next of kin" (any blood relative, in order of kinship);

- If you still have none of the above, then to the parents of a predeceased spouse, if any;

- If you still have none of the above, then your hard-earned property Will escheat (be transferred) to the state.

Unfortunately, million of dollars in property every year escheats to the state in this way — because the decedent had no relatives or they cannot be found. *Do not let the state decide how your property will be given away — do the smart thing and establish a Living Trust and pour-over Will as soon as you can.*

Appendix D

REVISED 2005 TAX RATE SCHEDULES

	If TAXABLE INCOME		The TAX is		
	T H E N				
	Is Over	But Not Over	This Amount	Plus %	Of the Excess Over
SCHEDULE X					
Single	$0	$7,300	$0.00	10%	$0.00
	$7,300	$29,700	$730.00	15%	$7,300
	$29,700	$71,950	$4,090.00	25%	$29,700
	$71,950	$150,150	$14,652.50	28%	$71,950
	$150,150	$326,450	$36,548.50	33%	$150,150
	$326,450	—	$94,727.50	35%	$326,450
SCHEDULE Y-1					
Married Filing Jointly or Qualifying Widow(er)	$0	$14,600	$0.00	10%	$0.00
	$14,600	$59,400	$1,460.00	15%	$14,600
	$59,400	$119,950	$8,180.00	25%	$59,400
	$119,950	$182,800	$23,317.50	28%	$119,950
	$182,800	$326,450	$40,915.50	33%	$182,800
	$326,450	—	$88,320.00	35%	$326,450
SCHEDULE Y-2					
Married Filing Separately	$0	$7,300	$0.00	10%	$0.00
	$7,300	$29,700	$730.00	15%	$7,300
	$29,700	$59,975	$4,090.00	25%	$29,700
	$59,975	$91,400	$11,658.75	28%	$59,975
	$91,400	$163,225	$20,457.75	33%	$91,400
	$163,225	—	$44,160.00	35%	$163,225
SCHEDULE Z					
Head of Household	$0	$10,450	$0.00	10%	$0.00
	$10,450	$39,800	$1,045.00	15%	$10,450
	$39,800	$102,800	$5,447.50	25%	$39,800
	$102,800	$166,450	$21,197.50	28%	$102,800
	$166,450	$326,450	$39,019.50	33%	$166,450
	$326,450	—	$91,819.50	35%	$326,450

Appendix E

ASSET QUESTIONNAIRE

Personal & Confidential Information

Name: _____   Birth date: _ _ / _ _ / _ _ _ _

Spouse Name: _____   Birth date: _ _ / _ _ / _ _ _ _

Occupation: _____   Income: _____

Spouse Occupation: _____   Income: _____

Address: _____

City/State/Zip: _____

Work Phone: _____   Fax: _____

Home Phone: _____   Email: _____

# of Children: ____ Ages: _____ # of Grandchildren: _____ Ages: _____

Yrs. until retirement: ____   Monthly (after tax) income required during retirement: _____

What long term rate of return do you expect to realize on your retirement investments:_____

Business/Practice Information: Gross Revenue: _____ # of employees _____

Accounts Receivables: _____   Annual income tax deduction desired: _____

Balance Sheet

Asset (or Liability)	Fair Market Value	Date Purchased	Equity	Held in own name, LP joint, living trust, LLC?
Pensions, IRAs, Profit Sharing Plans			n/a	
Primary Home				
Other Real Estate Holdings				
Brokerage, annuities, Bank Accounts, CDs				
Business Interests, Ltd. Partnerships, etc.			Basis	
Disability Income Insurance Coverage	Monthly Benefit:			
529 Plans, UGMA or UTMA				
Life Insurance	Death Benefit:		Cash Value	
Long-Term Care Insurance	Daily Benefit:			

Prior Planning

Document	Y/N	Year Last Updated
Last Will & Testament(s)		
Revocable Living Trust(s)		
Irrevocable Life Insurance Trust(s)		
Qualified Personal Residence Trust(s)		
Family Limited Partnership(s)		
Family Limited Liability Company(ies)		
Charitable Lead/Remainder Trust(s)		
Split Dollar or Buy-Sell Agreement(s)		
Other: _____		

Concerns

Please rank each concern on a scale of 1 to 10. (1 = not concerned, 10 = very concerned):

_____ **Minimizing Income Tax Liabilities**

_____ **Reducing Capital Gains Taxes on Investments**

_____ **Diversifying an Investment Portfolio**

_____ **Planning for Retirement**

_____ **Protecting Family Income against Disability/Death**

_____ **Protecting Wealth from Potential Lawsuits**

_____ **Protecting My Pension from the 83% Tax Trap**

_____ **Life Insurance Needs**

_____ **Reducing Estate Taxes**

_____ **Business Succession Planning**

_____ **Planning For Parents/Elders**

_____ **Charitable Planning**

Professional Advisors

If we work together, we may wish to coordinate the planning with your other trusted advisors. This can often make the planning seamless and less expensive for you. We will not share your information on this form with them without your permission.

Your Accountant

Name: _____   Firm: _____

Address: _____

City/State/Zip: _____

Work Phone: _____   For how long: _____

Your Attorney

Name: _____   Firm: _____

Address: _____

City/State/Zip: _____

Work Phone: _____   For how long: _____

Your Investment Advisor/Broker

Name: _____   Firm: _____

Address: _____

City/State/Zip: _____

Work Phone: _____   For how long: _____

Your Insurance Agent/Broker/Financial Planner

Name: _____   Firm: _____

Address: _____

City/State/Zip: _____

Work Phone: _____   For how long: _____

Estate Distribution Analysis

DIRECTIONS:

At the time of your death, how much would you like to leave to the following entities?
Please fill out how much in dollars ($$$) and as a percentage (%), that you would like to
leave to Charity, Children, and Taxes.

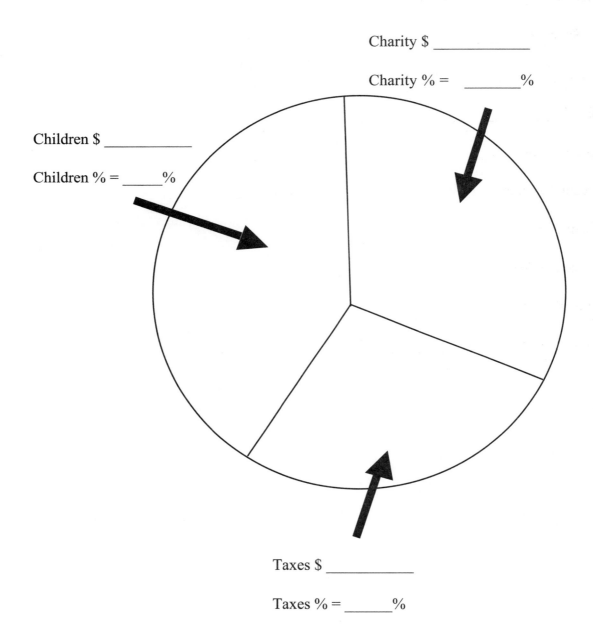

Charity $ _____

Charity % = _____%

Children $ _____

Children % = _____%

Taxes $ _____

Taxes % = _____%

Medical Malpractice Insurance Information

Name: _____

Address: _____

City/State/Zip: _____

Phone: _____ Fax: _____

Email: _____

Current Carrier: _____

Medical Specialty: _____

Effective Date: _____

Retroactive Date: _____

Limits of Liability: _____

Annual Premium: _____

Appendix F

SAMPLE EMPLOYEE CENSUS FOR RETIREMENT AND OTHER BENEFITS PLANNING

Wealth
Protection
Alliance

Please complete and fax to (888) 317-9896

Information Checklist for Qualified Retirement Plans / Tax Reduction Strategies

1.)   Name of Employer: _____

        Date of Incorporation: _____

2.)   Name of Plan: _____ Retirement Plan
        ( )   New Plan
        ( )   Pre-existing plan named: _____
              Which was originally effective as of: _____
              Value of YOUR plan assets (statement will be helpful) _____

3.)   Employer Address: _____

                         City _____ State _____ Zip _____

4.)   Employer Telephone: _____

5.)   Employer Facsimile: _____

6.)   Employer Tax Identification Number: _____

7.)   Name of Stockholders, Principals and Percentage of Ownership:

        Name _____ _____%
        Name _____ _____%
        Name _____ _____%
        Name _____ _____%
        Name _____ _____%
        Name _____ _____%
        Name _____ _____%
        Name _____ _____%

8.)   Employer Fiscal Year: _____ to _____

9.)   Main Business Activity: _____

10.)   Plan Fiscal Year: _____ to _____
        must be 12 consecutive months, not same as fiscal year

11.) Plan Agent for Legal Services: _____

12.) Plan Administrator (if other than employee): _____

13.) Plan Trustee(s): _____   _____
    _____   _____

14.) Accountant: name _____
    address _____
    phone _____

15.) Attorney: name _____
    address _____
    phone _____

16.) Do stockholders/principals own any interest in another business entity? If yes, please explain:

17.) Does the business lease/share any employee with another business entity? If yes, please explain:

18.) Please complete the attached EMPLOYEE CONFIDENTIAL CENSUS.

19.) For professionals (doctors, lawyers, dentists, accountants), date first received professional license:
    Month _____ Day _____ Year _____

20.) On a PRE-TAX basis, how much would each participant wish to put into a tax-deductible strategy?

Name of Person	Retirement Plan ($35,000 max)	Other Plan (unlimited)
_____	$_____	$_____
_____	$_____	$_____
_____	$_____	$_____
_____	$_____	$_____
_____	$_____	$_____
_____	$_____	$_____
_____	$_____	$_____
_____		

This form completed by: _____ Date: _____

Request for Pension Proposal (Part II)
Fax to (888) 317-9896

Name of Business_____

Tax Status: Incorporated_____ Unincorporated_____

Date business began_____

Date of Incorporation_____

Tax Year End_____

Approximate Contribution Desired $_____

(percent of pay or dollar amount)

Any current pension plan in force? Yes____ No____

(If so, supply details on a separate sheet.)

Do the owners have ownership interests in any other firms? Yes____ No____

(If so, supply details on a separate sheet.)

Additional Comments:

Confidential Employee Census

Name	Date of Birth	Date of Hire	Salary	See note below and check if:			
				Part Time	Non Smoker	Ownership percentage	Officer

Note: "Part time" means that the employee works less than 1,000 hours per year. Check "Non-Smokers" if known. List "Ownership Percentage" of all owners.

Appendix G

SCHEDULING A CME SEMINAR FOR YOUR GROUP, ASSOCIATION OR HOSPITAL

The authors have provided educational programs for hundreds of medical groups, hospitals, PPOs, pharmaceutical companies and medical associations and have written articles for over 250 medical periodicals.

An abbreviated list includes: International College of Surgeons, American Society of Internal Medicine, Society of Gynecologic Oncologists, Long Beach Community Health Center, Los Angeles Metropolitan Medical Center, Numerous Tenet Hospitals, Ventura County Medical Association, Iranian Medical Society, Orthopedic Special Edition, Strategic Orthopaedics, American Association of Physicians of Indian Origin (APPI), American Association of Neurological Surgeons (AANS), Anesthesiology News, American Medical News, General Surgery News, Cardiology Today, Neuropractice, American Society of Interns and Residents, American Medical Women's Association, West Virginia Medical Association, Alliance of the International College of Surgeons, American Society of Oncology Fellows, Tennessee Medical Association, American Phillipino Physician Association, Texas Medical Association, Fairfield County (CT) Medical Association, Florida Medical Association, www.Medscape.com, and many more.

Typically, our seminars are scheduled three to nine months in advance. However, we are dedicated to helping our clients address their timely needs. For this reason, we often accommodate requests for seminars within 30 days.

Wealth Protection Alliance members can offer seminars as part of grand rounds, a national or local medical society meeting or to a practice and its partners. There is typically a fee for the seminar and all attendees receive copies of our books, including 6.25 of CME credits from the Risk Management monograph.

To book us for a seminar call (800) 554-7233 and speak to Todd or Tricia. We will be happy to discuss particulars and negotiate an appropriate price with you. We may be able to offer continuing education credits for the attendees.

Wealth Protection Alliance Books

Fax to (888) 317-9896

Risk Management for the Practicing Physician is nationally accredited for 6.25 hours of Category I continuing medical education (CME) credits in risk management. Co-written by a practicing physician, an attorney and a financial advisor, this 75-page monograph includes chapters on: providing care in today's malpractice environment, liability and the doctor-patient relationship, managing diagnosis-related liability, minimizing risks of miscommunication, managing high risk communication areas, managing the dangers of drug therapy, nonmedical liability risks for the practicing physician, and liability in the new health care delivery system. Regularly $59.95.

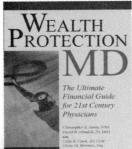

Wealth Protection, MD: The Ultimate Financial Guide for 21ˢᵗ Century Physicians is the first financial and legal planning book that tailors its recommendation to the physician's individual situation. It is also the first book to integrate financial, tax, legal and investment advice into a single text. By completing a Yes/No questionnaire, you can customize the book to fit your specific needs in the areas of Income Tax Reduction, Investing, Asset Protection, Practice Planning, Insurance, Retirement & Estate Planning. Regularly $50.

# of Books	Item	Cost	Subtotal
_____	Risk Management for the Practicing Physician	$30	_____
_____	Wealth Protection, MD	$25	_____
	Subtotal		_____
	Shipping & Handling ($5 per book)		_____
	Total (check payable to Guardian Publishing or Credit Card)		_____

Name: _____

Address: _____

_____

City/State/Zip _____

Phone _____

Email _____

Credit Card _ _ _ _ _ _ _ _ _ _ _ _ _ _ _ _   Exp. Date _ _ / _ _

Signature _____